ALAN
THE
IN W
BOOTS

ALAN BALL
THE MAN
IN WHITE
BOOTS

The biography of the youngest
1966 World Cup hero

DAVID TOSSELL

HODDER

First published in Great Britain in 2017 by Hodder & Stoughton
An Hachette UK company

This paperback edition published in 2018

1

A CIP catalogue record for this title is available from the British Library

B format ISBN 9781473660373
eBook ISBN 9781473660403

Typeset in Baskerville by Hewer Text UK Ltd, Edinburgh
Printed and bound in Great Britain by Clays Ltd, Elcograf S.p.A.

Hodder & Stoughton policy is to use papers that are natural, renewable
and recyclable products and made from wood grown in sustainable
forests. The logging and manufacturing processes are expected to
conform to the environmental regulations of the country of origin.

Hodder & Stoughton Ltd
Carmelite House
50 Victoria Embankment
London EC4Y 0DZ

www.hodder.co.uk

CONTENTS

PREFACE:
ITEMS OF A LIFE

'And should we need a memory, there's Wembley's masterclass
Where Bally's deft, determined feet touched every blade of grass,
Then Hurst is in the middle as the swelling voices sing
And a sparky lad from Lancashire is racing down the wing'

– from a poem sent to the Ball family, author unidentified

The socks. Red, rolled down around ankles as the legs they once covered set off yet again towards the right corner flag. Short-sighted Nobby Stiles has barely seen the run, yet a flash of ginger hair acts as a beacon and he delivers a long ball down the wing. Exploiting the space offered by West German defenders wearied by the demands of extra-time, Alan Ball never breaks stride. He crosses first time for Geoff Hurst to turn and score what will be the most debated as well as the most important goal in his country's football history. England will soon be the 1966 World Cup winners; 21-year-old Ball – a boy offered a career at Blackpool after his hometown club Bolton Wanderers told him he was too small – their youngest hero.

'He was probably the best player that day and if it had not been for his impact the result could have been totally different,' Bobby Charlton argues, while Stiles remembers that 'he covered every blade of grass; he was unbelievable'. For younger sceptics needing modern-day statistical proof, when football analysts Opta study the game in 2014 they find that Ball has made more effective attacking passes than anyone else in the match.

The boots. White. Painted, we find out later, because he doesn't like to wear the model he is being paid to use, and with which he quickly becomes synonymous. It's a sunny afternoon at Stamford Bridge when he unveils them, helping new League champions Everton to victory over FA Cup winners Chelsea in the Charity Shield. By now, Ball is operating at the peak of his powers, the heartbeat of one of the most celebrated midfield trios in English football.

More than four decades later, as you approach Goodison Park from the south, Stanley Park on your right, the flank of the Main Stand will greet you with a huge poster celebrating the 'Holy Trinity'. Ball is flanked by Howard Kendall and Colin Harvey, the way in which they most often lined up, with Ball given licence to move forward to score 79 goals in 251 games for the club. To watch Ball on a good day at Everton is to feel as though you are spying on a session of one- and two-touch training, his sharp mind, innate sense of his surroundings and his snooker player's eye for angles allowing him to decide on his delivery before the ball arrives. Lawrie McMenemy, his future manager, observes, 'In his early career he was a runner, a scrapper, a fighter. At the end of his career he became the best one-touch footballer in the game.'

On this day at Chelsea, the speed of his footwork is emphasised by the bright boots that will initiate a fashion trend, even though Ball himself wears them for only two seasons. The first goal, a shot from the edge of the box by Alan Whittle after an Everton break, typifies Ball's contribution. It is he who carries the play from one end to another, receiving the ball from his defenders, playing it second touch to Harvey, sprinting diagonally to take a return pass and laying it, third touch, to Whittle on his left.

It is the perfect example of Ball's style. Not for him the pause and then the languid 40-yard pass beyond the full-backs. One touch, pass, move into space for a return, first-time ball. Move on again, further and further up the field. If the 21st-century purveyors of the defence-splitting pass from deep are often likened to American football quarterbacks, then Ball is the running back: advancing his team relentlessly a few yards at a time; picking away at the defence, exposing vulnerabilities; never retreating, never resting. It is not so fanciful to imagine him playing 'tiki-taka' alongside Iniesta and Xavi in the Barcelona midfield that will redefine the game in the 21st century. 'It was really Alan who made the partnership with me and Colin work as well as it did,' Kendall will testify.

The suit. Thick and woollen for a winter's day. As he leans back in his chair in the Highbury boardroom, Ball reveals a six-button waistcoat topped by a fat-knotted silk tie. The perfect attire for a young man completing an important piece of business: his £220,000 transfer to Arsenal; a move that – as inexplicable now as it was in 1971 – breaks the hearts of Everton fans.

A disclaimer here. Ball's signing is one of the most exciting things to happen to a young Arsenal fan like me. Aged 10 when I hear of his arrival at Highbury, I already harbour a soft spot for Everton because the primary school team I play for wears the same colours; blue shirts with white collar, white shorts, white socks. I've pestered my parents into buying me a pair of the white Hummel boots endorsed by Ball. Now Arsenal are taking the kind of flashy, impulsive action I have never previously witnessed from them by breaking the British transfer record. The debate that will continue to rage among fans of my vintage is whether the presence of a touch player like Ball forces the Gunners to abandon, mistakenly, the direct style that has brought them the Double, or whether they persist with such methods too much to maximise his presence in their midfield.

'In my opinion he was one of Arsenal's greatest players of all time,' says Liam Brady, whose influential Highbury career is launched alongside Ball. 'Although we didn't win any trophies when Alan was here, he was still a fantastic player.'

The shirt. White, but trimmed with blue and red and bearing an Admiral logo; the manifestation of a new England era led by the commercially astute Don Revie. Ball, damp but delighted, is pictured sharing a joke with debutant Alan Hudson at the end of his first match as national captain, another Wembley win against West Germany.

Ball was in his prime when England went out to their old foes in the quarter-finals of the 1970 World Cup. Three years later he became his country's first player sent off in a World Cup match during a defeat in Poland that proved ultimately ruinous for Sir Alf Ramsey. After a period out of the team, Revie brings him back, makes him captain for an unbeaten six-game run that begins by beating the world champions and ends with a thumping of Scotland. And then he sacks him, without telling him, terminating a 72-game England career.

The shorts. Tight and black. And short; this being the early 1980s, when nylon seems to be in scarce supply at football kit manufacturers. So short that, as Ball stands at McMenemy's left shoulder in a 1981

Southampton team line-up, the lace that pulls them tight hangs down to the lower hem like a sporran. The legs protruding from them are stockier than those that gambolled across Wembley in 1966 and by now Ball uses them to take up deep positions from where he can probe and prompt, rather than racing all over the field. They can still deliver a decent cross, though, like the one that helps set up a goal in Southampton's victory over Stoke City in March of that season, extending their stay at the top of the First Division.

Ball first arrives at The Dell late in 1976, leading them back to the top flight and to a League Cup final. After his first unsuccessful venture into management at Blackpool, he has returned and, with Kevin Keegan as skipper, Southampton reach the summit of English football for the first time. 'I played with him when he was 36,' says Keegan. 'I'd already been European Footballer of the Year twice, but he could teach me things I never even thought about.'

Southampton's title challenge doesn't last much beyond that win against Stoke, but the final significant stop on Ball's playing career has been a triumph; another club where few all-time teams will be compiled without the inclusion of his name. It is not a new phenomenon. An internet site devoted to Blackpool will name him the ninth greatest player in the club's history. Similar projects at Everton regularly place only Dixie Dean alongside him in their particular pantheon. Even at Arsenal, where he won no medals, the club's official website places him at number 45 in a list of historic greats voted for by digital-age fans.

The watch. 'We're up. Kill this game off. Do whatever you can.' The fateful words that Ball, manager of Manchester City, rasps out at midfielder Steve Lomas as he sees time running out on the final day of the 1995–96 Premier League season.[1] Having witnessed his team fight back from two goals down against Liverpool, Ball has been informed that Southampton are losing at home to Wimbledon, a result that means City's point is enough to save them. Following orders like the good trooper he is, Lomas gains possession and heads to the corner flag with a singleness of purpose; to waste as much time as

1 The tournament was officially known as the FA Carling Premiership that season, but for ease I will refer to it throughout as the Premier League.

possible. But Ball's information is wrong. Niall Quinn, watching events unfold on a television in the changing room, knows it. He races back to the dug-out to scream that Southampton are not losing and what precious little time remains needs to be used in pursuit of a goal, not running down the clock in the corner.

It is too late. City are relegated and the episode becomes as symbolic of Ball's managerial career as the white boots of his playing days. Ball will even adopt it as a staple of his after-dinner routine: 'I saw an old lady in Manchester struggling with her shopping, so I went up and asked her, "Can you manage, love?" She said, "A bit better than you!"'

In its rundown of the worst coaching performances of recent years the *Guardian* writes, 'Alan Ball is quite simply an awful manager.' It is a harsh assessment. Ask Portsmouth fans what they think of him or prompt Southampton followers to recall a great Premier League escape, and you will struggle to believe they are discussing the same manager of whom Manchester City supporters have such painful memories.

Yet it remains a fact that Ball has seven spells as manager of six clubs and five times his teams are involved in relegation seasons, although he is not always still around when the final points are lost. That there are promotions and survivals along the way merely emphasises that his days in charge of football clubs are mostly spent a rung or two down the ladder from the heights of his playing career. For someone who defines himself as 'a winner' – and has the medals to prove it – it is a difficult reality to deal with. 'He was unlucky in his timing,' says his son, Jimmy, referring to his stints at Stoke City and, in particular, in Manchester. 'That club was at the stage when it was going to go down. It could have been anyone and the outcome would have been the same.' As Joe Royle, himself a future Manchester City manager, puts it, 'Alan was caught up in a very political club at that time.'

The cap. Flat, in Harris Tweed. Placed forlornly on top of the flag of St George that is draped over Alan Ball's coffin. It has been a fixture of his managerial career and now it is a poignant symbol of his premature death at the age of 61. A death that occurs by heart attack while he is fighting a late-night garden fire at his home; a heart that has already been broken by the loss three years earlier of Lesley, the childhood sweetheart to whom he was married for 37 years. She was diagnosed with cancer while daughter Mandy was already fighting an ultimately successful battle against the same wicked disease. It is easy to assume that it has all been too much for Ball to take; ironic when one remembers the warrior-like qualities that were as much of his game on the field as his instinctive touch on the ball.

On a bright spring day in 2007, thousands stand outside Winchester Cathedral, many in the shirts of Ball's old teams, as a roll call of British football's hierarchy make their way inside for a funeral. 'He had a great aura about him; he really was a smashing chap,' says Francis Lee, Ball's former England teammate and his boss at Manchester City. 'A superstar without any ego,' asserts McMenemy. 'You don't get many of them. It wasn't an effort to be nice; he was genuinely nice.' Former international and club colleagues, adversaries and managers are followed into the cathedral by the coffin, topped by that cap. To some it seems an odd choice; the emblem of the more challenging part of Alan Ball's career.

If only they could have found the boots. Those beautiful white boots.

Such flashbacks come thick and fast on a June morning in 2016 that does nothing to dispel Manchester's meteorological reputation. Rain is falling as the doors of the National Football Museum are opened for the launch of an exhibition to honour the team that won the World Cup 50 years earlier. A couple of hours ago, the nation's attention was half a mile away at Manchester Town Hall for the formal announcement of the European Union referendum result – a 'Brexit' outcome that has left half the country believing it can now return to those days when it did indeed rule the world and the other half fearful of ensuing years of hurt.

Yet nostalgia shoves politics to the sidelines as 1966 heroes Sir Bobby Charlton, Roger Hunt and Jimmy Armfield arrive at the museum; joined by Alan Ball's children, Mandy Byrne, Keely Allan and Jimmy Ball, and four grandsons. The family members gather on the plaza outside the glass-fronted building to inspect the bronze-coloured paving plate bearing Ball's likeness, one of 11 laid on the venue's new 'Walk of Fame' in recognition of the players who beat West Germany at Wembley. Other stars of the sport are similarly honoured, from Best and Pelé to Zidane and Messi, but it is the men who played for Sir Alf Ramsey – who, of course, has his own memorial – who are the stars of today's event.

Not that one character would necessarily agree with that. As the Ball family are being pictured and filmed, they are photo-bombed by long-haired Willie Nelson lookalike and renowned sporting artist, 82-year-old Paul Trevillion, the man whose distinctive drawings have been reproduced on the commemorative plates. 'He was the man!' he screeches from under his leather cowboy hat. 'He never stopped running.'

Safely inside, away from the persistent drizzle, the dignitaries are taken off for their own private tour of the exhibition. The Ball family walk respectfully behind the ex-England players, although Keely takes a discreet photo of her two sons with Sir Bobby, and Armfield chats in the lift about being at Alan's wedding to Lesley. He can't fail to recognise 16-year-old Louie, with his red curls, as a direct descendant of his former Blackpool and England teammate.

The exhibits are a delight. The tournament mascot, a lion called World Cup Willie, has his own section, complete with a reproduced magazine advert declaring that 'Bobby Moore Plays Willie Football'. Alongside all the memorabilia and artefacts, the displays relating to the major matches, a graphical timeline of 30 July and various video presentations, there is a wall-mounted glass cabinet devoted to each member of the World Cup-winning team. In Ball's display case is an international cap and the white number seven shirt in which he scored his first England goal in Sweden in 1965. Underneath it is reproduced a quote from the great journalist Hugh McIlvanney: 'His energy observed no natural law. The more he expended, the more he appeared to have.'

Once the tour is over, attention turns to the stage in the museum's entrance hall, in front of which a mixture of England fans and puzzled-looking tourists are standing and waiting. Ball's son and daughters are invited to sit to one side of event host Geoff Shreeves, to whose right are seated Charlton, Hunt and Armfield. After Shreeves has urged the audience to put the 'overnight uncertainty' behind them, he explains that the Walk of Fame inductees have been voted on by the public and drawn by the man who became known to football fans in the 1970s largely for his 'You Are The Ref' illustrations in *Shoot!*, the magazine for which Ball was a columnist for several years.

Invited to the microphone, Trevillion makes proceedings sound like a political rally. 'I saw these men play,' he bellows. 'I was there.' Always the showman – he worked as a stand-up comedian and was even responsible for the famous sock tags worn by Don Revie's Leeds United – he ends up shaking and crying with emotion as he yells his pride at sharing the stage with such illustrious figures; his passion as evident as his skill with a pencil. 'Alan Ball was my best friend in football; he was man of the match in 1966,' he screams, microphone superfluous at this point. He turns towards Jimmy, Keely and Mandy and urges, 'Come on, stand up.' They shift uncomfortably, rising slowly and reluctantly.

Eventually, Jimmy is invited to explain to Shreeves what the 1966 final had meant to his father. 'It passed him by so quickly,' he says. 'But he was immensely proud of his part in it.' Shreeves then tells the audience, 'Alan Ball was the finest after-dinner speaker I ever saw. For 40 minutes, without a note, he portrayed perfectly what [winning the World Cup] meant to people in the squad. By the end, there wasn't a dry eye in the house.'

The event breaks up. Fans disperse to visit the exhibition; the younger Ball family members head off to outscore each other on the museum's interactive penalty shoot-out; and Jimmy chats to various members of the media. The morning has reaffirmed the place Alan Ball continues to occupy in the fabric of his country's football history. Elsewhere, rehearsals are taking place for a play, *Ball of Fire*, that will relate the story of his life to theatre audiences in the north-west.

'In makes me proud but makes me very sad as well,' says Keely. 'It makes me miss him even more.' Yet she has seen her father kept alive in the exhibits; the memories they provoke and the strong feelings they stir. Jimmy concludes, 'I was emotional in a couple of places, but not sad. We are pleased that some people who wouldn't even know who he is will see the exhibition. Young kids might see this and ask their parents, "Who was Alan Ball?" For us as a family, that legacy is something that makes us very proud.'

And that, as Trevillion would undoubtedly concur, is something to shout about.

1

BIG DREAMS

'Even the smallest person can change the course of the future'

– J.R.R. Tolkien, *The Fellowship of the Ring*

TIME, along with town planning, has done its best to brush over the footprints of much of Alan Ball's early life. Farnworth Grammar School, where he spent his time in the classroom dreaming of life as a professional footballer, no longer sits alongside the A6053. The school closed in 1983 and was demolished five years later. On that same stretch of road, which sends residents of Ball's hometown on their way to Bolton two miles to the north, the locals used to be able to drink in the Rose and Crown, the pub run by his father. But, having later become the RAC Club, it stopped pulling in pints in 2010 and began painting toenails instead when a beauty salon moved in. Even the patch of recreation ground where one of England's World Cup winners learned the fundamentals of his trade in endless matches with his mates now bears the sign: No Ball Games.

But just as Ball was a renowned fighter in life, challenging those who thought he was too small to amount to anything in football, so, in death, he has defiantly re-established a presence on the Farnworth landscape. In 2008 a commemorative blue plaque, funded by his former clubs, was placed by Bolton and District Civic Trust on the house where he was born; a semi-detached home in Brookhouse Avenue that used to be owned by his grandparents.

Meanwhile, just beyond the town hall and library, a short walk north-west from where his father's name once sat above the pub door, the words 'Alan Ball House' now appear in large white capital letters on the red bricks of what used to be the Evangelical Baptist Church. Constructed early in the twentieth century, the building had sat unloved and vandalised for several years until developers converted it into a block of twelve apartments. Paul Lister, who was given the blessing of his hero's family for the proposed name, has done Ball's memory proud. As well as retaining the stain-glassed interior dome and renovating the high-arched timber-framed windows that look out to the park across the road, the building also displays an England three-lions shield, a football and, delightfully, a facsimile of a pair of white Hummel football boots. And the fact that it is a Grade 2 listed building means Alan Ball is now officially part of the country's architectural heritage as well as its sporting history.

Alan James Ball arrived into the world the same bundle of red-haired energy that he would remain throughout his 61 years, on 12 May 1945, four days after VE Day had signalled the end of six years of war in Europe. Britain was still in the midst of the kind of collective national celebration that it would not see again until Ball and ten teammates achieved another victory over the Germans, sporting this time, 21 years later.

That football was to be the biggest factor in his life was never in doubt, given that his father was obsessive about the sport. 'All he wanted me to be was a footballer because of his love of the game,' Ball would recall. 'I never met anyone as fanatical about football as my dad.'

A wing-half or inside-forward of limited natural gifts, James Alan Ball, aged only 20 when he became a father, would get no further up the professional ladder than some reserve-team games for Birmingham City and a handful of matches for Southport, Oldham Athletic and Rochdale. Known as Alan − 'senior' being added once his son's renown exceeded his own − his ambition for a top-level career on the field was transferred to his first-born from the moment word of his arrival reached him while on military duty in Germany. 'Within minutes I had decided to make him a great footballer,' Ball senior admitted. 'When I got home and saw his little red head, I knew immediately what I wanted him to be − a perpetual motion player. And everyone seeing him moving all the time because of that red hair.'

Nothing was left to chance. Family members would be contacted before birthdays and Christmas with instructions that presents should be selected with the furtherance of young Alan's sporting education in mind. Football boots were purchased almost as soon as he could walk; later came the Newcastle United shirt he wore proudly while playing with his mates.

'I knew at birthdays and Christmas what Alan was going to get,' recalls his sister Carol, two years younger than her brother. 'I knew it would be a round parcel, or kit or cricket bats. Anything to do with sport. That was the way Alan wanted it. He loved his cricket, he boxed when he was a young lad and he liked swimming. But it was mainly football.'

Few would deviate from the approved gift list. In fact, not many would argue with Alan senior about anything once he had set his mind on a particular course. Even when he first met his future wife and was told her name was Violet Duckworth, he declared, 'What sort of a name is that? You'll never be a Violet to me. You will always be Valerie.' Thus, she was Val for the whole of her married life.

Carol paints a vivid picture of life in the Ball household, where competition was never far from the surface. 'Dad was always doing mini games. Maybe if he had a weekend off it would be, "Right, we are going to race." He even got my mum into it as well. He would make us race up the side street and then he would make a long-jump pit, which I was good at; better than Alan. He didn't like that, our Alan. Dad would laugh at him and say, "Your sister is better than you!" He was very competitive, but we loved it. It wasn't like he forced us into it.'

Ball senior's view of parenting, as explained to Val, was 'a girl for you, a boy for me'. Carol doesn't contradict that entirely, but makes it clear that she never felt neglected by her father. 'He did take an interest in me, especially if I excelled at something. Later on, when I was in senior school, I started to do long jump and running and he turned up at school sports days, which I was thrilled about. He did encourage me. He took me up to Bolton Harriers, and when I took to horse riding he used to come to the stables to watch me ride. But in the early days I was with my mum more than my dad, and Alan was with him all the time.'

Ball spent some of the time while his father was away in the armed forces living in the same house as his uncle Trevor in Bentinck Street, Farnworth. His dad's brother was only six years older than young

Alan and their relationship was more that of brothers than uncle and nephew. 'He used to follow me around,' Trevor recalled. 'He was very young when he started showing promise as a footballer. He never did anything else but kick a ball around and even as a child he was focused.'

While barely more than a toddler, Alan would spend an hour every evening kicking a rolling ball back to his father, a ritual that continued until he was five. It was then that he was taken to the family doctor for a thorough check-up, including tests on his heart, to reassure his father that 'he would respond to anything I asked him to do in training'.

By that time, Ball junior, a pupil at St Peter's Church of England School, was already experiencing his first taste of professional football, taken along to watch his dad play for Southport and plonked on the bench.

The one thing his dad could not control, though, was physiology. Alan junior was a sprite. 'I knew him from when he was about eight,' explains Carl Davenport, a year older than Ball as they grew up in Farnworth. 'I used to go down to a park near us, Doe Hey, where they had posts, and I said, "Come round one morning." We had a goalkeeper and we had Alan on the wing crossing to me. He was useless. I said, "Don't bother coming again." He was only small and he couldn't lift the ball into the middle. We did play together a few more times after that, but he was too small for anyone to think he was going to be any good.'

Ball senior simply accepted that what his son lacked in height and strength would have to be compensated for by heart and skill. The less Alan grew, the harder he was pushed by his dad. He happily suffered deliberate kicks on the shin from his father – 'that is how he learned to stand up to everything in the tough midfield areas' – and was forced to endure hours of heading practice until he could execute this skill without shutting his eyes. 'I remember him heading that ball until his forehead was bleeding slightly,' said his dad, the kind of remark that would alert social services these days, but was indicative of the commitment of both teacher and pupil.

'I remember once Dad tied Alan's leg to a drainpipe,' Carol laughs. 'He couldn't kick the ball very well with his left foot so he was rolling the ball to him and he could only kick with one foot. My mum went out and they had this unholy row. Alan was going, "Mum, I am OK.

I need to kick with my left foot." People must think my dad was so cruel, but Alan loved it. Alan used to run up and down the stairs when we lived in a two-up, two-down. We would be sitting around playing board games and next minute he would get up. They were very steep stairs in those old houses and he would be up and down and it was really annoying. Dad used to tell him to do that because it would strengthen his legs.'

Even paper-rounds were viewed as an opportunity for extra training, Alan being instructed to deliver the newspapers on foot rather than taking the easy option of using his bicycle. 'His dad used to frighten the life out of me,' admits future Blackpool colleague and housemate Hugh Fisher. 'Sometimes, Bally used to say to me after games, "Do you want to come back to Bolton and we will have a night out?" In the car, his dad was always on his case, telling him he had to be better. He looked a hard guy, but Bally always spoke highly of him and he obviously thrived on it. Alan was a very strong character, even from a young age, and could deal with it.'

It would have been easy for the son to rebel against his father. How often does a child push back against the force with which a parent shoves them down a certain career path? Yet where others might have found resistance and resentment, Ball revealed to his father only determination and dedication. 'My mentor, coach, adviser, critic, psychologist, disciplinarian and caring father,' was how Ball came to describe his dad. He took pride in telling the story of his mum getting angry at him for wearing the sole off one half of a new pair of sandals by playing football in them, only for his father to offer easy forgiveness when he discovered it was the shoe he wore on that weaker left foot that he'd damaged through diligent practice.

In a 1999 interview with the BBC, Ball admitted that 'the demands of my father were very, very high'. Yet he continued, 'He was my Svengali. He was quite fantastic in moulding me into what he wanted to be. I think he just failed in being a real top player and he wanted, as a lot of people have said, to live his life through his son. I didn't really have a childhood other than football.' Ball remembered his father explaining to him, 'I always took the big stick to you, but if you had not responded I would have gone another way to get out of you what I could see in your ability.'

Carol confirms, 'They had a fantastic relationship. When Dad was out or at work, Alan used to sit at the window with his ball waiting for him to come home. My dad genuinely believed he would be a top player one day, but he never told Alan. He wouldn't say anything to me because he didn't want Alan to know, but my mum told me later, "Your dad really believed Alan would make it because he committed himself. He didn't want Alan to think he was going to be a top player in case he stopped everything." He obviously had talent, but it didn't come that easily. Once or twice, Alan wanted to go off with the lads and he wasn't really allowed to. But he wasn't right keen on doing that anyway.'

So legendary did that father–son relationship become that it is easy to overlook the role of Ball's mother in creating a stable home environment amid the typical upheaval created by a husband pursuing a career in football management. 'My mum was a very gentle person, complete opposite to my dad,' Carol explains. 'She could be strict, but not very often. She was pretty quiet; a pretty shy person. She would not go out if you got into trouble on the street. You might have a bit of bother with someone, but when you went to see her she would just say, "Well, go out and hit them back." Some other mothers would come out screaming at you, but she would never do that. She was a lady. She did teach us a lot about values in life, about right and wrong. And she always had everything very clean. If you took one thing off at night, it would be there ironed and ready for you the next morning. She always gave us a lot of hugs and was very warm and loving. Alan loved his mum.

'We lived by Dad's rules and my mum went along with that. My dad was a man's man and I hardly ever saw her argue with him. But they were brilliant together. He used to do funny things, like the weekend he had been away on football and he came back on the Monday morning and he'd brought her these crystal glasses. "There you are, Val," he said. "Some lovely wine glasses." She said, "I know where you got them from. You get them with so much petrol down the road." That was my dad, but she used to laugh at it. Dad used to take the mickey out of my mum and she gave him as much back, but it was all in fun. They were great parents. My dad was fantastic to be with. When he was out of his football crowd and it was just the four of us in the house he was really funny. We used to really belly laugh at him. I loved that part of him. He wouldn't act like that outside; he was quite a hard man out of the house. But he had us all laughing.'

Far from being driven to shy away from football, Ball junior couldn't get enough of it. When the family went on holiday to Spain, he was immediately arranging matches between their hotel and the neighbouring ones, eagerly pinning team sheets up on the notice board. Forced sometimes to look after his younger sister, he even got her involved in his games of football. 'I am very sporty anyhow,' says Carol, 'but I was usually the goalpost. I used to have to stand there with one of my friends. I used to join in when I could, but when he didn't need me to make a side up I had to go.

'He was always the best kid in the gang. But when we used to pick sides he always picked the poorest players. He would even sometimes have me. Usually, when you pick sides you want the best players, so I asked him about it years later and he said, "Dad always said to play against the best. That is how you will learn."'

Once Ball senior had moved the family to Oswestry for a three-year stint as player-manager, which he coupled with running the King's Head pub, his son's immersion in football became even deeper. Even though only nine years old, young Alan was allowed to change and train with the team and even – something unthinkable in modern times for any number of reasons – share the communal bath with them.

It was a welcome distraction, given that he went through an understandably unsettling period in the early days of his residency in the town on the Welsh border. 'It was the only time it was difficult having a dad who kept changing jobs,' Carol recalls. 'When we went to Oswestry we had this broad northern accent and they didn't take to us; they thought we were foreigners. In those days, people didn't go very far away from home and we thought we were in a foreign country because of the way they spoke. We weren't very happy at first and didn't have many friends. I remember one incident when Alan was in the playground playing football and he got in a fight with a boy because he was just too good for them. A teacher grabbed Alan by the jersey and picked him up and threw him into the school. I didn't know why he had done that because both boys were to blame. Anyway, the whistle went and we were back in class and the next minute the door opened and Alan walked in and he said, "Come on, Carol, we are going home," and we walked out. When I told my dad why were home, he marched up to the school and told them that we felt we were being picked on because of our accent. But as time went on we made friends and fitted in quite well and our accents changed. When we went back to Lancashire, people said, "Don't you speak funny?"'

Natural brightness, rather than any great resolve in the classroom, saw Ball pass his 11-plus examination and take up a place at Oswestry Boys High School. At a grammar school like this the teachers were unimpressed with a pupil who had thoughts of nothing but football. According to school friend John Foster, 'The teachers would say to us, "What are you going to do when you leave school?" and, of course, you hadn't got a clue really so you'd say something that might impress them. But Alan would say, "I'm going to be a professional footballer and I'm going to play for England," and it was – whack! – "set your sights on something realistic, lad."'

Foster explained after his friend's death that 'Alan was something special because you just couldn't get the ball off him. Although there were 30 chasing him, the ball was stuck to his foot.' But despite his obvious ability and a general athletic prowess that saw him running in cross-country events for his school and swimming for Shropshire, his lack of stature meant that a place in the school football team was not immediately forthcoming. He even had a go at boxing, explaining that 'it meant I could look after myself' and somehow helped my footwork on the football pitch'. His ring coach, Jock Shaw, told his father that he displayed enough natural timing and talent to have a promising future.

Meanwhile, membership of the Oswestry Parish Church Choir at least gave Ball the opportunity to turn out for their football team. 'We were playing one day,' said Foster, 'and Alan's dad came to watch him. Young Alan said to me, "Dad's going to give me sixpence for every goal I score." He scored fifteen goals, which in old money was seven and six, and his dad gave him three half-crowns.'

His school team could not resist for much longer. Future Blackpool teammate Glyn James, another Oswestry pupil, recalls, 'We had a sixth form there so we had boys up to 18 in the team. I got in there in the third year, but Bally got in during the second year. He was streets ahead of anybody there. His size didn't really make a lot of difference in my view. He might not have been very tall, but he was the perfect build and he could put himself about. I don't mean he would go over the top on anybody, but nobody would bully him on the pitch. He was the best I ever played with.'

As teenage years approached, Ball moved back to Farnworth after his paternal grandfather was taken seriously ill with emphysema, which would soon bring about his death. Ball senior took over the running of the Rose and Crown pub and then became manager of Ashton United in the Lancashire Combination, while his son found his talents recognised at school by sports master John Dickinson and was appointed captain of Farnworth Grammar. 'At 14 years old, Alan scored every goal in a 6–0 win for the school,' Dickinson would recall. 'I knew he was something special.'

There were further disappointments looming, however. Ball's trial for Lancashire Schoolboys in Southport lasted only 15 minutes before he was substituted, his size again creating a bad first impression. Then there was rejection by Wolverhampton Wanderers, who had invited him to play for one of their junior sides on Saturday mornings on the recommendation of a scout, George Noakes.

Risking the wrath of Farnworth Grammar by skipping school matches to wear the shirt of the team that had won three League three times in the previous decade, Ball recalled that 'everything about [Wolves] produced a tingle of excitement'. During school holidays he spent every day training at Molineux, staying in a boarding house run by the mother of England wing-half Eddie Clamp. Feeling he was holding his own among experienced players and enjoying being recognised by the senior figures at the club, Ball said that 'there weren't enough hours in the day for me. I never wanted it to get dark'. Yet when a heartbreaking letter arrived, explaining that Wolves would not be inviting him back, size and strength were once more cited as the decisive factors.

Ball senior, who was still insisting that two hours of ball work needed to be completed every night before homework, warned his son as he entered his final year of school that perhaps he ought to focus on passing his GCE O-level exams. Yet at the same time he continued to plot Alan's path into football, reminding him of the success of smaller men such as Blackburn Rovers and England winger Bryan Douglas and Bolton Wanderers' Dennis Stevens, both among Alan's own favourite players.

And he went one better than comforting words. He put his belief in his son on the line by selecting him to play for Ashton United, even though he was only 15 years, three months and 13 days old when he made his debut, becoming the youngest player to appear for the club. His first match was a 3–1 victory in the Lancashire Combination Cup at Glossop, where two of the goals were scored by forward Alf Arrowsmith, who would go on to win a League Championship medal with Liverpool. Ball played seven games for his dad's team, scoring one goal – against Northern Nomads – and concluding his stint with defeat against Cheshire League team Mossley in the final of the Manchester Intermediate Cup. A boy among men, his most vivid memory was 'a big left-back playing for Hyde United trying to kick me over the stand'. And he added, 'I learned plenty about the intensity of professional football even if my fellow teammates were bricklayers, electricians or van drivers.' The postscript to Ball's Ashton United career was the club being fined by the Football Association for irregular payments, including the few shillings a week Alan picked up in spite of his schoolboy status.

Throughout that same 1960–61 season, Ball had been invited to train on Tuesday and Thursday evenings as an amateur at his local club, Bolton Wanderers, along with future Professional Footballers' Association chairman and chief executive Gordon Taylor and Coventry City midfielder Ernie Machin. Once more, it would be stretching things to say that he left a mark on too many people. 'I was 17 and was there as a full-time apprentice,' recalls boyhood friend Davenport, 'but, funnily enough, I can't remember him being there. I was in Ireland on holiday with him not long before he died and he said, "Can you remember playing in the A team at The Cliff against [Manchester] United?" I said that I could and he said, "I played that day and you scored a hat-trick." But I just couldn't remember him.'

Future England teammate Francis Lee, an apprentice at the club, knew Ball from games against him in the Bolton Boys Federation. 'He was always a good player,' he remembers, 'but always very small. He was in and out of the colts and B teams.'

Lee describes the man who would decide Ball's fate, manager Bill Ridding, as 'a pain in the arse who treated us like shit'. And when Ball – having flunked his school exams after he continued to spend evenings kicking a football rather than revising – sought out Ridding to discover whether he was to be offered an apprenticeship, he was offered the opinion that the only apprenticeship to which he was suited was 'as a jockey'.

Again, size was everything. Again, the ability that he felt had made him the best player in every team he played for was considered irrelevant. And again, Ball senior asked his son if he remained committed to football and would not rather get a proper job instead. When the promise came back, 'I'm going to play for England before I am 20,' the search began for another club.

Letters were sent requesting trials and Ball's father spoke to Blackpool manager Ron Suart. Accounts differ on whether a simple misunderstanding or some economy with the facts led Suart to believe he was watching a 16-year-old called Alan James, as Ball had been christened according to the family tradition of every first-born male bearing the name James. The youngster was quickly rumbled, but needed only one half of a trial match to persuade Blackpool to offer him an apprenticeship. 'You've been handed a great chance,' his dad told him. 'Make sure the only thing they can do is to give you a professional contract. That takes hard work. It takes sacrifice.'

That aspect held little fear for Ball. It was enough for him that, at last, potential on the field had been considered more important than potential for physical growth. The fact that he would never rise above 5ft 6in didn't matter. Hard work, he was convinced, would overcome. Alan Ball, just as he had always dreamed, was on the way to becoming a professional footballer.

2

LOVE ME DO

'Almost everything that is great has been done by youth'

– Benjamin Disraeli

THE 16-year-old apprentice with the shock of red hair received the ball, glanced to his right and slipped it diagonally behind the opposition left-back. It was, thought Alan Ball as he released the pass, weighted perfectly for the most illustrious player in the history of Blackpool Football Club, perhaps the whole of English football, to run on to. Stanley Matthews stood where he was on the training ground, watched the ball dribble out of play and pointed to the patch of grass in front of him.

'When you play the ball to me, play it to my feet,' Matthews barked at a teammate 30 years his junior.

'When I play it front of you, get your fucking feet moving and get there,' Ball fired back. Never mind that the sport's pecking order meant that he was responsible for keeping Matthews's hand-made leather boots clean, Ball felt those shoes should have been moving – and wasn't afraid to say so.

'You do not talk to me like that,' Matthews grumbled, while manager Ron Suart didn't hesitate in pointing out the error of the young man's ways. Yet other teammates couldn't help but be impressed by the audacity of the lad who had appeared in their midst only a few weeks earlier. 'Bally seemed to have no respect for Stan,' says goalkeeper Tony Waiters, 'He certainly wasn't afraid of him. He was such a confident person that he didn't let anyone overawe him.'

Ball's antipathy towards Matthews never subsided. 'He might have been one of the greatest footballers of all time, but I hated him,' he wrote more than a decade later. 'Never at any time did he give me one word of encouragement that a senior player usually gives young lads.

Matthews didn't bother me, although he could have crushed someone with a different personality. I've never been overawed or nervous.'

Club captain Jimmy Armfield can attest to that. 'Alan didn't care about reputations,' he states. 'He would have a go at anybody. No one spoke to the great Stanley Matthews like that. But that passion made him into what he was.'

'The thing with Bally,' ventures Blackpool defender Barrie Martin, 'was that he was a terrible loser. I have known him to sit and cry in the dressing room when we lost. But with it he was so confident, irrepress-ible. I remember the first time my wife met him. Alan was just coming out of Bloomfield Road and he shouted, "Hiya, Baz," She said, "Who was that little squirt?"'

Hugh Fisher, who would begin his own apprenticeship at the club a few months after Ball, recalls, 'He was always bubbly and such a confi-dent lad. We youngsters were all a bit quiet, a bit reserved. We would look and learn and weren't too sure what was going on. Bally was the one shouting from the rooftops that he would play for England.'

Ball would describe himself as 'never the nicest person around a football club', adding, 'I could never tolerate being second best.' He was, he said, 'subservient and respectful to all my elders off the field' but he confessed that 'my attitude changed completely once I stepped on to a football pitch'. Martin continues, 'He argued with everyone and he tried it on with me during a practice match at Squires Gate. He kept having a go and in the end he put his studs down the back of my leg. I turned round and had a go back and shoved him. But you understood that was him and you made friends with him.'

Defender Glyn James has another memory of Ball's competitive fire. 'When we played five-a-side, Tony Waiters loved to play out of goal. He was a big carthorse and Bally used to take the mick out of him. He would show him the ball and drag it away and Tony would be running around in circles. We had a great laugh at things like that.'

It was easy to forgive someone so driven to do well, both for himself and for his team. 'He had such a will to win,' according to Fisher. 'He spoke in the dressing room, which was unusual for one so early in his career around senior pros. He used to throw his boots about and wasn't afraid to have a go at somebody.'

Martin recalls something else that caught people's attention, as it would throughout his life. 'We used to call him "The Mouse",' he relates, 'because he didn't talk, he squeaked.'

But it was not just Ball's vocal characteristics and his willingness to speak out that made a mark. His commitment to self-improvement had not gone unnoticed, especially to people such as Martin, who recalls that 'no one could have believed he was going to be such a good player'. Waiters explains, 'I would stay for extra training in the afternoon, and so would Alan. One of the things he worked on was his speed because he was not particularly quick. He was quick in his head, but not physically quick. Bloomfield Road had one of those cinder tracks around the field and we would put on the old spiked running shoes and spend 45 minutes or so just working on fitness over 10 or 15 yards. He trained himself to become faster.'

Fellow midfielder Graham Oates remembers the galvanising effect Ball could have on the most mundane of training sessions. 'His enthusiasm was unbelievable and his stamina was incredible,' he recalls. 'Life was never dull with Bally around and he was totally immersed in football. He made your day. He could lift you because sometimes you didn't feel like it, but you did it because Bally did.'

And, of course, his talent was evident to all, particularly to Suart. Adopting the shin-kicking methods of Ball senior, the manager assigned Fisher to apply the next painful stage of his development. 'You had to try to get close to him,' Fisher explains. 'In training, Ron used to put me against Bally and tell me to kick him. I used to follow him in practice matches trying to have a dig. If I did catch him, Ron would never give a foul. He said it was part of Bally's education.'

Fisher admits that it was not often that his friend had to worry about ending up with bruises. He had usually gathered the ball, distributed it and moved on before the assault arrived. 'What a fantastic player. He was a great believer that two touches was too many. He was a good passer of the ball, he could see people, his first touch was usually excellent and his second was invariably a good pass. He very rarely gave the ball away.'

Ball incorrectly related in his autobiographies and after-dinner speeches that it was injury to Matthews that allowed him to make his first appearance for Blackpool. In fact, the man who would become football's first knight left the club ten months before Ball's debut, returning to Stoke City. But it was two days after Matthews played his final game for Blackpool, aged 46, that Ball began capturing the attention of Seasiders fans. On 9 October, he scored the final Blackpool goal in a 6–3 win against Chester in the first round of the FA Youth Cup. When Ball's team knocked out Preston North End the following month, the *Blackpool Gazette* highlighted his 'insatiable appetite for work' and described him as 'a veritable human dynamo with the confidence and skill to draw and beat a man and promising flair for positional play'.

But by the time the 1962–63 season approached, there was little to suggest that Ball, who had signed as a full-time professional on his 17th birthday – initially earning £7 per week, rising to £15 as a first-teamer – had anything more to look forward to than a run in the Blackpool A team, the club's third eleven. As the August editions of the local paper rolled off the presses with their pictures of crowded beaches, advertisements urging dancers to join Reginald Dixon at the Blackpool Tower and reports of West Indian cricketer Rohan Kanhai racking up record scores for Blackpool in the Northern League, Ball was absent from any discussion of the prospects for Suart's team. On 9 August, reporter Don Creedy warned, 'With the playing strength hardly at comforting level, Blackpool Football Club will no doubt be hoping to escape the crop of injuries which the rush of fixtures at the start of the season usually brings.' But as the reporter ran through possible options should those fears be realised, Ball never merited a mention.

Creedy's eyes were opened a couple of days later, however, when Ball played for the first team in a 1–1 draw against Bury in a friendly, the report of which carried the headline, '17-year-old does well.' Creedy wrote:

> He is 17 years old, rather slightly built but with a man-sized heart. He still has a lot to learn, but if he is willing to learn it he will surely establish himself in Blackpool's first team one day. His name is Alan Ball and in last night's practice match with Bury at Bloomfield Road he looked surprisingly at ease in first-team company.
>
> There were times when he clung to the ball a fraction too long. Put this down to his unquenchable enthusiasm to be in the game at every

opportunity. Some of his centres and crosses should have been made better use of by his colleagues, while one of his shots at goal was knocked out by goalkeeper Harker, who knew little about the save.

Blackpool's big sporting event in the week leading up to the start of the Football League season was local heavyweight Brian London's victory over American Howard King. Rain waterlogged the outdoor ring in Stanley Park and forced both men to fight bare-footed in sawdust thrown down in an attempt to make things less treacherous. Observers likened the whole occasion to a return to the days of bare-knuckle boxing.

Two days after that throwback event, Blackpool's football team took a bold, decisive step into the future after Steve 'Mandy' Hill, the man who had been wearing the number seven shirt since the departure of Matthews, suffered what was simply described as a 'ligament injury' in training. 'Blackpool Debut for Boy Winger,' was the *Gazette* headline above news that Ball, who had never even played in the Central League for the reserves, had been promoted to make his debut in the season opener at Liverpool. Creedy called it a 'spectacular selection'.

Ball couldn't wait to share news of his elevation, as Carl Davenport recalls. 'When he left Bolton and went to Blackpool, I signed to Preston. We used to catch the same train at Bolton every morning and I would get off at Preston. I'd had a few first-team games and was playing in the reserves regularly and one morning he said, "I wish I was you. You have got it made." On this particular day, coming back from Blackpool, he is hanging out of the window at Preston station shouting at me, "I'm in the first team!"'

In August 1962 Liverpool was poised to rival Manchester as the cultural capital of the north, perhaps the country. A group of four lads, going by the name of The Beatles, were setting pulses racing at the Cavern Club and were about to record their first single, 'Love Me Do'. They would be joined at the top of the charts by local acts such as Gerry and The Pacemakers and Cilla Black, while comedians Ken Dodd and Jimmy Tarbuck were becoming staples of television's light entertainment schedules. In football, Everton were embarking on a season that would see them win the First Division title, while Liverpool, reinvigorated by the growling charisma of manager Bill Shankly, were back in the top flight after an eight-season absence and getting ready to accumulate all manner of trophies. Little did Alan Ball know that he would become one of the city's pivotal characters in a few years' time. For now, it was enough that – on the same day that The Beatles dropped drummer Pete Best from their line-up in favour of Ringo Starr – he had been named as an unknown teenager to do battle in front of the Kop.

Wearing a new suit, bought by his mum at Burton's, Ball duly reported for duty two days later. His dad, kept away from the game by his commitments as manager at Nantwich Town in the Cheshire League, had sent him off with the instruction to 'go out there and do your job', just another worker clocking on for a regular day in the factory. A 51,000 crowd, however, would ensure that this was a some-what more nerve-racking first day than that experienced by most employees.

Not that anyone would have known it from the way Ball rose to the occasion. 'Playing in front of big crowds was a stimulus for him,' says Oates, while Ball would write of the atmosphere on his Anfield debut, 'I wasn't overawed or even impressed by it at all. I was determined, as usual, to show whoever was watching that Alan Ball was as good as any other player on the park, and better than most.' The comment demonstrates both the chip on the shoulder he carried around in the early stages of his career, and the habit he quickly developed of refer-ring to himself in the third person – a trait that became a deliberate strategy when he became a manager delivering team talks.

Ball used to joke in his after-dinner routine that, as he'd stood in the tunnel before the game, Liverpool full-back and future manager Ronnie Moran handed him a piece of paper that read, 'Evening Menu – Liverpool Royal Infirmary.' More exaggeration, no doubt, but indicative of the false expectation among the opposition that Ball would be swallowed up by the occasion. 'He played well,' Martin remembers. 'Moran was a good player, but Alan gave him a bit of a chasing.' Ball proved he was not going to be shoved around by getting tangled up early on with local hero Ian St John. Then he went on to play his part in a 2–1 Blackpool victory – a 'smash and grab win', as the *Blackpool Gazette* described it. This time, Creedy reported:

> Manager Ronnie Suart was right in predicting that Ball would not be overawed by the electrifying atmosphere. The searing pace was too much for him at times, but there was no lack of effort and he showed some wonderful touches. He well merited his place.

'This is for me' was Ball's recurring thought during an afternoon that saw goals by Ray Parry and Ray Charnley earn his team both points. 'You could see then how good he was going to be,' says Waiters. 'To make your debut at 17, to go out and play well at Anfield with a sell-out crowd, you could see he was something special.'

Returning home in a daze of euphoria, he told his dad, 'You should have seen me today. I told you I would make it.' Alan Ball senior, the man who had striven for 17 years to ensure that his son fulfilled all the ambitions he had been unable to achieve for himself, was not going to risk, even for a moment, that Ball saw this as anything other than small step along the way.

'Made it, son?' he sneered. 'Don't come in this house telling me you have made a footballer until you have played about 15 games and every time you put your shirt on everyone knows you are going to be good enough for Blackpool Football Club. Don't tell me you have made a footballer until you can go into work every day and your manager and your teammates know exactly what they are going to get from Alan Ball. There's no highs and lows in your performance; they are not scratching their heads wondering what they are going to get from you today. Everyone can trust what they are going to get from you. Until then, don't come in telling me you have made a footballer.'

Ball remembered that 'the man I loved most in all my life had absolutely slaughtered me'.

Two days later, he made his home debut in a 1–0 win against the League champions, Ipswich Town, who had John Compton opposing Ball at left-back. Creedy, who had gone from neophyte to expert on the subject of Alan Ball in a matter of days, was impressed once more:

He faced one of the best full-backs in the game, but he tormented him all the time. That I expected, knowing this little red-haired terrier. What one did not expect was to watch him taking the ball up to his full-back, swerving past him, taking it inside; playing, in brief, as a good wing forward should play, and in this unfamiliar position – for essentially he is an inside forward – showing that he is something a lot more than one of those bish-bash boys.

'Bally had everything,' says James. 'He would get the ball and he was always in space. It always looked as though the person marking him was having a bad game. He always found space, which is probably the hardest thing to do. If you were looking for a get-out he was always there. He made those playing against him look like bad players.' Oates pays a similar tribute by noting, 'Even if he was marked he could lay it off and play a one-two. He took over matches.'

As The Beatles put it while recording that first single, Blackpool had indeed found 'someone to love, somebody new'.

The man who had given Ball his big break, Ron Suart, had become Blackpool manager in 1958, accepting the thankless task of following a club legend in Joe Smith. Failing health had brought to an end Smith's 23-year reign, during which – led by Matthews – Blackpool had become one of the most exciting teams in the country. But the regular goal-scoring of Charnley could not disguise the decline as the last few remaining members of the 1953 FA Cup-winning unit were phased out and, by the early 1960s, relegation battles had replaced cup campaigns as the staple of a typical Blackpool season. The abolition of the maximum wage in 1961 made it even tougher for a small provincial team with shrinking attendances in a town which, by its nature as a tourist resort, had a more transient population and fluctuating fan base than many clubs.

'During the illuminations we would get 20-odd thousand,' recalls James, a one-club man who has remained in Blackpool throughout his life. 'But as soon as the illuminations had finished we dropped back to 12 to 15. Manchester United were getting 40 or 50 thousand. It was hard to compete.'

As promising as his early games were, Ball was powerless to effect any kind of instant reformation. A run of four matches in the first team ended with a 5–2 defeat at Ipswich Town and, although he was soon back for another loss at Nottingham Forest, that was it for the season. 'You've got a great future but we don't want to rush you,' Suart told him. 'Too many games will be bad for your development. You're still growing.'

Ball might have lost his first-team place by the time 'Love Me Do' was released in October, but it was obvious to all that he had a First Division future. The jibes about becoming a jockey could be consigned to his repertoire of anecdotes.

In the meantime, the elevated status of Ball, who was splitting his nights between home in Farnworth and a Blackpool boarding house run by a landlady called Mrs Mawson, offered a practical benefit for his housemates. 'We were in digs together with Emlyn Hughes,' says Glaswegian Fisher, who must be the only Scot in the game to have begun his career living with two future England captains. 'Bally was the first one to break into the first team, which meant he was the first to have a car. It was a big, long Ford Zephyr. You could just see his eyes over the steering wheel. Wherever he went, we went.'

Ball always insisted that he rarely went out during his formative years at Blackpool, preferring early nights to save his body for the exertions of training. 'In a place like Blackpool there is always someone asking you to have a drink or a night out,' he explained. 'I believe that to get to the top in football you have to make sacrifices. For me, smoking and drinking are out. If I come in at half past ten, Dad says, "What time is this to come in?" He keeps a grip on me. I like staying in. We talk soccer, watch television, play chess or play records.'

According to Martin, 'Alan would have a night out occasionally, but he wasn't a big player on the night scene. But of course we didn't get a lot of money in those days to keep going out.'

Competition was at the heart of everything Ball did, which, says Oates, included placing a bet whenever he could. 'He was a big gambler and would bet on anything. If we went bowling he would have to run a book on it. But that just showed the confidence he had. It was, "Right, that is going to win. I'm a going to bet on it."'

But even gambling was a mere distraction to fill time between matches and training. Armfield says that 'he had nothing else in his life; only to be a footballer', while Hughes recalled that even car journeys were more educational than recreational. 'We all used to look up to Alan,' he recorded in his autobiography. 'He talked football incessantly. I would hang on every word Bally said. He was always keen to improve his game and in the afternoon we would be back at Bloomfield Road, heading, turning, sprinting.'

The Ball family had been keen to ensure that young Alan found himself a stable domestic environment in Blackpool, a home away from home that would offer him comfort and security rather than driving him out of the house to find trouble in the fleshpots of a seaside town. Mrs Mawson offered exactly that. 'He was well looked after,' says sister Carol. 'My mum asked Dad to take her to meet the woman he stayed with. She was a lovely little old lady and she loved Alan. Mum did miss him, though, and Dad used to say, "Don't be so soft, woman." He did used to nip home a lot as well because he had met Lesley by then and he missed her.'

Alan also had a new entertainment system he wanted to make use of. 'He loved his music,' Carol continues. 'He loved Trini Lopez and then of course he liked The Beatles. I remember the first record he ever sent to Lesley was a Trini Lopez song. With his first signing-on fee at Blackpool he bought a record player; an old-fashioned cabinet one. It cost £50, which was a lot of money then.'

Meanwhile, back on the training ground, the young Hughes, who would relish the nickname 'Crazy Horse' during a career most notable for future achievements at Liverpool, quickly learned a valuable lesson about commitment. When the ball ran loose during a practice match, he challenged Ball, who was two years his senior, and caught him late on the ankle. 'He went down in agony,' Hughes remembered. Suart and trainer Wilf Dixon raced on to the field, fussing over their future star. 'What the hell do you do things like that for?' spluttered Dixon in the direction of Hughes. 'You don't do things like that in practice matches, especially to players like him.'

A few minutes later, the same situation presented itself. Hughes, who 'felt like a criminal' backed off on this occasion, conceding possession. Ball raced after him at the next break in play. 'Don't you ever do that again, whoever you're playing against,' he scolded. 'If you pull away like that then there's nothing in football for you.'

Ball, of course, was still learning the game himself, notably from Pat Quinn, a Scotland midfielder who spent one season at the club after a transfer from Motherwell. Waiters recalls that 'Pat was similar to Bally in that he controlled the middle of the field and he helped him learn his trade', while Ball said that Quinn possessed 'the brain of a fox'. He explained, 'He taught me what he called "the yard" on the pitch; change your body, change the picture, change your angle and open your body' – all vital lessons as Ball progressed towards his status as arguably the best one-touch passer of his generation.

And there were other teachers. Ray Parry took the opportunity of a car journey to warn Ball not to let his youthful confidence spill over into selfishness, while Bruce Crawford chipped in with, 'You can't win a football match on your own.' Meanwhile, Ball would be glowing in his praise for Bobby Finan, a Blackpool goal-scoring legend who had joined the coaching staff and under whose influence he 'grew up as a footballer'.

Playing in 27 Central League games, the majority of them in his preferred inside-right position, Ball scored eight goals, while the first team were finishing 1962–63 in 13th place in the First Division. Inevitably, there were times when his failure to break back into the senior team depressed him. 'If things go on like this even a little longer, I'll have to pack up the game,' he told his father when his mood was at its darkest.

Impressive again in the build-up to the following campaign, and confident that he was ready to grab his chance on a permanent basis, Ball was re-introduced to the senior side for the seventh game of the 1963–64 season. This time his contribution to a 1–0 win against Manchester United was enough to convince Suart to give him the number eight shirt for the next three years. 'He was a good player,' says Armfield, placing an emphasis on the adjective in order to imply a superlative. 'His work-rate and energy were very high. He was demanding of others, short-tempered and passionate and believed that everybody should be the same. He would do things that would annoy me when I was captain. On one occasion, he sat on the ball in the middle of the field when we were winning 4–0. I had a go at him, but that was him. It is about the blend. I don't think you can cope with eleven of them like that. They would drive you barmy.'

Oates adds, 'He did cause problems. If the game was going nicely and you were winning 2–0, he would want to go on and win 5–0, bang, bang, bang, no stopping. He would wind somebody up on the other side and it could become a bit of a battle. If you are a seasoned pro, at 2–0 up you just settle down and make sure you don't do anything silly to let them back in the game. But you couldn't calm him down.'

James has a similar memory. 'I remember we played Leeds on the Saturday and again at Blackpool on Monday night,' he explains. 'Bally dribbled around some people and sat on the ball. Jack Charlton and Norman Hunter were storming back at a hundred miles an hour and as they got back he back-heeled it into the net. You have got to have some confidence to do that. If he had got caught he would never have lived it down.'

Hunter has his own painful recollection of his initial encounter with a future England colleague. 'He was playing for Blackpool as a young-ster and Don Revie said to me, "Pick up this lad Ball." I said, "Gaffer, it's Blackpool. I don't need to pick him up." He said, "Pick him up." I was a little bit annoyed and the first pass Bally got I hit him a bit high and he bounced up like a rubber ball. That little fella absolutely destroyed me. He was up and down, running all over the place.'

Given a free role by Suart – 'a lovely man who encouraged me to enjoy my football' – Ball finished as top scorer with 13 League goals as Blackpool struggled to 18th position in his first full season in the side. It was a similar gloomy story a season later (11 League goals for Ball, 17th place in the First Division) and in 1965–66 (16 goals, 13th position). And in three seasons as a Blackpool first-teamer, he would fail to win a single FA Cup tie. 'There were a lot of good, experienced players there,' says Fisher, 'but whether it was the mix of young play-ers coming in and experienced ones just going over the top, we struggled.'

Waiters, capped five times by England in the build-up to the 1966 World Cup, adds, 'We didn't have good enough players. Jimmy Armfield was fantastic and Ray Charnley was a very good striker, but overall the standard wasn't good enough.' Having gone on to manage Plymouth Argyle before becoming a successful coach in the North

American Soccer League, Waiters concludes, 'It helped my coaching, but it didn't necessarily help my playing career. I became an expert in fighting relegation.'

Suart, meanwhile, did not necessarily possess the personality best suited to a dog fight. 'He was a nice guy,' says Oates, 'He was quite knowledgeable, but sometimes he was a little bit soft. You never saw Ronnie lose his temper. He was a gentleman. Probably he wasn't hard enough.'

Regardless of his team's struggles, Ball was forcing himself into the headlines more frequently, for better or worse. In the days when players almost had to commit grievous bodily harm to earn a booking, Ball was cautioned twice in the opening few weeks of the 1964–65 season. Having been sent off for the first time aged 12 for arguing back to a referee in Oswestry, he was becoming familiar enough to opponents that they recognised he could be easily wound up, incited to say or do something in retaliation that would bring him to the referee's attention.

'That was a side of the game I had to learn about, and I'm afraid I got into some trouble,' Ball recalled later in his career. When he was cautioned again on 24 October in a 3–0 defeat at Birmingham City, the *Daily Mirror* reported that 'the third booking of the season threatens the international career of the man they call England's Denis Law', although Suart complained that Ball's opponents were trying to 'knock the football out of him by hacking and kicking'. Ironically, it was Law with whom Ball was at the centre of another controversial incident when Manchester United visited Bloomfield Road three weeks later. Ball, dishing out the kind of verbal assault he was used to receiving himself, recalled telling Law, 'You're finished, you're old, step aside,' as he ran past him. He claimed that Law had then gone into a tackle late when the ball was next between them. In the ensuing fracas, heated words were exchanged and referee Peter Rhodes sent off Law when he believed that some of those expletives were directed at him.

'Alan was very fiery,' says Martin. 'You target that, especially defenders. You play against certain players and you think you can wind them up. I used to do the same with Francis Lee at Bolton, saying to his teammates, "How do you play with this fella?" Bally could do it too.

Denis Law getting sent off at Bloomfield Road was Bally's fault. He was niggling at him and the next thing Denis is marching off.'

A week later, Ball achieved a domestic landmark by scoring his first Football League hat-trick in a 3–3 draw at Fulham, but even though it was described by one reporter as 'a powerhouse performance', his temperament ensured again that the day was not all joy and laughter. Alan Mullery, who played against Ball for Fulham and Tottenham, recalls, 'He was the master at winding people up. He could start a fight in a phone box.' On this occasion, Ball refused to sign autographs for Fulham supporters after the game. Displaying an immaturity that was not present in his play, he admitted that he was 'still feeling cut up about the fact that before I scored that hat-trick, I was considered a nobody' by the Craven Cottage crowd.

Of greater immediate concern was the further booking he collected for throwing the ball away in a show of dissent. As a result of that caution he found himself up before the FA disciplinary commission and received a 14-day ban.[1] In the *Daily Mirror*, Ken Jones described it as 'a crisis point in a career already punctuated by controversy' and warned that Ball's 'bursts of temper could destroy him'.

Ball addressed his concerns about his own record after a defeat at Tottenham Hotspur, by which time he had further added to his tally of cautions. 'I've been booked five times this season,' he sighed. 'I just can't afford to get into more trouble. Opponents realise this and I keep copping it. But the referee [Tommy Dawes] helped me today. I was beginning to get upset after a few fouls against me when he said, "Just carry on playing. I'll look after you."'

Even celebrity magazine *Titbits* ran an article focused mostly on Ball's disciplinary problems, while support came in the unlikely form of *Daily Express* thunderer Desmond Hackett. At the start of

1 Such was Ball's reputation at the time that he came to remember things as being far worse than they actually were. In his 2004 autobiography, he wrote about being sent off in the matches against both Manchester United and Fulham, when in fact he had only one booking to show for the two encounters. Mind you, he also recalled the Fulham game being a day after President Kennedy's assassination in 1963 rather than a full year later, so the minutiae of his career were clearly never his specialist subject.

the 1965–66 season he wrote a piece that began with, 'Ball's accent is as Lancashire as Blackpool Tower and hits a pitch that makes you wonder why the lad is already wearing long pants. But put him in a pair of short soccer pants and you have a very adult player.' Hackett defended Ball by suggesting that 'the red hair pinpoints him' and made it easier for any misdemeanour to be picked up by the referee. Nonsense, of course, but at least someone was speaking up for him.

All the talk of Ball's temperament could not be dismissed as mere fodder for those looking to fill their columns. There was an underlying significance to such debate. England players in the 1960s were held to high standards of on-field behaviour by the media and the blazer-wearing committee men of the Football Association. What Ball needed was an England manager who would not be influenced by such chatter. Fortunately, as would be proved famously in 1966, he had one in Alf Ramsey, who was reported to have had Ball watched twice as early as October 1963.

Invited to join the England Under-23 tour to Hungary, Israel and Turkey in the summer of 1964, Ball's elation at his squad selection was, typically, centred largely upon his father. 'Dad didn't achieve any international recognition,' he said. 'But even if he had, I don't think he'd have been so happy about it as he is about this.' Yet excitement turned to frustration as he watched the games without getting on the field. Squad member Geoff Hurst recalls, 'He was left out of the final game and he was so incensed. I was having a drink with him and Nobby [Stiles], who was always his roommate, and he threw his boots against the bedroom wall in disgust and anger.'

Ball's elevation to the Under-23s' starting eleven finally came in a 3–2 win against Wales in Wrexham the following November, when he was one of eight new caps. The occasion marked his first encounter with Ramsey, and from the moment that the England manager took the trouble to say 'thank you for coming' Ball was smitten. 'I don't think there was ever a sour moment in our relationship from that day onwards,' he recorded. Three weeks later, he scored his first goal for the team in a 5–0 victory over Romania at Highfield Road, Coventry, where the appeal of Young England, as they were called, was proved by a crowd of more than 27,000.

Ball played in all six England Under-23 games during 1965, but it was the three additional times he wore the England shirt during the spring of that year that mattered most to him; his first appearances for the senior national team.

The knowledge that he was getting closer to a full cap had been deepened by his selection for Ramsey's Football League team against the Scottish League at Hampden Park in March, a game notable for Ramsey picking the Charlton brothers together for the first time. Weeks later came the real thing, allowing Ball to fulfil the promise he had made to his father that he would win his first cap before his 20th birthday. He achieved it with three days to spare, against Yugoslavia, on 9 May 1965.

Having been selected for the senior squad's European tour before he would join up with the Under-23s for their own summer matches, Ball assumed he was merely there to gain experience around the big boys. But Ramsey approached him in Belgrade with the news that 'I am going to throw you in at the deep end', assuring him that 'I know you won't let anyone down'.

England drew the game 1–1 and, while remembering the thrill of the occasion, Ball's own performance was unspectacular. 'Up to the interval he was largely a lost Ball,' said *The Times*, while the *Daily Mail* concluded, 'He was never quite able to control the centre of the pitch or stamp the game with the influence of his still-maturing class.'

'I don't think I played very well' or 'I played a decent role', were his own verdicts, depending on which autobiography you are reading. He was harder on himself, however, when recalling his debut for *Alan Ball's International Soccer Annual*, published in 1969 as the first of a four-year series. 'I was lost,' he confessed. 'I was frightened to do anything wrong. I played negatively and didn't go into the positions I should have done.'

Despite his own misgivings, he had done well enough to play against West Germany three days later, one of only two non-defenders to be retained. It was always the back four about whom Ramsey felt greater certainty, with the quartet of George Cohen, Jack Charlton, Bobby Moore and Ray Wilson keeping their places – as they would throughout the World Cup finals a year later. Ball played alongside Arsenal's delicate, skilful schemer George Eastham, describing the experience as 'taking a lesson from a professor'. More at ease during the 1–0 win in Nuremberg, he recalled that 'everything came off for me' and would even describe it some years later as 'my best-ever game for my country'.

As usual, the impression he had made on new teammates was immediate and profound. 'He seemed like a very young boy; immature if you like,' Cohen remembers, 'but he had the brain of a real professional. He was quite extraordinary. He tried to do everything right, but he had this flair that meant he could turn an impossible situation into something. He didn't over-simplify or do silly things; he did the right thing all the time – push and run, one-touch football.'

Bobby Charlton was amazed that someone so young could be 'so alive, so aware of everything that was happening around him'. He explained, 'He saw points of conflict incredibly early, he anticipated them and responded ahead of the rest. But never stupidly. You could be in a very tight situation, needing a little time and space, and you looked up and he was there.'

Hurst continues, 'My first impression of him had been what a dedicated player he was, probably the most passionate I have ever seen about playing for his country. He wanted to be the best and he was so serious about his football. After a few games he said to Alf Ramsey, "If you want my shirt back you are going to have to tear it off my back." But he was also very humorous, great fun to be in the company of. He was always mucking around and cheered the party up.

'On the coach sometimes he would stand up in the middle and sing a song, *Catch a Falling Star*, and he would do all the actions, catching a falling star and putting it in his pocket. I've no idea why he did that. That was Bally. And he was continually winding up Jack Charlton. Jack wore old-fashioned clothes – fishing clothes, checked jackets, long braces. As soon took he took them off in the changing room and hung them on the peg, Bally would gather everybody round. He'd say, "Look at these. Do they still wear these where you come from?" and wind Jack up. I remember once, many years later, being at a dinner and Jack was sat at a lower table, while Bally was up speaking. Jack said, "Look at him up there, the flash git. We know him for the little shit he really is." But they had a wonderful relationship and Jack loved him.'

Hunter adds, 'He was full of fun, very serious on the field and passionate about the game, but one of the lads. He liked a laugh and was always taking the mickey.'

Ball played again four days later against Sweden in Gothenburg, opening the scoring after nine minutes as England triumphed 2–1. 'I was put clear in the penalty area and as the ball bounced I hit it as hard as I could,' he said simply. He would miss the next three England internationals, sent back to the Under-23s in the meantime. But Ramsey had seen enough. Ball would be back in time to play his part in English football history.

That was if, in the meantime, his continuing disciplinary problems didn't ruin everything. When he arrived on the Under-23s' tour as a newly-capped senior, more trouble was looming. In the first match, against West Germany, he was booked for kicking the ball at the referee. Then, in the third and final game against Austria in Vienna, he was sent off. Booked four minutes earlier after clashing with the home team's left-back, he was dismissed after 61 minutes for hurling the ball in the direction of Hungarian referee Gyula Gere because he refused to allow a quickly taken free-kick. Even though his throw never made contact, Ball was physically bundled towards the touchline by the indignant referee before being led away by England trainer Les Cocker. He had become only the second player to be dismissed while playing for England's Under-23s, after Sunderland's Stan Anderson in Bulgaria six years earlier. Noting that Ball had been booked nine times in the previous 18 months, the *Daily Express* argued, 'He plainly has the ability for international football but equally plainly he has not the temperament.' The FA fined him £100 for his misdemeanours.

Despite keeping him out of the full team for the rest of the year, Ramsey clearly had no belief that Ball was unmanageable. He had cautioned him a day after his dismissal in Austria that he would have to 'face up to a lot more problems like this, especially if you want to keep on playing in international competition'. The England manager subsequently allowed him to make a two-goal contribution to the Football League's 5–0 win against the League of Ireland at Hull, a week before he scored his second goal for his country's junior side in the last of his Under-23 appearances, a 3–0 defeat of France at Carrow Road early in November.

A week later, Ball was a non-playing member of the full squad for the game against Northern Ireland. He was back in the fold just as the biggest occasion in the sport was looming on the horizon. Yet there was a big question to be answered: for which club would Alan Ball be playing by the time the 1966 World Cup rolled around? As the 1964–65 season ended, he had submitted a transfer request, to which Blackpool responded by giving him a pay rise and holding him to the 12-month option clause in his contract. Ball always maintained that any desire to leave Bloomfield Road was nothing to do with 'grabbing after money'. He said, 'It was because I was hungry for success, for the honours that a player can win with one of the top clubs. I also wanted so desperately to be recognised as a great player.'

Yet he would have to wait. 'There will be no question of Alan Ball leaving this club if we can prevent it,' Suart told Blackpool's annual general meeting. The final five words were significant. Could they honestly prevent it if the player wanted to leave and someone offered the kind of fee that would turn the heads of a club of Blackpool's stature? For a while it appeared that they could. Everton manager Harry Catterick contacted Suart in November 1965, but was told 'Ball is not for sale'. The Blackpool boss denied press reports that a bid in excess of £100,000 had been made. 'Complete and utter nonsense,' he called it.

Renowned Italian agent Gigi Peronace admitted to scouting Ball for various clubs and, to complicate matters further, Ball would soon start receiving anonymous phone calls claiming to be on behalf of Don Revie, the man who had led Leeds United from the foot of the Second Division to a position challenging for the game's top honours. Newspapers had already reported late in 1965 that Revie was set to offer Blackpool a six-figure sum. Eventually, Ball was persuaded to meet the Leeds manager in private on Saddleworth Moor, a somewhat macabre setting for a business meeting in the immediate aftermath of the discovery in that area of the bodies of children murdered by Ian Brady and Myra Hindley. Revie told Ball that when he left Blackpool, which was becoming increasingly inevitable, he wanted him to team up with Billy Bremner and Johnny Giles in his midfield.

Versions of what exactly happened next are once again contradictory, depending on whether one reads *It's All About a Ball*, published in

1978, or *Playing Extra Time*, released quarter of a century later. The gist, however, is the same: Ball started to receive payments of £100 per time from Revie. In his first book he said Revie handed him the cash in person during subsequent moors meetings, telling him that it was to enable him to fund a pay dispute with Blackpool. By 2004 he was saying that the money arrived via anonymous delivery to his home. Whatever the truth of the forgotten detail, Revie was determined to get his man, while Ball, he would admit, was 'unworldly' to accept the money.[1]

Meanwhile, the fast-approaching summer of 1966 was not only bringing the world's finest footballers to England, it also signified Ball's coming of age. Football League regulations allowed players the right to negotiate new contracts once they were within three months of their 21st birthday and as Ball received 'the key of the door' he also had a new pay package presented to him by his employers. 'It is indeed a generous [offer],' said Suart cagily, while refusing to confirm reporters' suggestions that it amounted to £100 per week for two years, plus a £10,000 signing bonus. Ball said merely that he was 'thinking it over', but as the global sporting community turned its attention to England he put such thoughts out of his head for a few weeks. There was a World Cup to be won.

---

1 When Ball first revealed his acceptance of such payments in 1978, he was fined £3,000 by the FA. Ball professed himself 'staggered' by the fine and his solicitor, Tony Wilson, argued, 'The FA have failed to listen to the mitigation put forward on Alan's behalf. We consider that the fine is out of all proportion to the offence and unjust. The fact that it was upon Alan's own admission that these proceedings were brought and that he pleaded guilty and that the offence was in 1966 when Alan was just 21 would seem to have shown that leniency could be granted. We feel that the commission has failed to act in the best interest of the sport.'

Ironically, the same sitting of the FA's disciplinary committee banned Don Revie from football for 10 years for quitting the England manager's job in 1977 for a £340,000 job in the United Arab Emirates.

3

THE WORLD AT HIS FEET

'Here's Ball, running himself daft'

> – BBC's Kenneth Wolstenholme in the build-up
> to England's third goal in the World Cup final

'**G**ET out of my sight.' Alan Ball felt Alf Ramsey's words hovering above his head like the blade of a guillotine as he, Nobby Stiles and John Connelly made their way down the corridor away from the England manager's room. Could they really have just blown their chances of playing in a World Cup in their own country for the sake of a single pint of beer?

On previous occasions during this two-week pre-tournament training camp in the rural surroundings of the National Sports Centre at Lilleshall in Shropshire, Ramsey had allowed players to visit the bar at the local golf club. This time, no such permission had been granted, yet Ball and his colleagues had ventured out regardless. Overcome by guilt and fear, they quickly downed their first drink and headed back to the stately-home accommodation of Lilleshall Hall. Upon arrival, they were greeted by Stiles's former Manchester United teammate, Wilf McGuinness, one of the coaches assisting the team's preparations. 'You're in deep shit,' he told them. 'Alf knows you went down to the bar.'

Ramsey had, famously, once put the frighteners on a group of players who had gone for a prohibited drink before an overseas trip by placing their passports on their unoccupied beds, making them sweat about whether they were to be sent home. This time, he simply ordered the trio to his room, where he explained that, although he had not said they couldn't go for a drink, he had expected that they would not. Ball and Stiles, stricken with fear, offered sincere apologies; Connelly chose to protest that there was no harm in a single pint after training, to which Ramsey's response was to bark a dismissal at them. They would have to wait before discovering whether their indiscretion would be held against them.

Ramsey had seen enough fear in the faces of Ball and Stiles to know that the two men who would become such a pivotal force over the coming weeks could be trusted. Instead of taking further action he warned the squad the next day, 'We are here for a purpose. I just want to say that if anyone gets the idea of popping out for a pint, then they will be finished with the squad forever.' Ball said a silent prayer of thanks. He would not have to explain to his father how he had got himself expelled just as he was becoming an established member of an England squad on the threshold of the greatest opportunity of their lives.

Having been left out for three full international matches while he continued his Under-23 career early in the 1965–66 season, Ball had been back in Ramsey's senior team for a 2–0 win in Spain in December. The result raised optimism over England's World Cup hopes and had seen them take the field without a recognised orthodox winger. Stiles recorded in his autobiography, *After the Ball*, 'Bally had put in a phenomenal performance, running magnificently into the open space left by full-backs who [were] repeatedly pulled out of position.'

Ball retained his place for a home draw against Poland at Goodison Park and a 1–0 Wembley victory over West Germany. He played in two of the next four games, wins in Scotland and Finland, where he had a penalty saved, and suddenly the World Cup was looming large.

Then came Lilleshall, with England's hopeful 27 players holed up and left to sweat on Ramsey's selection. 'The one anxiety was to get into the final 22,' Ball told David Miller for his book *The Boys of '66*. 'We all worked so hard. I was so fit. The training was so competitive.' Indiscretions at the golf club forgiven, Ball seemed unlikely to be one of the five men facing disappointment. Mercifully for him, Ramsey announced the squad to the hopeful players in alphabetical order, meaning his was the first name confirmed. Anxiety alleviated, Ball recalled nothing of the remainder of the meeting and would regret being so caught up in the moment that he neglected to commiserate with those whose names were not called. Ball proceeded to play in the final two warm-up matches at the beginning of July, victories in Denmark and Poland.

No one could be sure of Ramsey's selection plans for the tournament, the last World Cup to be played without substitutes. But Ball had experienced enough of the England manager to have complete confidence in the man who had played 32 internationals as a thoughtful right-back and then masterminded the incredible feat of guiding Ipswich Town to the League Championship in 1962, one year after promotion from the Second Division. 'When you looked at Ipswich's title,' said full-back George Cohen, 'you had to ask how it could possibly happen. It had to be down to the manager.'

What Ramsey lacked in public charisma and charm – despite his elocution lessons – he made up for with the kind of strategic pragmatism that had been the key to Ipswich's triumph. Appointed to the England role in the wake of that success, he had also demonstrated fierce loyalty towards his players, which was returned in equal measure. 'The fellow was complete,' Ball told Miller, 'tactically aware, thorough, had his own idea how the game should be played, was approachable, could put you right.'

In his second *International Football Book*, Ball wrote, 'All the England squads that I've been in have given him 100 per cent, and the reason for this is quite simple. They each know they are getting 100 per cent back from [him].'

According to Ball, Ramsey possessed 'a keen sense of humour' that was rarely exposed to the public 'and is glad to share it with the lads. Just because a man does not go about slapping people on the back does not mean his reaction to a joke must be a frown.' Ball's tribute concluded by highlighting Ramsey's 'almost fantastic quality to make players not only believe more in themselves than they do already, but to turn all those individual hopes into a collective team of character, courage and ability'.

Notwithstanding the theft of the Jules Rimet Trophy, recovered by a dog called Pickles, World Cup preparations went smoothly enough for England to arrive at their first game in a confident frame of mind, even if the media remained sceptical about whether Ramsey could make good on his promise to win the tournament. At least the *Daily Express* could always be relied upon to launch the tournament with a patriotic back page, chief sports writer Desmond Hackett – never afraid to say something for effect – declaring that 'this is the greatest England squad I have ever rejoiced upon', little more than a year after he'd been writing off their chances.

In order, Uruguay, Mexico and France would be England's group opponents, with all the games in the comfortably familiar surroundings of Wembley Stadium. Ball was picked for the first match and spent the time in his hotel room before the team bus departed for Wembley listening to a Walker Brothers LP. Children paraded in team colours, the Queen declared the event open, and the country sat back to spend their Monday evening biting their fingernails.

The teamsheet graphic before kick-off suggested to television viewers that Ball would be operating on the left of a three-man midfield behind winger Connelly. For much of the first half, though, while Ball played narrow on the left, Connelly operated wide on the right. Half-time brought a swap, with the Manchester United man now out on the left, but neither alteration was able to prompt an England breakthrough.

In front of a crowd of 87,148 – tickets were available to those walking up on the evening – Uruguay's massed defence kept the hosts at bay and frustration swept around Wembley. Watching a recording of the game, there is a lovely, revealing moment five minutes from the end: Jack Charlton wins the ball in the air in Uruguay's box and it drops towards the head of Connelly to the left of the penalty spot. As Connelly draws back his head to send the ball against the top of the crossbar, Ball is seen near the bottom of the screen, so immersed that he mirrors his teammate's heading motion in the manner of a fan sitting in front of the TV.

Fifteen corners against Uruguay's one was indicative of England's dominance, but for the first time in 52 Wembley internationals since the war, the home team were held goalless. The final whistle found the Uruguayans jumping around and punching the air, their ambition of a point achieved. 'I imagined that all teams would be going out to win,' said Ball. 'Yet for an hour and half we had to batter away at a defensive wall.'

As the nation's thoughts of becoming champions dipped from doubt to downright dismissal, Ramsey sought to lift morale with a visit to the Pinewood Studios, where Sean Connery was filming the new James Bond movie. It would take more than an encounter with 007, however, to lift the morale of England's number seven when he was left out of the next two games. Ball watched Southampton's Terry Paine (against Mexico) and Liverpool's Ian Callaghan (versus France) given an opportunity to patrol the right wing, while West Ham United's Martin Peters slotted into the left of midfield. Stiles, billeted with Ball in a room at the top of the Hendon Hall hotel, remembered his room-mate returning one day and dancing on a pile of five pound notes he had won at the bookies' and declaring, "Fuck Ramsey." Yet he recognised that Ball 'was really breaking up inside'.

Hurst was another one on the sidelines during the group stages, but doesn't recall much conversation among those on the fringes about their chances of selection. 'It wasn't an issue for me,' he insists. 'I was just happy to be there. Bally had been in the side for a year so was a more regular member, but I was just happy to be sitting on the bench as one of the best 22 players in England. There was no whingeing, we were a very professional outfit. Even though I know how passionate Bally was to play for England, he didn't show me he was upset. We all had enormous respect for Alf and his decision was final.'

England duly topped their group with a pair of 2–0 wins, but Ramsey had clearly not yet settled on his personnel or playing pattern for the knockout games. And if he had, then he was certainly not going to share it with a media corps with whom his relationship was consistently prickly. 'I suggest you wait and see until the next team is selected,' he said when asked whether he would continue with a winger.

'To be honest, he winged it,' Jimmy Greaves told the BBC in 2016, although the choice of verb is ironic given the decision he was about to make. For the quarter-final against Argentina, runners-up in Group Two behind West Germany, at least one change was needed because of the badly gashed shin suffered against France by Greaves, goalless in three matches. The injury brought in Hurst. If FIFA and the FA had had their way, Stiles would have been missing as well after the outcry over his late tackle on France's Jacques Simon, even though it went unpunished in the game. FIFA urged the FA to drop Stiles; the FA relayed the message to Ramsey; and Ramsey, in effect, told them to get stuffed. If Stiles went, he went. In training, Ramsey approached the man who acted as his back four's shield and asked him, 'Did you mean it?' When Stiles admitted only to mistiming rather than malice, Ramsey told him he would play.

And Ball would be joining his roommate in the team. Having tried three different orthodox wingers in three games, Ramsey finally opted to play Ball and Peters in midfield either side of Charlton. The 'Wingless Wonders', as the team would be dubbed, had finally arrived in the World Cup. It was a line-up destined to go down in history:

Banks

Cohen   J. Charlton   Moore   Wilson

Stiles

Ball   R. Charlton   Peters

Hurst   Hunt

Ramsey had, of course, experimented along the same lines before. In the victory in Spain the previous December and the home draw against Poland the following month, Eastham had played in the Peters role. 'We can attack with eight and defend with eight,' Ramsey had said of his tactics in Madrid. At home to West Germany in February, Hurst's debut, it had been Norman Hunter on the left of midfield. But then came five more matches that featured an orthodox winger, before the 1–0 win in Poland became the first in which the four-man midfield unit of Stiles-Ball-Charlton-Peters was employed. A week later, the World Cup kicked off and the revolving door of wingers was reinstalled.

But not any longer. Rationalising Ramsey's selection for the quarter-final, Ball told Miller, 'He thought Marzolini at left-back needed watching and it was my job to stop him coming forward.' He added, 'A winger couldn't have done it. A winger wants the ball and then to go with it.'

To right-back Cohen, it mattered not whether Ramsey selected an orthodox winger ahead of him or used Ball to offer width when the situation allowed, such was the esteem in which the 21-year-old was held. 'Everybody had a great deal of confidence in him. There was no thought that this was a young fellow who had just come into the squad. Alf wouldn't have picked him if he couldn't do the job. He could see Alan's potential; an old head on young shoulders. Personally, I loved him. If you were a full-back, having to cover across the middle, you knew damn well that you didn't have to look over your shoulder to find out who was in the real estate behind you. He was always there. He had tremendous energy and enthusiasm for the game and a high amount of skill. He was one of those guys you could count on because he knew the game. It was very comforting to know he was behind you on the far post. He was absolutely marvellous at that. And he had a great combination with Nobby.'

Miller noted in his retrospective chronicle of the tournament that 'two essentials of Ramsey's eventual formation were the versatility of Ball and Peters, and the use of Stiles as a plug in front of the defence.' Meanwhile, both Ball and Stiles – and many others – would enjoy, in future years, relating the tale of Ramsey discussing the nature of dogs to chase after balls and sticks when thrown, before returning them to the owners' feet. 'That's what I want you two to do for Bobby Charlton,' the manager said.

'Nobby and Bally epitomised the spirit and defiance of Alf's team,' Martin Peters recorded. 'They chased every lost cause and ensured everyone else did their share of the work.' He concluded that they 'looked as though they had spent a lifetime playing in the same team'.

According to Ball, 'Nobby and I died so Bobby could live. Bobby was different, a world-class player. Nobby and me were there to give him the ball, to give him time.'

Ball and Stiles were the Fred Flintstone and Barney Rubble of the squad, as close off the field as they were conjoined by ambition and purpose on it. Ball described himself as a 'white stick' for his short-sighted, accident-prone friend. It had been Stiles, himself a relative newcomer to the team, who had instigated a practical joke by way of initiation on the eve of Ball's full England debut. Having trained in the stadium in which England would be facing Yugoslavia the next day, Ball returned to the dressing room to find his trousers missing. 'I realised there and then what sort of mettle Alan Ball had, and what kind of character he was,' Gordon Banks remembered. Instead of putting on some tracksuit bottoms, Ball scoured the stadium in his underpants. Banks even recalled him asking bemused local officials, 'Has anyone seen my trousers? Somebody has nicked them – grey flannels with a brown belt.'

Hurst states that 'Nobby and Bally were the heart and the soul of the side' but adds that 'the whole team blended; all the different kinds of players and attitudes added up to a fantastic team'.

And Cohen is keen to stress that, as close as Ball and Stiles were, they never removed themselves from the overall team dynamic. 'I don't believe we had any sort of cliques,' he says. 'Alf stopped all that when he took over and, quite honestly, it was a major move towards winning the World Cup. Those two knew each other's responsibilities. You act as a team. You go up as a team, back as a team, over and across as a team, and those two next to each other were the two who made the centre of the field very secure because they were coming back into the gaps. This is what Alan was very good at. Nobby was there as a policeman, if you like.'

Such was Ball's all-round ability that Cohen believes his role in the team could have expanded even further had the need arisen. 'I have often said that if Bobby Charlton had got injured we had two guys with Alan, and perhaps Martin Peters, who could take his place on the pitch in that role. Certainly, Alan had that sort of talent.'

As much as Stiles was delighted by his pal's reinstatement for the quarter-final, he had expected nothing else. 'I just couldn't see Alf going into a match like this without Alan's energy and bite,' he said. So, with a week of the World Cup remaining, England, their shorts white for easier identification on television, faced up to Argentina's style of what BBC commentator Kenneth Wolstenholme described as 'the walking football that is so popular in South America'. It soon became evident that another aspect of the game stereotypically associated with that part of the world would be to the fore.

Ball's first run was ended by a firm tackle and when he was sent tumbling inside the box after five minutes the crowd's boos were unequivocal in relaying their belief that a foul had been committed. Three minutes later, Ball stepped in to keep the peace after Stiles clashed with Roberto Ferrero. The tone had been irreversibly set.

Ball chased, snapped at heels and looked for interceptions. 'Nobby would go and win the ball off the other fella with a crunching tackle, but Bally would just nick it off you,' Jack Charlton recalled. It was Ball's creative ability that surfaced after 11 minutes, embarking on a gliding run and laying the ball into the path of Roger Hunt to cross on to the roof of the net. When Ball broke after a pass by Stiles three minutes later he was clipped from behind. Seeking pastures new, he turned up to make a tackle in the left-back position, breaking down the inside-left channel and placing his pass just too far ahead of Hunt.

All this time, the tall Argentinian captain, Antonio Rattín, a sublimely gifted footballer when the mood took him, had been committing his share of fouls and being a constant, unwanted presence on the shoulder of German referee Rudolf Kreitlein, who eventually cautioned him after 31 minutes for an attempted trip on Bobby Charlton. The official's gestures appeared to indicate that he was not far from being sent off, although he let him off three minutes later when he clattered Hurst from behind. But when Roberto Perfumo brought down Hunt, Rattín was once again in the official's face. Kreitlein's patience ran out. Wolstenholme reported that he was 'dicing with death' and, once Charlton had shot wide, the cheer that rose from the crowd indicated their realisation that Rattín was being sent off. According to BBC analyst Jimmy Hill, the offence was 'violence of the tongue'. It took eight minutes for Rattín to depart, during which time Argentina threatened to walk off. Finally, England were left with a one-man advantage. 'Bally always used to say that Rattín was a lovely man.' Hurst laughs. 'He would kick you in the balls, but then he would help you to look for them.'

Argentina reorganised effectively and restricted England to long shots by Peters and Charlton. 'I felt they were quite prepared to gamble on a toss-up at the end of a drawn game, rather than trying to win it,' Ball would note. At last, after 77 minutes, Peters floated a cross from the left and Hurst, as he had done hundreds of times on the West Ham training ground, met the ball at the near post with a glancing header past the goalkeeper. Ball was first to leap into the scorer's arms and, 13 minutes later, was celebrating a place in the World Cup semi-finals.

Much as Portugal's fate in the European Championship half a century later would appear inextricably linked to Cristiano Ronaldo, so the key to halting England's next opponents was stopping the brilliant Eusebio. A member of the great Benfica side that challenged consistently for Europe's top honours throughout the decade, the Mozambique-born striker had been the star of the World Cup. The four goals he had scored in the quarter-finals to drag his team back from three down to beat underdogs North Korea 5–3 had taken his tally for the tournament to seven. If ever a job was made for Stiles, this was it. Eusebio would endure a frustrating night, desperately trying to evade the smothering attention of his marker, sometimes wandering out to Portugal's left wing, where Ball picked him up. FIFA would conclude in its technical report of the match:

> In this game R. Charlton's support play was outstanding, and Stiles effectively shielded the attacks of Eusebio. The physical condition demanded of this fast tactical interchange between attack and defence was typified by the play of Alan Ball, who one moment was defending and the next attacking or unselfishly running to provide openings for other players.

Despite the focus on stifling Eusebio, the 96,000 crowd at Wembley – watching a game originally slated in the tournament schedule for Goodison Park – saw England play their best football of the competition. Ball contributed fully, turning up on the left to deliver a low cross that led to scramble in which Hurst forced a low save by José Pereira. Then he slid a neat, quick pass in from the right to allow Bobby Charlton to set up Hurst for another attempt on goal. With Eusebio rarely able to get behind Stiles, Portugal made do with long-range efforts and England took a deserved lead after half an hour when the goalkeeper, in denying the onrushing Hunt, could only send the ball to the right foot of Bobby Charlton, who glided it past him from the edge of the penalty area.

Eusebio finally found room to force a save out of Banks with a right-foot volley, but even though Portugal found a way to press more in the second half, Charlton doubled the lead with his second goal 10 minutes from time. Hurst battled to get behind his marker after Cohen's long ball and laid back a pass for his teammate to crash in a rising right-foot shot. Hurst's determination to turn what looked like a misdirected pass into a goal-scoring opportunity was exactly the contribution that Ramsey would weigh up in the days that followed as Greaves approached fitness once more.

Not that England's place in the final was quite secure yet. There was still time for Eusebio to convert a penalty after Jack Charlton's nervous handball. That Banks dived left while Eusebio placed the ball low to his right was something for which the keeper blamed Ball, who had been pointing to his keeper's right as the ball was being placed on the spot. Portuguese captain Mário Coluna saw Ball's signals, said something to Eusebio and, Banks claimed, forced him to re-think which way he was going to dive – on the assumption that Eusebio was also changing his mind. Banks maintains that 'but for [Ball] I could have had a clean sheet'. Still, no one was going to fall out over what, eight minutes later, proved to be a mere footnote to England's victory.

'A great match played in a wonderful atmosphere,' was the recollection of Ball, who reckoned that 'euphoria' was not a strong enough word to describe the atmosphere around the team as they headed back to Hendon Hall. The players had two beers each, ate sandwiches together and were sent to bed.

Over the next three days, the question that occupied the minds of most observers as England prepared to face West Germany in the final was whether or not Greaves would be back. A couple of weeks earlier, the prospect of England choosing to contest the final without the greatest goal scorer of his generation was unthinkable. Greaves now accepted it as inevitable, even if neither Hunt nor Hurst were taking their places for granted.

Ball recalled being too young and too concerned with his own potential selection to pay any attention to the debate, although he would explain, 'With Geoff I could always bounce the ball off him, build something. He would help to get you into the team. With Jimmy, you had to play for him. Geoff could do more for our team.' Ramsey came to a similar conclusion. As the players arrived at the cinema on the eve of the final, Hunt and Hurst were told they were playing the next day.[1]

---

1 The recollection of various players differs in whether Ramsey took them to see *Those Magnificent Men in Their Flying Machines* or the First World War movie *The Blue Max*. The release dates, June 1965 and June 1966 respectively, make the latter appear more likely.

As the night hours brought kick-off closer, Ball explained to room-mate Stiles how he planned to get the better of West Germany's powerful left-back, Karl-Heinz Schnellinger. He recalled that neither he nor Stiles had 'an ounce of fear in our bodies', although his colleague was up at the crack of dawn to find a Catholic church in which to say his final prayers – not an easy task in the predominantly Jewish community of Golders Green.

Once Ball had heard his place in the team confirmed, he called his father, who had insisted that he would not bother to put petrol in his Morris Minor and travel down to the game unless Alan was playing. Pride and excitement poured down the telephone line as Ball senior issued orders that his son enjoy the occasion, take in every moment and return home with a winner's medal, concluding with the reassur-ance: 'You'll be good enough out there today'.

Ball was the one member of the team not to have had his place confirmed by Ramsey the night before. No explanation for Ramsey's reticence was ever offered, although Hurst recalls Ball speculating that the manager was giving Greaves an extra few hours to heal and might have considered leaving him out in favour of a three-man forward line had his star striker been healthy enough.

With time to kill before departure for the stadium – and the intru-sive age of celebrity yet to be born – Ball was one of several players who spent the morning shopping unmolested in Golders Green, treat-ing himself to a £300 watch from the £1,000 he had just received from his boot suppliers Adidas. Such an excursion would be unthink-able in future years, yet Ball would write, 'We were part of the people. We were the English football team. We were approachable . . . we were ordinary lads.'

As the hands of his new acquisition approached kick-off, Ball was ready for whatever fate might throw at him. Ramsey had run through the opposition players and pressed home to his men their 'responsibil-ity to win something for the people of England'. The manager's belief in his team had never wavered for a moment. In a crowded and chaotic dressing room, Ball sat quietly with his own thoughts – an unusual state of affairs for someone who would normally talk, frequently clown around and often do impressions to pass the time. He looked around at the men heading to the field with him and saw world-class performers such as Bobby Charlton, Bobby Moore, Gordon Banks and Ray Wilson. He knew there were those like himself and Stiles, Hurst and Hunt who were prepared to work, fight and run themselves to a standstill around such superstars. He saw one of the greatest of all, Jimmy Greaves, heading to a seat in the stand, unable to earn a place in the eleven. And he sensed powerfully the 'desire and passion to win something for this country' that ran throughout the whole squad.

Ball walked up the incline of the Wembley tunnel and into the most famous afternoon in English football history. In the fourth edition of *Alan Ball's International Soccer Annual*, he offered this description of the journey to the playing arena:

> You file down the tunnel towards the field of play, and as you emerge into the daylight, you suddenly become aware of a sea of faces, a vast multitude of people . . . and you are being greeted by a roar, a crescendo of cheers. It brings a lump to your throat . . . you would have to be completely without a heart, utterly without any sense of occasion, devoid of all emotion, not to be affected by that huge throng and the atmosphere it generates.

Third in line, Ball had the red number two shirt of Cohen in his immediate eye-line, Banks walking behind, and the white-shirted Germans on his left. A strong breeze kept the national flags flying horizontally above the stands, while rain had softened the playing surface in many places. Even the Queen, renowned for her ambivalence towards football, appeared to be fighting back an excited smile as the band of the Royal Marines played the national anthems. 'I was too young to have nerves,' Ball would reflect. 'It was the most instinctive game I've ever played. I didn't play to any orders. I just worked and ran.'

And changed his life forever.

The initial tension gripping the crowd, along with the placement of the BBC's effects microphones, means that players' voices can be heard in the opening minutes of the television coverage. The shout of 'Bally' is clearly audible as he gets the ball for the first time. When Ball over-hit a pass with his second touch, Wolstenholme, a fellow Farnworth Grammar old boy, pointed out that it would take a while for the players to get used to a surface made slick by earlier rain.

Ball's interchange with Jack Charlton on the right after 10 minutes led to Peters cutting in from the left to force the first save from German keeper Hans Tilkowski. A minute later, Ball and Peters swapped positions, Ball carrying the ball out of defence on the left before sliding it across for Peters to try another long-range shot. And then, with 12 minutes played, Wilson made a hash of a headed clearance and the ball dropped at the feet of Helmut Haller to fire past Banks. Yet England were behind for only six minutes before Hurst drifted into space to head Moore's quick free-kick down into the German net.

As it became obvious that Bobby Charlton and the great German schemer Franz Beckenbauer had been assigned to mark each other and were eliminating themselves as significant factors, so it also became clear that Schnellinger had been instructed never to stray from Ball's vicinity. Even on the occasions when Ball switched flanks, the German full-back went with him, eliciting groans from the crowd when they felt he had taken Ball out illegally near the left corner of the box. 'He ran Schnellinger into the ground,' says Hurst. 'His performance was no surprise to me. I knew what a strong character he was when it came to the big occasion. He was always going be there and doing the job.'

Ball spent a good portion of the first half on the left, cutting inside his marker to send low deliveries into the penalty area. On other occasions he would set a move in motion from deep on the right before advancing on a diagonal route and sending in an eventual cross from the opposite corner of the field. And it was Ball who was first on the scene in the six-yard box in the 34th minute after Tilkowski failed to hold a low effort from Hurst, although the unhelpful angle worked against him. The only thing that threatened to disturb him were decisions by Swiss referee Gottfried Dienst, who prompted angry gestures when he twice penalised Ball for fouls inside his own half.

As heavy rain greeted the players for the second half, Ball was instantly back into his stride, as if someone had merely released the pause button on the playback of the action. He knocked a neat ball outside the defence for Stiles to cross and then had to be brought down in order to prevent him setting up another opening. With 13 minutes remaining, Ball shot low from an angle on the right of the penalty area and Tilkowski pushed the ball behind for a corner. Ball took the kick himself and saw it drop to Hurst 20 yards out. His shot looped into the air off a German boot and dropped for Peters fired England into a 2–1 lead.

As chants of 'We want three' and a chorus of *Rule Britannia* circled the stadium, Ball sliced inside Schnellinger and laid the ball off for Hurst to shoot over the bar from distance. It was becoming impossible to keep up with Ball's whereabouts. On the left once more, he jinked inside a tackle and clipped a reverse pass back down the wing for Hunt to combine with Hurst. Then it was his interception on the edge of his own area that broke up a German attack. No one had earned their winner's medal more than Ball.

And then it was taken away.

As anyone with a passing knowledge of English football history knows, Wolfgang Weber equalised for West Germany after a free-kick in the dying seconds. All England could do was kick off before the final whistle went, prompting Stiles to boot the ball the length of the field in frustration. Ramsey's words at that point have assumed Churchillian renown. Ordering his players not to sit down so as not to betray any tiredness to the Germans, he told them, 'You've won the World Cup once; now go out and win it again.'

Ball rolled down his socks and responded to Ramsey's rhetoric with his finest half-hour. In the stands, reserve defender Norman Hunter could barely believe what he was seeing. 'If anybody ensured that we won that World Cup in extra-time it was Alan Ball,' he remembers. 'He had an abundance of energy. He was awesome. He was all over the place and he just ran and ran.'

After a minute of the World Cup final's first-ever overtime period, Ball received a pass on half-way, swerved into the middle of the field, advanced towards the box and unfurled a dipping shot that Tilkowski pushed over the bar. Before long, he was sending over a cross that led to Bobby Charlton skidding the ball against the foot of the goalkeeper's left post. The delivery from right-back Cohen looked weary, however, after Ball had beaten two men and laid a pass at his feet.

Cohen resolved to put his colleague in possession whenever possible. 'Alan wanted the ball,' he recalls. 'He wasn't comfortable without it. He wanted to play. He took Schnellinger on every time he could. He was pretty accurate with his crosses, he understood where he should be and what he should do at the right time.'

Interviewed for the 20th anniversary of England's triumph, Ball explained, 'Obviously I felt very tired in games because I am a human being, but in this particular game I can honestly say I was crying at everybody to give me the ball because I knew that I had the beating of this chap and knew I could cause problems.'

With 10 minutes of extra-time played and Wolstenholme telling viewers about the ticket arrangements for a replay three days hence, Ball chased a pass from Stiles down the right wing and pulled the ball back first time into the box, aiming for the near post. Hurst, who had begun his run a little too soon, found the ball arriving behind him, but controlled, swivelled and fired a right-foot shot against the underside of the bar. Enough print and air time has been devoted to the subsequent 50-year debate about whether or not the ball bounced down over the line to be able to skip all but the basic detail here: Azerbaijani linesman Tofiq Bahramov said it was a goal and England were 3–2 ahead.

'It was a good ball by Nobby,' Hurst recalls. 'It looked like it was going to go out, but Bally chased it down. Playing with him in the Under-23s helped then because he knew that at West Ham we liked the ball to the near post. He didn't wait to stop it or get it back on the other foot; he just whipped it into the near post and knew I would be on the end of it. Coming through together, you get an understanding of what people like and what service they want.'

Ball wanted more. 'Here comes Mr Perpetual Motion again,' said Wolstenholme like a proud uncle as England's number seven flew at the Germans. 'He's run himself mad,' he chuckled early in the second half of extra-time as Ball went at it again. Even now, Schnellinger was still being dragged all over the pitch, twisting this way and that as Ball tormented him with another dribble that ended with Stiles delivering a cross. 'I had him on toast,' was the way Ball would describe his mastery of his opponent. Only with a minute left did he show any sign of tiredness, playing the ball too far ahead of Peters.

What happened in the final seconds of the game has gone down in English football folklore, complete with its own soundtrack;

Wolstenholme's famous 'some people are on the pitch . . . they think it's all over . . . it is now!' as Hurst gathered up Moore's flighted pass, bore down on goal and smacked in a left-footed shot that almost broke through the Wembley net. Less obvious is the part Ball played. Having given the ball to Moore to begin the move, he had defied the exhaustion he could see all around him by sprinting upfield in the inside-right channel. Fearing that Hurst would square the ball to him, German defenders backed off, unsure of their next move.

'Look at the way Bally made up land when Geoff scored his third goal,' Cohen purrs. 'He is screaming for the ball. If you look at those two centre-backs facing Geoff, one just pulled away to his left to Bally and left Geoff one-on-one. He should never have gone that early, but he was covering for Bally coming up very quickly.'

Of course, if Ball had had his way history would now look different. The only man to score a World Cup final hat-trick explains, 'I heard this high-pitched voice shouting, "Hursty! Hursty! Give me the ball." Bally calling for it really upset the German defence. But me not passing to him, well, the little bugger never forgave me for the next 40 years.'

'I still think Geoff should have given it to me,' Ball said in 1986, 'but his strike on goal was unbelievable. It was a typical case of, "Give it to me. Give it to me. You . . . oh, great goal!"'

Ball was again the first to leap at Hurst. This time the scorer was too weary to lift him. Seconds later, the final whistle confirmed England as world champions.

Exhaustion and emotion combined to send red-shirted heroes to their knees as a nation rose to its feet in front of television sets and took to the streets or, in Trafalgar Square, the fountains. Ball had been born in the wake of similar celebrations 21 years earlier, and England's opponents in the World Cup final had made this day all the more poignant for those who had lived through six years of conflict.

'He'll be running half an hour after the finish, will Alan Ball,' Wolstenholme had said at one point during extra-time, and he wasn't far wrong. While older teammates such as the Charltons and Wilson wept in acknowledgement of the magnitude of their achievement, the youngster of the team darted around, jumping into colleagues' arms and shaking hands with the non-playing members of the squad. He looked up to the stands for Lesley, who, he discovered later, had fainted when West Germany had scored their late equaliser.

Eighth up the steps to receive his medal, grinning all the while, he thought about the parents who had made it possible for him to be part of this glorious day. Every kick on the shins his father had given him to toughen him up; every extra hour of training he'd been pushed through; all the advice, criticism and encouragement he'd been force-fed had helped to propel Ball around Wembley and into football history. Every kit his mother had washed uncomplainingly, each meal that had been delayed while he and his father stayed out kicking a ball around had moved him a little closer to where he now found himself, on top of the world. Before the day was out, he had presented his winner's medal to his mum and dad.

While Ball recognised his debt to his family, so the country had much to thank him for, although it was only years later that modern-style match statistics were produced to confirm what anyone with even the smallest, fuzziest black and white television had seen with their own eyes: that he'd had a hell of a game. The match analysts from Opta revealed that Ball was tied with Beckenbauer for the most successful passes in the final third of the pitch, (21), but noted that Ball's passes were into more dangerous positions, with a greater percentage into the penalty area. Sky Sports' analysis of the game in 2016 made a case for Ball being the most influential man on the field, ranking second in shots on target (two), fifth in successful passes (49), second in chances created (two), second in dribbles (two), and first in free-kicks won (five).

Ramsey, someone who would have trusted his own instincts more than a statistical package, made little differentiation between his play-ers. To him they were all heroes and he left them alone to do a lap of honour that is remembered mostly for the gap-toothed Stiles skipping around holding the Jules Rimet trophy on his head. 'What a day this is,' sighed Wolstenholme as the pictures went around the world.

The day ended for the players with dinner at the Kensington Garden Hotel – wives condemned to eat in a separate room – before Ball and several others, and their spouses, headed to the club of enter-tainer Danny La Rue in Hanover Square.

And the following day it was back to ordinary life. 'Nobby and my dad stopped on the way home on the M6 for egg and chips,' recalls Jimmy Ball. 'Nobody bothered them. No one asked for an autograph.' Yet that one extraordinary day at Wembley was about to be followed by events that would define Alan Ball as a club footballer.

4

SCHOOL OF SCIENCE

*'The flame-haired inside-forward is the most contemporary figure of
the game; as representative of his times as op art, Carnaby Street, the
electric guitar and LSD'*

– *World Sports* on Alan Ball, April 1967

ALAN Ball couldn't help but feel like a fraud. It was six days after
the World Cup final and he found himself at Blackpool Town
Hall listening to tributes falling around him. The mayor, Councillor
Robert Brierley, in whose chamber a celebratory civic reception was
being held in honour of Ball and England squad member Jimmy
Armfield, handed both players a set of gold cufflinks. 'We were all
emotionally involved following you in the last few weeks,' he declared.
'We were very proud that we in Blackpool had a share in the triumph
through two such fine footballers.'

Addressing Ball directly, Cllr Brierley continued, 'Someone once
said to me that you had poetry flowing from your boots. We were
thrilled by the way you performed on the field. I can only add that
everybody in this room is proud you belong to Blackpool.'

Listening with a degree of embarrassment, part of Ball knew that
those words were fully justified. There were now people in all corners
of the globe aware of the town, thanks to his role in making England
champions of the world. Yet how fully did he still 'belong' to Blackpool?
The welcome he had received from thousands of people when he'd
gone back to his birth place of Farnworth had been unambiguous and
easy to enjoy. But how deeply would these people in his professional
hometown feel let down if he left to chase ambitions of club glory?

It was all very well for the likes of Roger Hunt, Bobby Moore and
Bobby Charlton to accept unconditionally the tributes coming their
way from their clubs. They were older, had reached the heights of

English football with their teams and had no great desire to go anywhere else. But for Ball, here we are in Chapter 4 and the World Cup has already been won. The story of his playing career is less about striving to reach the top of his sport than it is the tale of what happened after he got there.

As he offered thanks for his 'wonderful present', the reality for Ball was that he would, in effect, be playing out his career in reverse. The natural progression, followed by other teammates, was to become established in League football, challenge for domestic honours and achieve crowning glory via the World Cup. Ball had taken that final step while only 21 years old. With the exception of George Cohen, who had served his time loyally at Fulham, all of Ball's Wembley colleagues had already won winners' medals, even if Jack Charlton's had only been in the Second Division. Ball, having earned international football's greatest prize, now had to prove himself in the club game.

'The position hasn't changed,' he told reporters when asked about his contract. 'I still want to move. I have not accepted Blackpool's new offer and there is little likelihood of me doing so.'

Two days after the final, the *Blackpool Gazette* wrote a piece urging him to address his future quickly, although the paper resisted the kind of subsequent daily speculation that would be inevitable in the modern era of 24-hour rolling news. There were no camera crews trailing him when he headed to the Lake District for a break after appearing in a friendly at Preston North End on 8 August. When Blackpool's pre-season team picture was taken without him, the local paper simply printed it on 11 August with a note that Ball was 'absent owing to indisposition'. Of far greater interest to the *Gazette* that day was The Beatles' departure for America on what would prove to be their final tour.

By Monday 15 August, Ball was back at work, several days earlier than scheduled. Restless and bored, he couldn't wait any longer to start preparing for the new season – wherever he might find himself playing – so he turned up for training hoping to take part in that night's return friendly against Preston. There had been reports of a formal £105,000 bid from Leeds United, while Stoke City manager Tony Waddington had been telling reporters of his interest. The club had even told Ball that his situation was attracting attention from Italian clubs. But he had no inkling of what was now unfolding.

While having lunch at Collinson's Café, he received a telephone call instructing him to return to the ground. 'I've been trying to get hold of you,' Ron Suart told him upon his reappearance at Bloomfield Road. 'Harry Catterick has been on the phone from Everton and has made an offer. I know you will want to talk to your dad.'

Catterick had made a previous bid of £105,000, but would explain later that the intention was to make Leeds think that he would go no higher. 'Don't let anyone know,' he had told Suart, 'but this isn't our final word.' Yet Suart 'had no idea the offer was coming' on that particular day. In a late-morning phone call, the Everton manager tabled a bid reported at the time to be £112,000, but which the course of history has rounded down to £110,000. Blackpool were told that the deal had to done by early evening in order to meet Everton's deadline for registering players for the European Cup Winners' Cup.

As Ball spoke to his father, a quick drive to Blackpool was undertaken by Catterick and Everton chairman Edward Holland Hughes in order to hold further discussions with Suart and Blackpool chairman Richard Seed and to talk terms with their transfer target. Later reports suggested that Ball was offered a £10,000 signing bonus. There was one further twist when Don Revie, having got wind of Everton's bid, called Suart to match it on Leeds's behalf, although he had to content himself with making his final appeal to Ball on the telephone rather than in person.

With Everton's deadline approaching, Ball committed his future to them. 'It is a big club with big crowds and great traditions,' he explained. The transfer represented a record fee, the first six-figure deal agreed between two British clubs.

Catterick celebrated his capture and dispatched chief scout Harry Cooke to deliver the appropriate forms to the FA. Others were left to lick their wounds. 'I am disappointed,' admitted Revie, 'but it is not the end of the world. We have a good team at Leeds and we shall soldier on without him.' Indeed they would. Blackpool, though, had fewer alternatives in their midfield. 'I had hoped he would be playing for us next season,' said Suart, while Phil McEntee reported in the

Blackpool Gazette, 'Although Blackpool knew it was inevitable, this feeling of disappointment remains.'

'Losing him was massive,' says Armfield. 'We couldn't replace him. We were just a mid-table team and we had started losing some of our best players. It ended up happening with Tony Green, Tommy Hutchison and others.'

'It was almost club policy to sell a player every season,' says Glyn James, while Tony Waiters, an England international who had not been part of the World Cup squad, admits to feelings of envy. 'Bally was too good for Blackpool; he had to move on. I look at my own career and what I didn't have was someone who could advise me. Alan had that in his dad. If I had an agent he would have got me moved on.'

There is no evidence that Ball senior, by now coaching at Stoke City, had any greater involvement in the transfer than to act as a sounding board for his son, but Waiters contends, 'Alan, in effect, had an agent in his dad. He had quite an influence. He gave Alan advice, confidence and belief in himself.'

The club Ball was joining were FA Cup holders and had been League Champions three years earlier. Catterick believed Everton could already have added another title had they not been hit by the four-month prison sentence and lifetime football ban given to England midfielder Tony Kay after revelations by the *Sunday People* late in 1964 that he, Peter Swan and David 'Bronco' Layne had bet against their Sheffield Wednesday team two years earlier. What particularly irked Catterick was that Wednesday, the third club he had managed after his own modest playing career, had benefited from Kay's £60,000 transfer while Everton were the club punished by the ban. Kay's absence created a void in their midfield that would not be filled until Ball's arrival.

It had been Ball's performance against Kay in a match two years earlier that had first alerted Catterick to the talent emerging on the Fylde coast. He later told broadcaster Charlie Lambert, 'This little fellow kept going past Kay and at half-time Tony said, "I've clobbered him a couple of times but the little so and so keeps coming back – and he can play."'

Another Everton contest at Blackpool the following season had underlined Ball's blooming talent. It was a memorable day for centre-forward Joe Royle, making his Everton debut at the age of 16, but his recollection of the occasion is dominated by Ball. 'Even the Everton fans took to him that day,' he explains. 'He did his party tricks. He trod on the ball, he made to wipe his nose with the corner flag. The Everton fans knew he was pretty exceptional and on a frozen pitch that day he ran around for 90 minutes as though it was a normal pitch. And they beat us 2–0.'[1]

One month before Ball's transfer, Everton's modernised Bellefield training centre had opened, playing host to Brazil's World Cup squad. The club had first become known as 'The School of Science' in the midst of their successes of the 1920s, but Catterick, who had arrived at Everton in 1961, declared that the nine-acre site used by the club for the past 20 years did little to reflect such lofty standards. At a cost of £115,000, Bellefield had now evolved from a collection of wooden huts and bad fields into the 'football factory' Catterick demanded and which he believed was a greater legacy of his management than the trophies he won.

A north-easterner who had planned to be a marine engineer before football claimed him, Catterick was a man of straightforward values, based on military-style discipline, which led to ambivalence among his players. While contemporary managers and coaches such as Bill Shankly, Brian Clough and Malcolm Allison could inspire outright love among their men, Catterick was often hated, always feared and, at best, respected. 'His own staff loathed him,' recalled Howard Kendall, who joined the club a few months after Ball.

Winger Derek Temple, scorer of Everton's winning goal in the 1966 FA Cup final, had found Catterick waiting for him as manager after he returned to his hometown club following national service. Catterick could easily have been one of the officers he'd been serving under. 'He

1 The match entered Everton infamy when Harry Catterick was said by some to have been 'attacked' by fans angry that he had included Royle at the expense of crowd favourite Alex Young. The exact details of what happened are disputed, but somewhere in a melee of fans as the team left Bloomfield Road, Catterick ended up slipping, or being pushed, to the ground.

didn't like referees, he didn't like journalists, he was just a strange sort of guy,' he remembers. 'If you did your job he was OK with you, but I don't think he had a lot of friends.'

Colin Harvey, a home-grown player who would link so successfully with Ball and Kendall in Everton's midfield, felt that Catterick's need to frighten the life out of his players was born of insecurity. Rarely seen on the training field, the manager spent the majority of his time observing from his office, which sat at the top of a flight of metal stairs and over-looked the practice ground. The tracksuit would only come out for effect if the television cameras or the club chairman were around. Pre-season training was approached in the manner of an army boot camp; players forced to run up and down sand dunes at Ainsdale, while Catterick sat in his car watching, taking note of which players were being sick. Forward Ernie Hunt, who spent part of one season at Goodison Park during a well-travelled career, recalled 'the hardest training I'd ever experienced; more running than in any of my other clubs'.

Tactical nous, skilled man management and psychology; all were missing from Catterick's make-up. What he did possess was the ability to see which players, either from within the Everton youth system or via the transfer market, would blend together to make a good team. 'He used to get some great players in,' admits Temple. 'He would disappear up to Scotland for a day or two and come back with a player. And they could all play.'

'He bought good players,' Kendall recorded. 'That was it: simple,' although that does not do justice to a production line that saw the likes of Harvey, Royle and others emerge to join the big-money signings in a Championship-winning team.

Catterick had the good sense to let his men play to their strengths without confounding them with over-complicated strategy. John Hurst explains, 'Harry knew who to buy and who would fit in. That was his great talent. He was a great motivator, but as tactician he had very little to do with the team. I can't ever remember having a real conver-sation with him. Even when it came to signing a new contract, he would say, "I have had a hell of a battle to get you a £10 rise. I can't get any more, so sign this and off you go." '

Defender Roger Kenyon, signed by Catterick as an apprentice in 1964, echoes that memory. 'You all lined up at the end of the season, one by one, and he would tell you, "You are getting a fiver. You are getting nothing. You are getting sold." You said "OK" and walked out. He was a ruthless man. He was better if he had bought you, but with the likes of me, who came through the ranks, he would treat you as if you were still down below.'

Catterick was at least consistent with reporters, regardless of age or status. He distrusted them all. He insisted on trying to hide his formations from them, reciting his team on a Friday in strictly alphabetical order. The custom of giving centre-half Hurst the number 10 jersey, although done through superstition rather than deception, did occasionally fool *Match of the Day* into listing him in midfield on its pregame team sheet. 'He didn't like the press at all,' Hurst continues. 'He used to wind them up, keep them waiting and then he would go out the back way. The press found him hard work.'

A consistent record of top-six finishes and challenges for the FA Cup over the course of a decade appeared to justify his methods, while the adventurous style of football played by his team in the latter half of the 1960s contradicted his dour reputation and hinted at a more complex character than the one-dimensional disciplinarian. It also signified a change to the approach that had been drummed into his players in the early years of his reign. 'Harry worked on the principle of not giving anything away,' Temple explains. 'He used to say, "You are going out there with a point and I don't want you coming back with anything less." But he had a side that could play.'

A further paradox was that, as much as Catterick demanded state-of-the-art facilities for his club, his philosophy on some aspects of the football business could hardly be described as modern. That desire for his team and tactics to retain the element of surprise meant, for example, that television cameras would not be allowed into Goodison Park until the fourth season of *Match of the Day* in 1967–68. He even asked Everton's directors to create a non-cooperation pact against the BBC with their counterparts at Liverpool. Such a deal was rejected by the Anfield board, who immediately saw the promotional benefits of being seen by millions of viewers.

Even Catterick, though, eventually proved powerless to halt progress. Football's journey into the mainstream of Britain's cultural and media landscape, accelerated by the introduction of *Match of the*

Day to the Saturday evening schedules in 1964, was hurtling along at breakneck speed in the slipstream of the World Cup. Buoyed by the nation's response to Ramsey's men, the BBC had moved its weekly highlights programme from the regionally-restricted BBC2 to the vast audiences offered by BBC1. New, glossy additions to the newsstands, in the form of weekly magazines *Goal*, *Shoot!* and various short-lived imitations were on their way. When schoolboys weren't sticking colour posters on their bedroom walls they were in the playground swapping stickers for the new *Wonderful World of Soccer Stars* albums or the ever-brighter cards offered by A&BC chewing gum.

Ironically, given Everton's original stance on refusing to grant *Match of the Day* access to Goodison Park, viewers were offered an insight into life at the club via two fascinating pieces of television made during the early days of Ball's time at the club.

When Everton were drawn at home to Liverpool in the fifth round of the FA Cup in March 1967, the ambitious step was taken to stage the game at 6pm and to have it aired simultaneously on big screens inside Anfield. It meant a combined 'live' audience of more than 100,000, enough of a development for ITV's *This Week* current affairs programme to assign the lugubrious Clement Freud to present a half-hour special examining the passions involved in the most famous of cross-town rivalries.

'Liverpool is a city of fanatics,' Freud states as he introduces the programme from a bench in Stanley Park. 'Nothing causes more single-minded high-octane fanaticism than football,' he adds, in a manner as far removed from high-octane as it's possible to be. His nervous shifting and twitching on the bench suggests he is worried that he might be mugged. Having noted the size of the two audiences for the game, played before shooting this piece-to-camera, Freud concludes sniffily, 'That means more than 103,000 people watching 22 footballers kick a ball around a pitch in a match that was never going to be a very exciting football match.'

After interviews with fans, Ball is shown arriving for training in his soft-top sports car. On the training pitch, Freud blunders into his interview with Catterick by pointing out, 'As a footballer you never really made it, did you?' and follows up with, 'What impact has your lack of success had on you as a manager?' Catterick shifts uneasily and tries to resist the temptation to kick this buffoon out of his beloved facility. 'The fanaticism in this city is quite unusual,' Catterick ventures in stilted tones once Freud asks him a question he can actually answer. 'At times people take it much too much to heart. One must always remember it is only a game.'

Wearing a jaunty bobble hat, Liverpool manager Bill Shankly is, typically, much more at ease than his Everton counterpart. Asked how much football encroaches on his home life, he replies cheerily, 'It encroaches all the time, Clement. I don't know how my wife has stood it. I don't know why she doesn't leave me.' It is not the first, or last, time that the presence of Shankly across the way serves to make Catterick appear even more inscrutable.

Yet as impressive as Shankly is in front of the camera, his club's facilities don't excite Freud as much as the new Bellefield. 'Everton provide lunch – almost luncheon – and recreations like table tennis,' he gasps over shots of Brian Labone with bat in hand. The truth, however, was that games of ping pong were strictly controlled, with bats and balls having to be signed out by Catterick's secretary and woe betide anyone who failed to return them. Similarly, the one television on campus remained in a locked cabinet, opened only for suitable programming. No sitting around all afternoon watching horse racing for the Everton players.

Eventually Freud introduces a few minutes of action from the game by describing the event as 'three weeks of razzmatazz, culminating in 90 minutes of raggle, taggle football'. At one point he notes, 'This is the incident,' as Ball lies on the floor clutching his cheek after a punch thrown by Ian St John. Meanwhile, goalkeeper Gordon West leads the charge of Everton players looking for retribution. Everton fans would have been unconcerned at Freud's contemptuous commentary; certainly not after Ball pounced on a loose ball in the box as half-time approached and banged in the only goal of the game, his joy the perfect antidote to Freud's disdain.

Temple can partly understand the presenter's dismissal of what he had seen. 'I always found the derby games difficult,' he confesses. 'They were not great games to play in because there was too much riding on them, especially for local lads like me. They were easier for an outsider. Bally used to shine in the derby games, he loved them.'

Ball would recall this particular occasion a few years later by saying, 'When I got to my feet after scoring I shall never forget the look of devotion on the faces of so many people just a few feet away from me. I didn't realise exactly how emotional a Merseyside derby could be.'

Greater televisual energy and whimsy would be in evidence when the doors were thrown open again later that year, this time to the BBC for *The Golden Vision*, a film directed by Ken Loach and aired in 1968. Part of the production consists of dramatised scenes showing the importance of Everton to the lives of the working folks of Liverpool. Interwoven is a profile of Alex Young, the 'Golden Vision' himself, for which Loach was given behind-the-scenes access at Bellefield. Among the more instructive sequences are of Wilf Dixon, who had followed Ball from Blackpool to Everton, putting the team through fitness training, which, he explains, they focus on at the start of the week before concentrating more on football as match day approaches. In another scene, Catterick is shown moving counters around on a table-top football field to demonstrate formations for a game against Arsenal. There are also instructions on positioning at corner kicks, during which Dixon seems to contradict some of Catterick's thinking. The sequence was actually filmed after the game, but offers a glimpse behind the curtain nonetheless.

The film, which finishes with actor Ken Jones scoring for Everton in a dream sequence, is notable for some honest introspection by Young, who suggests that his chosen profession is not all it is cracked up to be and admits, 'Maybe there is something better.'

It is not a sentiment with which Ball would ever have concurred. One of the spin-offs of the new media attention being lavished on football in the late 1960s was the plethora of 'named' football annuals arriving in the book market and finding their way into Christmas stockings. George Best, Derek Dougan, Denis Law, Billy Bremner and Ball himself were among those signed by Pelham Books. Ball would take the opportunity, in his first offering in 1969, to outline a weekly routine that – even if one takes it with a pinch of salt – indicates a dedication to his profession that is undisputed by former colleagues.

Monday, he writes, 'is usually a free day, particularly if we have had a good result on the Saturday. I usually spend it relaxing, playing golf or going to a race meeting.' On Tuesday, the players reported around

9.45am. 'It is a hard morning on one of the three pitches we use – two outdoor, one indoor,' Ball notes. 'We do circuits, lapping, ball work and end up playing five-a-side in the gym. In the afternoon I usually go back to iron out a fault the manager or trainer has spotted in my game.' This is no exaggeration for his young readers, Ball being remembered by all who played with him for the amount of additional training he undertook.

Wednesday, he reports, was a lighter training day, consisting mostly of various games and ball exercises in the gym. 'I spend the afternoon at home, because I have a heavy night in front of me, playing snooker. I represent the local British Legion club.' It is hard to believe there was a more competitive player in the local leagues.

Thursday was 'a light morning with plenty of sprints and ball work, finishing up with a five-a-side game' followed by Catterick's blackboard discussion about Saturday's opponents. Such preparation was still considered new-fangled enough for Ball to feel the need to remind his readers that 'tactics play a big part in the modern game'. An evening out with his, by now, wife Lesley and friends was followed by an early night.

The morning before the weekend's game found many players working on their own specific needs and skills, concluding with 'a few dozen sprints' before an afternoon with Lesley and his baby daughter Miranda (Mandy). 'I always have difficulty getting to sleep on a Friday night,' Ball explains, 'because of the excitement of the match the following day.'

Unsurprisingly, given its contemporaneous nature, Ball's article makes no mention of the infamous Catterick 'clocking-in' system, something Everton players of the era talk about to this day. A notebook would be waiting in which the players had to sign their names on arrival at Bellefield. Sharp at 10am, the book would either be removed, according to some recollections, or the colour of pen and pencil changed, according to others, so that Catterick knew exactly who had arrived after the cut-off time.

That particular discrepancy in memory proves easy to resolve. Remarkably, Catterick's final signing-in book still exists, taken as a memento by Stewart Imlach, who joined Everton as youth team coach and ended up working with the first team. The former Scotland international's sons, Steve and Gary, have inherited this treasured piece of memorabilia, which features in the latter's award-winning book, *My Father and Other Working Class Football Heroes*. It was pencil for the punctual; red ink for the tardy. 'Along with the red-pen entries of the honestly late,' Imlach writes, 'there are some suspicious-looking efforts in pencil, where an apprentice has been bribed or threatened into forging a senior player's name.'

Catterick inspected the book regularly and anyone who had signed in the incriminating colour was fined, with no appeals and no allowances for such trivial matters as car breakdowns or roadworks. Shortly after her birth in 1968, Ball's elder daughter Mandy was unwell one morning, which required a return to hospital. Ball dared not tell Catterick or ask to be excused from training, entrusting arrangements to his neighbours and calling home for the latest news.

Imlach, meanwhile, recalls the spell cast by Ball over a youngster privileged, thanks to his father, to be granted access to a world that his schoolmates could only glimpse through the pages of the latest football magazine. 'He was my favourite player, a real hero to me. I just remember that it [football] seemed to matter so much to him. When you are a kid it is life and death to you and it seemed to matter as much to him. Not that the rest of the players gave the impression that it didn't matter; it just seemed to matter more to Bally. He was so intense.

'I remember doing the same thing as him with his socks. He didn't do a ridiculous full John Terry, but he had his socks really high and just up to the knee cap so I was very careful to do my socks like Bally. I remember the shock of first going to down to Bellefield and seeing the great man turn up, not in kit, but in actual clothes. I think it was some incredibly loud checked jacket with wide collars and I remember a big fat kipper tie with the biggest wings and knot I had ever seen. I was mesmerised by every detail of him.'

By the time Ball's less advantaged fans were reading about life at Everton in his first annual, he had already been persuaded to cash in on his heightened profile by issuing his first autobiography, *Ball of Fire*, published by Pelham in 1967. The 144-page volume is a standard offering for the period – career highlights and challenges, selection of a world eleven – but has the topical relevance of including a detailed, if not particularly revealing, account of the previous year's World Cup.

Ball was also present in the lives of football-mad youngsters via his placement on the box of *Soccerama* – 'the family football game with a difference', first produced in 1968. A board game in which players had to accumulate wealth by guiding their teams from the Fourth Division to the top of the First, Ball's endorsement declared it to be 'the best game I've ever played'. In fairness, it wasn't bad and Ball certainly never suffered from association with it.

Early in 1970, Ball would join England batsman Geoff Boycott on captain Cliff Morgan's team on *A Question of Sport* and, before the World Cup in Mexico, he would agree another significant deal. The start of the 1969–70 season had seen the arrival of *Shoot!*, a glossier, more design-led rival to *Goal*, which felt more rooted in the decade just finishing than the one that was to come. While Bobby Charlton wrote for *Goal*, Bobby Moore and George Best had been columnists for *Shoot!* since its launch; now the newer publication was adding a second World Cup winner in Ball, who was photographed meeting the magazine's editorial team in Mexico. Working with ghost-writer Christopher Davies he would produce his 'Soccer as I See It' articles for the next seven years.

'I did it on the phone when he was at Everton and then, when he joined Arsenal, I used to go to see him,' Davies recalls. 'He took it seriously and he would always call back if I couldn't get him. At Arsenal, they trained at Highbury on a Friday and I went along with a tape recorder, which was the size of a desk, and before we did the interview we had to go and see Stan Flashman, the ticket tout, at Edward Bond House, just off Gray's Inn Road. I have never seen so many locks on a door. Bally would go there to do some transactions and then we would do the column. He was very, very good. He was opinionated, but in those days you weren't looking for anything too hard-hitting and he didn't have to slag people off. It could even be something like "my favourite time to play football is a warm summer evening".'

Yet Ball's natural passion and sense of justice couldn't help but ruffle some feathers on occasions, such as the time when he had to explain to the FA his description of referees as 'a joke'. His column became required reading among the football reporters. 'In those days, the only way for the papers to get a quote from one of the top players was from *Shoot!*' says Davies. 'People never went to training grounds during the week. I would come up with the subject matter and most of it was his words. You didn't have to speak to him for long to get what you wanted. Bally was always very good. I think we paid him about £50 a week.'

The most lucrative media deal that would come Ball's way in that period was a three-article commitment in the *Sunday People* in 1974, set up by his friend Paul Trevillion. Ball was paid £4,000, a staggering amount for the time, equating to three or four months' basic salary. 'Other players couldn't believe it,' says Trevillion. 'Getting £1,000 was always seen as the big target, but Bally got four times that. Imagine how much that would be worth today.'

In truth, financial spin-offs from 1966 had been minimal compared to the riches that present themselves to modern-day World Cup winners. The players had earned a bonus of only £1,000 each from the FA, opting to split a pool of £22,000 equally among the squad instead of basing it on appearances in the tournament. It was no surprise that Ball should be foremost among Ramsey's heroes when it came to whatever commercial opportunities did exist – although he never got to feature in a TV sitcom like Colin Bell (*The Dustbinmen*) or Bob McNab (*On The Buses*). With no Messi-like magician or Ronaldo-sized ego in the 1966 team to monopolise attention, Ball, as the young-est player and one of the most recognisable and controversial figures, was obviously a main attraction. At the end of 1966, he'd been named seventh in the European Footballer of the Year voting, with winner Bobby Charlton and fourth-placed Bobby Moore the only Englishmen ahead of him. The appeal of those more statesmanlike figures was to a different demographic, their personalities more guarded.

'He is a modern hero who can be a model for the future,' *World Sports* magazine gushed in April 1967. 'He has experienced almost the whole gamut of football in less time than it took most of his elders to progress from the boot-room to a place on the reserves' bench with the second eleven.'

The same article insisted that Ball was more in control of his temperament than at any time in his career. 'In a few months he changed the character as well as the style of his play, particularly to fit in with what the England manager Sir Alf Ramsey expected of him,' Doug Gardner's prose continued. 'Today Ball is submerging his aggressive nature without losing his combativeness on the field.'

Impending marriage, it was generally assumed, was a contributory factor to the perceived enhanced maturity, with Ball tying the knot with his first and only girlfriend Lesley Newton at the conclusion of his first season at Everton. His father had done his best to dissuade him from the wedding, believing that he was too young to become 'tied down' and even cataloguing why Lesley was the wrong girl for him. Ball was not to be moved and sensed that his dad's opposition was born out of the realisation that his son was, for the first time in his life, making a major decision without him. He knew his father had nothing personal against the girl he'd first encountered when he was 15 – as a result of his sister raiding his wardrobe.

'Lesley was my friend,' Carol explains. 'She used to come riding with me at the stables. One time I was doing a gymkhana and I took one of Alan's ties to wear and he couldn't find it. He came over to the stables ranting and raving. In those days you only had one or two ties. Lesley was there so I introduced them. After that he kept coming over and it was about a 10-minute walk from the house. He'd come and say, "Your mum said tea will be ready in an hour." I used to think, "I know what is going on here. He wouldn't come over just to tell me that." The day I knew they had got together was when I was going home from the stable and I saw Alan and Lesley walking hand in hand up the lane.'

The fact that he'd had a girlfriend at home had made it even easier for Ball to resist the temptation of going out on the town in Blackpool. Unsure how his dad would feel about him having a female 'distraction', he made sure to keep the relationship from him. Ball senior was used to seeing Lesley around as a friend of Carol's and, Ball recalled, he 'never suspected what was happening under his own nose'. When Lesley visited his digs in Blackpool, they stayed in playing records rather being seen out together and she would be on her way home at 9pm. Ball senior was eventually put in the picture, but could hardly be said to have given instant approval, ignoring her when she was at their house.

'I remember after a night game at Blackpool, Mum and Dad were staying over there, but Alan came home because Lesley was staying with me,' says Carol. 'When he got home he said, "Mum and Dad don't know I am here." But they soon found out.' When, at 19, Ball became engaged to Lesley, he chose not to tell his dad immediately, leaving him to find out inadvertently when his grandmother placed a congratulations notice in the local newspaper.

Alan and Lesley married on 21 May 1967, at St Stephen's Church in Kearsley, enjoying a one-day honeymoon before Ball had to report for England duty. Even a wedding ceremony could not completely release him from the grip of his father's influence, though. When, early during married life, Ball was suffering a dip of form and receiving some stick from a group of fans, Ball senior waited outside his son's home in Worsley, on the outskirts of Manchester, one Saturday night and was furious when he and Lesley arrived back at 2.30am. 'You've become a bloody prima donna,' Ball was told.

Ball and his wife had become regulars on the Manchester social scene, enjoying nights out with players from various teams. Willie Morgan, who moved from Burnley to Manchester United in 1968 and became a close friend, recalls, 'You would play against each other and then meet up later. Bobby Moore always used to stay over in Manchester and come to the night clubs with us when West Ham played at Old Trafford. There was a lot of camaraderie between the players. It was a different world, a nicer world. Bally and I did lots of night clubs together, trying to avoid his dad in the meantime.

'Bally actually took me for my first Chinese meal, at the Mandarin in Wilmslow. He had booked a table for us and our wives, but I said I wanted steak and chips. I had ordered soup as my starter and it was low lighting, quite dark, and I tasted it and said, "This is absolutely shit, Bally. I am never coming out with you again." He said, "Willie, that is the water we use for cleaning our fingers."'

5

A GRAND OLD TEAM

'Once Everton has touched you, nothing will ever be the same'

– Alan Ball

JOE Royle scored more than 100 League goals for Everton, his hometown club; managed them to an FA Cup victory in 1995; and returned in recent years to work on youth development. As we conclude our chat, it seems appropriate to ask someone so embedded in Everton history why Alan Ball, whose record of five years at the club and one League Championship is hardly out of the ordinary, continues to be held in such reverence at Goodison Park, even by those whose only connection to the era in which he played is the enduring presence of the *Z Cars* theme tune as the team takes to the field.

'He was the best player ever to wear a blue shirt,' is Royle's unequivocal answer, delivered without a moment's pause. 'That's not a bad place to start.'

Ball's Everton debut, in front of fewer than 22,000 at Fulham's Craven Cottage, came three weeks after he'd performed for a worldwide audience at Wembley. Not that the size of the theatre ever made any difference to him. He treated every game as though it was opening night. 'I'm the world's worst loser,' he once said. 'In this I am like my dad. When we are playing against each other, whether it's cards, tiddlywinks or what have you, neither of us will concede best.'

A story from a little later in his career, told by football artist Paul Trevillion, illustrates that point perfectly. 'I had a portable putting green and Alan liked to stop on his way home from training at Arsenal,' he explains. 'There were three rows of holes, one with one hole, one with two and one with three. I said, "If you can get all three rows without missing you can have it." That was a mistake. If you said something like that to Alan, well, I knew I would lose it. He took up the challenge and on about the third visit he won it. I learned not to mention anything about art – there was always the chance he'd prove himself another Michelangelo!'

Derek Temple, who was on the left wing for Ball's first Everton match, recalls, 'The thing about Alan was that it didn't matter what game it was. He liked the big occasions – it was in his psyche – but he wanted to be a winner in any match. I have seen him in tears after we lost. He brought that winning attitude; he wanted everybody to work as hard as he did. He was very committed and competitive, but he was not going to go round kicking people. I could name a couple of players who you had to watch yourself against in training. Alan was not like that. He was just a very good professional.'

John Hurst explains that Ball 'loved his football and wanted to improve all the time', while Royle continues, 'Even in training, there was never any lack of effort, but there was always a smile as well. He loved what he was doing. That was the main thing about that side. We trained and played with a smile, but when there was any hard work to be done he was always the first one.'

Defender Roger Kenyon says, 'We had the making of a very good team, but Bally was one of the missing pieces. What shocked me was his enthusiasm, his fitness and his total determination in training every day. He made other players, whatever their reputation, work harder. He wouldn't entertain defeat, whatever the score. Even if it was five-aside, he wanted to win and he would rejoice in it. He would jump in the bath and have a laugh and make everyone on the losing side feel bad.'

Ernie Hunt recalled two off-duty incidents that proved how Ball had turned himself into one of the fittest players in football. During a night out in Southport he silenced some cocksure rugby players by challenging one to a race along the beach. 'Bally came jogging in with the rugby player nowhere in sight,' Hunt told author Chris Westcott. He also remembered being on holiday in Majorca a few years later when he and Ball were attacked verbally and, eventually, physically by a group in a nightclub. In the ensuing melee, Hunt had his nose broken before getting out and jumping into a taxi for the four-mile journey to their hotel, only to find that Ball had beaten him back there on foot.

Taking the field at Fulham with Ball in the line-up, Harry Catterick's team were looking to banish the disappointment of losing to Liverpool at Goodison Park in the Charity Shield a week earlier. That 1–0 defeat had been the final catalyst for Catterick to secure the signing of Ball. The new man's presence might not have been the only factor in Everton beginning their League campaign with a victory in London, but he did score the only goal of the match in the second half. On the journey home, the Everton fans sharing the train with their heroes left Ball in no doubt about how much they valued his arrival.

The story goes that, on hearing of the new acquisition at Everton, Bill Shankly sent Ball a message saying, 'Congratulations, son. You'll be playing near a great team.' Having proved, on his debut for Blackpool, his ability to silence Shankly, Ball would carry something of a sign over Liverpool throughout his career. In 13 Merseyside derbies he was on the losing side only four times, before winning on three consecutive visits to Anfield with Arsenal. He wasted little time in reminding Merseyside of the force now within its midst when, after suffering defeat to Manchester United on his home debut, he scored twice as Liverpool were beaten 3–1 in front of 64,318 Goodison Park fans four days later. 'There were no nerves,' Ball would recall. 'I was loving every moment of it, as if this was my stage. I knew this was what I wanted for the rest of my life.'

'The response to him from the fans was fantastic,' states Royle. 'They love a character. He was cheeky and they took him to their hearts straight away. And scoring in a derby game immediately endeared him to the Everton fans.'

Yet, as confident as Ball could appear in front of the packed terraces, there were understandable insecurities to be overcome as he sought acceptance from new workmates. Winning the World Cup, Ball feared, would count for nothing until he proved to Everton's players that he belonged in their company. He sensed an initial jealousy and an absence of camaraderie.

Kenny Swain, a teenage Evertonian at the time, was enthralled to hear his hero tell him about his early days at Goodison when he played under him at Portsmouth. 'I was like a rabbit in the headlights with my tongue hanging out,' he remembers. 'He told me about walking into the dressing room for the first time, wondering what on earth was he going to do sitting alongside all these great players like Alex Young, Roy Vernon and Brian Labone. He said, "I had my head down and I just made my way to Ray Wilson because I knew him and thought it would be great being under his wing." He said it was intimidating and Fred Pickering was looking around saying, "I wonder whose shirt you are going to take?"'

Interestingly, teammates were unaware of – or have forgotten – any of Ball's anxieties. Instead they recall the easy acceptance he achieved. Perhaps he merely imagined it all. 'We just thought what an asset he was going to be,' says Hurst. 'He was a hell of a player. We had already seen enough of him to know that. He didn't have to prove himself. All we expected from him was to improve us as a team. As a personality he was great in the dressing room.'

Temple has similar memories. 'We recognised what a talent he was. When you get a new player in a club you know what ability he has. It is just his character. Not everybody is going to like the new players and get on with them. But Bally fitted right in and I am not aware of any animosity.'

Jimmy Husband, a young forward fighting to establish himself in the first team, was struck by Ball's assertive personality. 'Alan was very good in the dressing room,' he recalls. 'He was a cheerleader; always had an opinion on tactics, always had a voice in discussions of games and opponents.'

Meanwhile, Ball's father, listening to his son's concerns, merely reminded him that if he helped his colleagues to pick up their win bonuses, he would become one of them quickly enough. It soon became obvious that few players would contribute more to the cause of Everton victories than Ball, especially once he had got what he felt was an early-season drop in form out of his system. 'Week in, week out, he was so consistent,' Royle confirms. 'The players used to joke that the man-of-the-match award was made on a Friday because he won it that often.'

Everton finished Ball's first season in sixth place, their new signing leading the way with 15 goals in 41 League games and adding three more in other competitions. A run of nine games with only one win before the turn of the year undermined any hopes of the title.

One of those games was at Manchester City, where the visiting fans erupted in violence after a disallowed goal. Although Everton were hardly among the country's worst offenders, the cloud of hooliganism would maintain a heavy presence over football during the course of Ball's playing career. As one of the game's most prominent figures, and one with the platform of a regular magazine column, Ball would frequently be asked what he and his peers could do to help to tackle the problem. If the authorities appeared powerless to prevent the violence that was becoming a staple of weekly football reporting, then Ball failed to see that there was much the players could offer. 'When it's suggested that we players should meet the trouble-makers, I just don't understand that,' he argued. 'Honestly, we're worlds apart. What could we say to persuade the punch-up artists anyway? I'm afraid it is simply a matter for the police, not for the players.'

Having gone out in the second round of the European Cup Winners' Cup to Real Zaragoza, Everton began their defence of the FA Cup with a replay win against Burnley before a televised draw at promotion-bound Wolves in the fourth round. Footage of the game reveals Ball accepting the opening kick-off from Jimmy Gabriel and immediately curling his right foot behind left to knock a 'rabona' pass back to Hurst. There was no messing around, however, when he stepped up confidently to score the equalising penalty 11 minutes from time after he had been bundled over in the box.

A 3–1 win in the replay was followed by the fifth-round Merseyside showdown that left Clement Freud so cold. Then the quarter-finals brought a quite magnificent roller-coaster of a game at title-chasing Nottingham Forest that even Freud could not possibly have failed to appreciate. Husband's two goals, the first set up by Ball's defence-splitting pass, were not enough to overcome a hat-trick by Forest's mercurial Ian Storey-Moore. With the crowd threatening to burst out of the heaving terraces and commentator Kenneth Wolstenholme struggling to make himself heard over the excited din,[1] Storey-Moore eventually headed in the late winner at the fourth attempt

---

1 At one point a crash barrier collapsed, causing one fan to be injured, while further crushing and fighting in the second half led to another spectator being stretchered away. Reflecting the attitude towards crowd safety that existed more than two decades before Hillsborough, Wolstenholme casually referred to 'the inevitable casualties of cup-ties'.

after being denied by a defender's block, the goalkeeper's save and the crossbar.

Ball's participation in that game had been in doubt until the FA's disciplinary commission showed leniency when he appeared before them in March after accumulating three more bookings. A World Cup winner's medal and a change of club environment had clearly done little to anaesthetise Ball's hyperactive on-field personality, whatever *World Sports* magazine might have thought. As well as the cautions, he'd given one of his typically crass demonstrations of on-field gloating when Everton beat West Ham United 4–0 in February; on this occasion sitting on the ball and making as if to tie a bootlace.

'I used to hate myself sometimes on the pitch,' he confessed in a BBC interview in 1999. 'The things I used to do; the things I used to say to other players. I watched myself on television after one game and thought, "That can't be me, surely." My mother and my wife said, "You used to be awful on the pitch." But as soon as that was over I hope I was the first to the bar to have a drink with [the opposition].'

Temple recalls, 'He would take the mickey out of players if he could, and if we got a couple of goals up he would take the ball into the corner flag and sit on it, and that would wind the opposition up. I remember him doing that once and then passing me the ball, and they were all trying to kick lumps off me. But it was in him to say, "We are much better than you." You couldn't change him.'

'Bally was a bit of showman,' says Kenyon. 'And he was entitled to be because he was a world-class player. A lot of teams would man mark him and he would love to deride them whenever we were on top.' Everton colleagues had quickly come to understand what teammates at Blackpool and England had discovered: that, as George Cohen states, it was 'all part of the will and desire to win'.

Typical of the manner in which he could make a target of himself is a story related by Jack Charlton, who heard Ball instruct Johnny Morrissey to 'get the big bastard' during a game at Elland Road. Charlton deliberately took Ball out a few minutes later, looking down at his prostrate figure with a warning to 'mind your own business'.

Yet Hurst is sympathetic of Ball's need to find ways to combat the aggression he was confronted by week after week. 'He used to dictate games in the days when you were getting kicked all over the back.

Players used to receive the ball laid up to their feet and defenders would come right through them. It never bothered Bally. He was a great player anyway, but imagine him today knowing he was not going to get kicked every game. He was targeted. People used to think, "If we can kick Bally and keep him quiet, half the job is done." He had a fiery little temper on him, but that was his will to win. He wasn't the biggest of lads, but nobody frightened or intimidated him. The bigger they were, the more he would stand up to them.'

The martinets of the FA disciplinary commission were the only ones who appeared to have a problem with Ball's approach to his profession. Even Harry Catterick shrugged it off. His description of Ball to journalist Mike Langley – related in Rob Sawyer's biography of the Everton boss – was that he was 'a player who was decidedly right-footed, limited in terms of pace and always in trouble through his temperament, but I would still classify him as a world-class player'.

Unqualified praise comes from Royle, whose autobiography cited Manchester United's Roy Keane as a modern-day equivalent of Ball and who describes his teammate as one of the first 'box-to-box all-action midfielders'. Royle argues that his tireless running and 'infectious enthusiasm' were only part of what he brought to the Everton team. 'Alan would come and get the ball and he could actually run a game, dictate the pace of play,' he explains. 'He was one of few players I have ever seen able to do that, like Paul Gascoigne or David Silva now. He was a full 90-minute player and his one- or two-touch would kill people. He quite regularly had a man marker on him, trying to make it ten versus ten. If that did happen he would take them into false positions where they didn't want to be and the rest of us would benefit. And when his chance did come, he was deadly. He would either do them with a killer pass or put a terrific cross in.

'On top of that, he scored goals. In that part of his career he was prolific. We would work on set plays and we had a free-kick routine between the pair of us. I would sort of walk away disinterested and, as I turned, he would be on the ball in one stride and giving me a yard in front of people. We did quickly strike up an association.'

The most famous association of Ball's playing career developed from another shrewd Catterick transfer in March 1967. Howard Kendall had made headlines in 1964 when, aged 17, he'd become the youngest player to appear in an FA Cup final, right-half in the Preston North End team beaten by West Ham United. For £85,000, Catterick secured the services of a man whose tackling and work rate would provide a platform for the midfield creativity of Ball and Colin Harvey.

Kendall made an inauspicious start, a home defeat to Southampton on his Everton debut, in which he said he 'froze'. Up against him was Ball's former Blackpool housemate Hugh Fisher, who was playing his first game for his new club. 'I think we crossed the halfway line once and scored,' Fisher recalls. 'It was like the Alamo.'[1]

With Jimmy Gabriel maintaining his place in the team, Kendall played only four games in what remained of the season after his transfer and, like Ball, felt intensely the need to be accepted in the dressing room. He recalled having to stand on a table to sing a song as part of his initiation and being picked on by club captain Brian Labone before he finally told him enough was enough. 'It was Alan Ball who was the greatest help to me in those early days,' he recorded in his autobiography. Kendall remembered being impressed by Ball's insistence that he would own his own house by the time he finished playing – the extent of most players' material ambitions in the early years after the abolition of the maximum wage – and heeded his advice to be careful around the fearsome figure of Morrissey during training.

Kendall was not kept waiting long to make the number four shirt his own. 'One of the great things that Harry did,' says Husband, 'was that, after they won the FA Cup with virtually the same team that had won the League in 1963, he decided he was going to build a new team. The likes of Jimmy Gabriel, Dennis Stevens, Derek Temple, Alex Young, they weren't actually finished, but Catterick decided to build on youth, with the likes of Tommy Wright, Joe Royle, Colin Harvey and me coming through the system. It was a new era. He blended the team extremely well, like Alf Ramsey did with England. The team that won the World Cup weren't exactly the best players in

---

1 Fisher remembers an occasion when Ball gained revenge during a game at Arsenal. 'Something happened in the box and the ball rolled to me. The referee gave Arsenal a free-kick just outside the box and Bally shouted, "Hughie!" Of course, I automatically picked up the ball and chucked it to him and he took a quick free-kick and they scored.'

each of their positions but they were the best blend. Harry had the same approach.'

With Kendall in the team for good from the start of the 1967–68 season, one of the most celebrated midfield units in English football history was in place: Kendall on the right, Harvey on the left and Ball taking a more advanced position in the centre. The 'Holy Trinity', as Goodison Park fans would come to remember them, had been conjured up by the sound football sense of Catterick, but the alchemy that dazzled fans and opponents over the next few years was a natural phenomenon.

Harvey recalled that Catterick 'just let us get on with playing' and could not remember him ever discussing the manner in which they should operate. The manager saw enough in the way they blended in small-sided training games to know that he was better off leaving them to it. 'They really worked at it,' Catterick said. 'You wouldn't see them passing nonchalantly at any time.'

Kendall agreed that 'our brand of football was about retaining possession, passing quickly and incisively, and moving into space. It was largely intuitive, perfected over endless, joyous games of five-a-side.'

Ball explained that 'instinct and understanding took over' when they entered the field of play, maintaining that 'we could have found each other in the dark'. The key to their success, along with the telepathy developed in training, was the complementary qualities each man offered to the collective. Kendall was a tackler and a sound reader of the game, happy to rein himself in and do the hard graft. Harvey was a visionary link man, deft of touch while being no shrinking violet when it came to the physical elements of the game. Then there was Ball, the attacking all-rounder. And all three could run; their contribution no less in the final few minutes than it was at the start. 'The first thing about them,' says Royle, 'is that they all worked like slaves. And then they were all so talented. The blend was terrific.'

According to Husband, 'All three were great individuals, but the balance was brilliant. Howard had no pace at all, but was a great passer over long distances and a good tackler. Alan Ball was everywhere; good, neat control and a great engine. He scored goals as well. Colin was a beautiful little neat player, hard to get the ball off. Give him a really hard pass and it was under control in a flash and he could turn quickly. Put the three of them together and you had a great combination.'

The fact that 'the three of them were opposites' temperamentally, Roger Kenyon believes, was an advantage. In his view, 'Howard was not very verbal as a player; Bally was the opposite, as we know; and Colin was one of those who, if you fired him up, he would get so angry he would lash out at anyone.'

Hurst elaborates further on the trio's tactical synchronisation. 'They just instinctively knew what they were going to do. Howard would go wide right, Bally would drop back and Colin would go wide. They rotated so well and would all react to each other. They had great foot-balling brains. All of them went on to be managers because they understood the game. Bally used to play in front of Howard and Colin and he would be the top one supporting Joe. But his energy meant he could drop back too. With Jimmy Husband wide right and Johnny Morrissey wide left, we were the first team to play a system like that.'

Husband is keen to stress that the midfield players were not so absorbed with their own pattern of play that they failed to blend with other components of the team. They clearly saw themselves as part of, not apart from, the greater collective. 'Me and Howard worked out the way we played together,' he says. 'I was a sort of right winger, but I didn't stay on the right wing; I used to cut across field and end up on the left if that is where I felt like going. If I did that, the left-back had the choice of passing me on to the next defender or following me. If he followed me there was a gaping hole on the right wing that Howard would come into. He would get a ball from Colin or Alan and he would have acres of space in front of him, with Joe taking up positions in the penalty area for a cross. It was me and Howard who worked that out, it wasn't coached into us.'

Opponents were no less in awe of the trio. Derby centre-back Roy McFarland, Ball's future England colleague, says, 'Ball-Kendall-Harvey was known throughout football as the best footballing midfield in the country. Alan's link-up play, his movement, was outstanding: have it, knock it sideways, get it again, move it forward. That midfield three was similar to Barcelona's now. It had those qualities. They never lost the ball and they drew people out of position.'

Derby teammate Alan Durban was part of a midfield unit – along with Archie Gemmill and John McGovern – that had many a battle with Everton's vaunted threesome. 'If Bally played central then it was always McGovern's responsibility to look after him,' he explains. 'It was similar when we played against him for Wales; we would let Terry Hennessey look after him. A lot of the pitches we played on then were mud, certainly at the Baseball Ground, and Alan was one of those people who could run over the top of it. You had to make sure he got picked up, otherwise he could hurt you. He became a much better player after '66. He slowed down a little bit in that he wasn't in such a hurry to do things and as result he saw a lot more, more through balls, more crosses.'

Everton installed a new first-team coach at the start of 1967–68 when Tommy Eggleston left to become manager of Mansfield Town and was replaced by Wilf Dixon, Ball's former coach at Blackpool. But Dixon was no more likely than Catterick to attempt to influence the midfielders' style of play. 'He was a fitness fanatic rather than a coach' was Ball's description, although Husband is a little more generous. 'He was an excellent coach, more motivational and talking to individuals than team tactics.'

History was made on the opening day of the season when *Match of the Day* was finally allowed entry to Goodison Park. Typically, Ball rose to the occasion with a pair of goals in a 3–1 win against the champions, Manchester United. Overall, though, Everton made a stumbling start to the season, winning only two of the next eight matches, although a run of seven consecutive victories in the spring saw them finish fifth. In the end, they won more games than anyone other than the top two, Manchester City and United. Playing in front of the newly-formed midfield trio, Royle benefited to the tune of 16 goals in 34 League appearances. Ball, meanwhile, scored 20 times in 34 First Division matches, a remarkable tally for a midfielder.

By the end of the season, the classic Everton line-up of the era was established; Royle flanked up front by Morrissey on the left and Husband on the right. The popular Alex Young had been reduced to occasional appearances and would soon be on his way to become a player-manager in Ireland. With the exception of Ray Wilson, this

line-up that contested the 1968 FA Cup final with West Bromwich
Albion would be the first-choice unit as Everton won the title two
years later:

West

Wright   Labone   Hurst   Wilson

Kendall   Harvey

Ball

Husband   Royle   Morrissey

Substitute: Kenyon

Everton's route to Wembley began with gentle wins over Southport,
Carlisle United and Tranmere Rovers, without conceding a goal,
before Husband's double set up a 3–1 win at Leicester City in the
quarter-finals. The semi-final draw paired Everton with a buoyant
Leeds United, whose recent victory in the League Cup final had seen
Don Revie's team land their first trophy after several years of near-
misses. Ball would be watching from the stands at Old Trafford,
suspended for five matches and fined £100 after being sent off against
Newcastle United. The injured Hurst was sat alongside him, but it
was Everton who advanced to Wembley after Morrissey's penalty
provided the only goal of an uninspiring contest.

Having beaten West Brom 6–2 in the League two months earlier –
Ball scoring four in the rout at the Hawthorns – Everton were favourites to win the FA Cup for the second time in three seasons, giving Ball
a first domestic honour to place alongside his World Cup medal.
Desmond Hackett went as far as telling *Daily Express* readers that 'Alan
Ball will destroy West Brom'. With a little less hyperbole, Tom Jagger
wrote in *Soccer Star* that Everton's 'entire success, their chances of trotting first up those stairs for those presentations, depend largely on a
real honest-to-goodness piece of Lancashire – Ball'.

Everton, however, gave a tense performance, a premonition of
which surfaced during the team's coach ride to the ground as Kendall
and Wilson argued over the choice of music on the radio. It was in
front of goal that the uncertainty manifested itself. 'We had scored 10
goals in two games against them,' Hurst sighs. 'We were odds-on

favourites. But we could have played an extra day and never scored. We didn't play well compared to how we had played all that season.'

Royle cites Everton's failure to properly meet the physical challenge posed by a West Brom team who 'set about us' and admits that 'we weren't firing properly'. Ball was, at various times, body-checked and tripped and, as Everton bit into some retaliatory tackles of their own, the crowd were frequently reduced to chanting, 'We want football.'

The best opportunity in the early stages fell to Husband, who missed the target, and a pattern quickly emerged; yellow Everton shirts doing more of the attacking and West Brom content to strike on the break. Neither tactic produced any further significant moments until Kendall shot just over after Ball slipped him a pass in the 40th minute, before Morrissey concluded the first half by forcing John Osborne to tip away his well-struck effort.

Yet Everton's endeavour led to very few clear chances. Ball had a speculative shot blocked and then saw Husband just fail to connect with a clean header after he curled in a free-kick. Inside the final minutes, Morrissey's cross glanced off the head of Ball and then Husband headed over, leaving Ball gesturing angrily that he had been in a better position.

The only goal of the game arrived three minutes into extra-time. West Brom centre-forward Jeff Astle, who had scored in every round of the tournament, had a long-range shot blocked, but then pinged the rebound back past Gordon West from the edge of the box with his left foot. 'We had one the one of our worst games of the season,' says Husband, 'probably one of the worst performances by that Everton team. I met Jeff years later and he admitted it was probably the only goal he scored with his left foot. Sad day.'

It was games like this where Ball most felt the absence of a top-class coach, someone who could teach him and his team the odd trick or two and come up with a tactical nuance that could decide a tight contest. He went as far as saying that he 'resented' Catterick's inability to think like someone such as Malcolm Allison, who was coaching Manchester City to the title that season.

Yet for the next two seasons Everton became arguably the most exciting team in English football. In 1968–69, their 77-goal tally in finishing third was 11 more than the total achieved by a Leeds United team in the process of winning the League with a record haul of 67 points. Leeds would outscore them the following season, but finished nine points adrift in second place as Catterick's team became more clinical and were beaten only five times in their march to the Championship, while increasing their total of victories from 21 to 29. The facts, impressive as they are, do a poor job of conveying the joy of much of Everton's football over that period.

'We had a goalkeeper and ten players who were good on the ball,' says Royle. 'Alan used to say before games, "If you want to play. we'll play you; if you want to run us, we'll run you; and if you want to try to bully us, we will take it and bully you back." Quite honestly, whatever way you wanted to play that side we could handle it.'

Hurst continues, 'We played some fantastic football and that is where the midfield trio came into their own. We were playing a different game to everyone else. No one was playing the kind of 4-3-3 system we were using.'

A sluggish start to the 1968–69 season – two defeats in the first three games – was followed by an unbeaten run of 16 matches, during which Ball scored another hat-trick against West Brom. That sequence was brought to a halt by a 2–1 defeat at Leeds, a game that featured one of the many tussles Ball fought with Billy Bremner over the years for club and country. Ball got his retaliation in first on this occasion, fouling Bremner inside the first minute. 'The feud I had with him never abated,' he would write. 'We would go at each other non-stop.'

Leeds defender Norman Hunter recalls, 'Bally made himself a great player. He wasn't the quickest but I have never seen a player control the ball and pass it better and he had such great enthusiasm. As time wore on, we used to mark Bally man-for-man and we used to put Paul Madeley on him. Paul was very quick and Bally used to get very frustrated, very emotional. Paul never gave him a kick and he was so frustrated he was in tears after the game.'

Everton wasted little time moping, bouncing back with a 7–1 thrashing of Leicester City. Failure to win more than four of their final 13 matches condemned them to remaining a safe distance behind Leeds, but in the meantime another assault on the FA Cup was being launched. Royle's winner in the quarter-final at Manchester United set up a meeting with Manchester City in the semi-final at Villa Park, before which Catterick announced that he had fined Kendall for comments to reporters. In fact, he had done no such thing. He merely put the story out in order to discourage Ball from making any careless remarks in the build-up to the match. For all the style and swagger with which City had won the title the previous season, they possessed, in Allison, a coach who could resort to pragmatism when needs arose. They had been one of the first leading English teams to employ a sweeper on a regular basis as they were fighting to establish themselves back in the top flight. Now, Allison recognised that the way to halt a quick, direct side like Everton – whose style was not dissimilar to his own team's – was to ambush their forwards through use of an offside trap. Frequently, the linesman's flag went up the moment the ball crossed into the City half and a goal by Tommy Booth was enough to deny Everton a return to Wembley.

No season would be complete without Ball attracting unwanted attention for a brush with authority. This time he was considered lucky not be sent off for throwing the ball at referee Norman Burtenshaw during a frustrating goalless draw against Manchester United. 'If I cooled down I wouldn't be the player I am,' he protested. 'This was the first time I've shown anger in six months and I've been kicked from pillar to post.'

Reprieve in the wider world of criminal justice came Ball's way a few months later when he was found not guilty by a jury of drink-driving. Stopped after leaving Blinkers night club in Manchester because of a faulty light, Ball was subsequently breathalysed and alleged to be over the legal alcohol limit. He was cleared when it was shown that his test had been administered only minutes after his last drink – in violation of standard procedures – causing alcohol residue in the mouth and saliva to give a falsely high reading.

Three days after Ball's day in court, the new season began, although he missed an opening-day win at Arsenal through suspension. By the beginning of November, no one could be in any doubt that this Everton team was a real contender for the First Division title. Fifteen wins and only a single defeat in 18 games made sure of that. Once again, a match against Leeds provided a benchmark of Everton's progress. This time, the cameras caught Husband, courtesy of a Gary Sprake error, and a Royle double giving Everton a three-goal lead at

Goodison. Leeds pulled two back, but their 34-match unbeaten run in the League was over.

November brought the scare of Harvey having to miss a couple of months because of inflammation of an optic nerve, while December saw a chastening 3–0 loss at home to Liverpool, a game remembered largely for a spectacular diving header into his own goal by Sandy Brown. Yet Everton's progress appeared to persuade Catterick to loosen up with the media, offering an uncommonly forthright appraisal of his team to ITV. 'We believe in quick play, accurate passing and possession until we can see an opening, and then striking as quickly as possible.' The public, he said, wanted to see 'attractive players', adding his belief that 'if you get too defensive-conscious your attacking flair goes'.

He launched into a glowing tribute to Ball by arguing, 'Whatever I can say about Alan Ball would indeed underestimate him because this chap has great ability on and off the ball. He's a good competitor, he trains as hard as any professional I know, or indeed have ever known, he wants to win, he has skills, he wants to win so much. Many skilful players get complimented yet you forget the time they've spent standing around. This boy never stands and he's always competing and creating.'

Given what was lurking around the corner, Catterick's further comment was prescient. 'Alan's temperament possibly has been his worst enemy in some aspects,' he said. 'But I've seen this boy take some terrible punishment physically on the field, with very little protection at times.'

In January, the optimism created by a new decade, two successful moon landings and England's impending World Cup defence was somewhat lost on Ball when he was suspended for five weeks by the FA and fined £100 after picking up his third booking of the season for a foul on Liverpool's Ian St John. He had unsuccessfully appealed against the second of those cautions, given for alleged time-wasting against Wolves. As draconian as Ball's ban sounds by 21st-century standards, some observers attending the hearing in Derby felt that disciplinary chief Vernon Stokes was going soft in giving Ball a sentence only one week longer than George Best received for the solitary act of knocking the ball out of referee Jack Taylor's hands. Ball was described as greeting news of his ban with a 'wry smile'.

A typically energetic Alan Ball in training at Blackpool in 1965. His father always wanted him to be a 'perpetual motion' player.

Wearing the tangerine jersey of Blackpool, the club who gave him his professional chance after rejection by Wolves and Bolton.

Prior to the 1966 World Cup, Ball was pictured revisiting the streets where he had learned to play football during endless training sessions with his dad.

Alan Ball needed an international manager who would look beyond the disciplinary problems of his early career. He found one in Alf Ramsey.

Restored to the team after missing two group games, Alan Ball is the first to congratulate Geoff Hurst on scoring the winner in the World Cup quarter-final against Argentina.

Alan Ball threatens the West German defence during the 1966 final. 'He was probably the best player that day,' Bobby Charlton recalled.

Ball takes on West German midfielder Wolfgang Overath.

Champion of the world at the age of 21, Ball joins Roger Hunt, Geoff Hurst, Jack Charlton, Bobby Charlton and skipper Bobby Moore as England's celebrations begin.

...and Lesley attract a crowd at their wedding at ...phen's Church, Kearsley, in May 1967.

...ey and Alan celebrate the arrival of the first of ...r three children, daughter Mandy.

Lesley was the practical partner in her marriage to Alan, evidenced by the fact that it was her name on their mortgage agreement.

'My mentor, coach, adviser, critic, psychologist, disciplinarian and caring father,' was how Ball described Alan senior, pictured here reading up on murder trials.

Members of the 1970 World Cup squad Jeff Astle, Alan Ball, Geoff Hurst, Bobby Moore and Peter Osgood off duty in Mexico.

Now one of the highest-profile footballers in the country, Alan Ball joins Manchester United stars Denis Law and George Best in launching their range of football annuals.

Ball became even more distinctive when he signed a deal to wear Hummel's revolutionary boots, even though he mostly wore his own preferred brand painted white.

Ball the family man at home during the third birthday party of daughter Mandy, right.

At England training in 1971 with Bobby Moore, a great friend who became 'Uncle Bobby' to his children.

Confrontations with referees were a recurring theme of Ball's career, even prompting questions from MPs when he was eventually made captain of England.

The happiness of teammates John Hurst and Roger Kenyon quickly turned to bemusement when they heard, later the same day, that Everton were selling their illustrious teammate.

Subsequently addressing the issue of suspensions in *Shoot!*, Ball aired his view that 'the way to get at an erring player is to hit him in the pocket'. He pleaded, 'Fine him, but don't take away his very life for what seem to be ever-increasing spells of suspension . . . what hurts so much is being cut off from a job which is also a way of life.' Yet in speaking of the pain of a suspension, Ball was demonstrating exactly why the administrators felt it was the most effective deterrent.

Everton won only one of four League matches in Ball's absence. The final game of his suspension, a 2–2 draw against Arsenal, had been scheduled for television coverage, but with the title in sight Everton's paranoia had returned. 'We have been over-exposed,' said chairman Jack Sharp in announcing another ban on the cameras. There were more serious concerns, however, when draws in the next two games allowed Leeds to take top spot in the First Division. Catterick called a team meeting at which he warned the players they were in danger of throwing away their shot at glory unless their performances improved. Club captain Brian Labone waited until the management team had departed before he delivered his own stern warning to his colleagues.

But while Leeds slogged away in an effort to win League, European Cup and FA Cup, Everton's third-round defeat to Sheffield United in the last of those competitions had left them a clear runway towards the title. With the season ending early to accommodate England's preparation for the World Cup, six consecutive victories during a busy March left Everton with only the formalities to complete. Don Revie, meanwhile, had been forced to send out reserve players in increasingly meaningless League games as he attempted to preserve his Leeds men for a three-match FA Cup semi-final against Manchester United and their heavyweight European semi-final against Celtic.

An additional spark had been introduced to the Everton line-up in the second half of the season in Alan Whittle, whose instinct for goal proved as eye-catching as his shock of blond hair as he either deputised for the suspended Ball or kept Husband out of the number seven jersey. By the time Everton prepared to face West Brom on the night of 1 April, the 20-year-old's 10 goals in 13 games included one in each of the previous five matches.

'It was very disappointing,' admits Husband. 'I got a slight thigh strain which meant I was going to miss about three games and then I would be fit again. But Alan came in and scored something like four goals, so when I was fit again Harry did what most managers would have decided: don't change a winning team. I was sat watching matches in a suit and tie and Alan carried on until the end of the season scoring goals. It was bitter sweet for me.'

Ball had been leading the team for a month because of Labone's injury and now he had the chance to be at the helm as Everton gained the final victory they needed to clinch the Championship with two games still to play. He buzzed around the Goodison Park dressing room, injecting his colleagues with an additional dose of his own enthusiasm. Catterick, meanwhile, offered a quieter reassurance.

Kenyon, who was deputising for Labone in the centre of defence, recalls, 'It was West Brom, of all people, the team who beat us at Wembley; everyone was waiting for it, there could be only one result. Everybody knew we would win. The feeling was that there was no way we were going to get beat. And we battered them. It could have been far more than 2–0.'

The irrepressible Whittle calmed any nerves by opening the scoring after 19 minutes and Harvey added a second mid-way through the second half when he cut in from the left and curled in a shot from the edge of the penalty area. The only question remaining was whether Catterick's purposeful march towards his players in the middle after the final whistle would see him arrive before they were lost among the mass of fans racing on to the pitch to celebrate. Ball received the trophy in the directors' box from the Manchester United chairman Louis Edwards and then left it behind for safe keeping as he joined his teammates for a lap of honour. 'It was just a euphoric feeling,' Kenyon continues. 'The celebrations afterwards were fantastic. We all went into town and painted it red.'

Catterick was enjoying the manner of Everton's success as much as anything. 'They won it by playing football,' he glowed. 'And I would like to believe we have entertained spectators all over the country in the process. We don't play assassin stuff.' When the club produced its official celebration brochure, Catterick reiterated, 'It has often been said that the end justifies the means – in other words it does not matter how you win as long as you win. But as far as I am concerned the way Everton achieve victory IS important.'

Ball, meanwhile, having added his country's highest domestic prize to the world's greatest international honour already in his possession, saw this as merely the precursor of even greater achievement by his club. 'This is the start of five great years for Everton,' he predicted. Yet by the time that period was up, Ball's career had taken some unexpected turns and Everton Football Club, and English football in general, would look very different.

6
END OF THE WORLD

'Look back over the past, with its changing empires that rose and fell, and you can foresee the future too'

— Roman Emperor Marcus Aurelius

THE sideburns look too bushy and the attempt at capturing his wavy hair has ended up creating the impression of a Victorian-era barrister. Still, Alan Ball's vivid colouring was never likely to receive full justice from a silver-coloured metal coin that you could pick up with four gallons of Esso petrol and then, if you'd paid your two shillings and sixpence, place into the blue mounting board with 29 of his international teammates. The FKS Mexico 70 sticker collection manages to offer up the full auburn head, although the crude colouring on the shirt suggests that the publishers simply painted white over an existing Everton shot rather than attempting to photograph him in England colours.

Handling these artefacts now is a wonderfully nostalgic indulgence, but at the time they represented must-have items for those schoolboys – and young at heart – who had been counting down the days between Sir Alf Ramsey's team winning the World Cup and defending it four years later. Many of those rushing down to the newsagent to spend their pocket money on stickers, or issuing strict instructions to parents about which garage to patronise, had been too young to recall July 1966 and therefore, knew nothing other than a world in which England was football's ruling nation. Their excitement might have been the most intense of all. The stories they had heard and images they had seen of Hurst, Ball, Charlton and the rest frollicking around Wembley had expanded to fill every corner of their daydreams about what would happen when pictures were beamed 'via satellite' into their homes from the other side of the world.

In truth, even those who had been paying closer attention to the England team in the previous four years than simply cutting out colour posters and swapping bubble-gum cards had found reason for excitement. Even though Alan Ball felt that the first eleven of four years previously was stronger, the squad for Mexico was, in the view of many, even deeper than the triumphant 1966 group. Yes, Bobby Charlton was slowing down; but Gordon Banks and Bobby Moore were still the best in the world; Geoff Hurst, Martin Peters and Ball had matured into craftsmen in their positions; and the likes of Alan Mullery and Francis Lee had hardly weakened the team by succeeding Nobby Stiles and Roger Hunt. And Colin Bell, Peter Osgood and others offered important options off the bench in an exhausting tournament in which substitutions were expected to play an important role. Of course, England had not received rave reviews in every match since winning the World Cup, but there was absolute trust in the now-knighted Ramsey to get it right when it mattered most. 'I'm backing England to win again,' wrote Albert Barham in the *Guardian*, while Desmond Hackett told *Daily Express* readers, 'The squad contains all the qualities to do it again.' And so on.

England's first task in the afterglow of the 1966 World Cup had been to secure a place in the knockout stages of the European Nations Cup, which would conclude in Italy in 1968. It was the first time England had entered the competition, although qualification didn't entail anything too unfamiliar, with UEFA deciding that two seasons' worth of Home International results would determine which British team advanced. Scotland went home from Wembley in the spring of 1967 as 3–2 winners and, in their eyes, world champions, but a 1–1 draw at Hampden Park the following year, plus a series of wins against Wales and Northern Ireland, ensured that England advanced to the last eight.

Bobby Charlton scored the only goal of the first leg against Spain and, not for the last time, Chelsea's Peter Bonetti found himself deputising in a major quarter-final after Gordon Banks was taken ill before the return match in Madrid. Even though Spain levelled the tie, Peters and Norman Hunter secured victory in what was considered England's best performance since the World Cup. Ball had revelled in the unusual role of playing as a centre forward, alongside Roger Hunt.

'There was this guy of about 5ft 6in playing centre-forward against an outstanding national side,' Mullery recalls. 'He just ran riot. He ran into spaces and popped up everywhere.'

In Italy, where they would face Yugoslavia in the semi-final in Florence, England discovered that sympathies were running strongly against them. Ramsey's 'animal' accusations directed at Argentina in 1966 were seen as a slur on all football of Latin origin and were thrown back at a team thought to be too reliant themselves on the physical elements of the game. England weren't helped by arriving wearied from a defeat in West Germany only five days before the semi-final and then found themselves victims of persistent rough play by the Yugoslavs, none more so than Ball. Hurst, watching from the sidelines, described 'one of the most violent games I can remember', with England opting to stand up to their opponents foul for foul. With four minutes remaining, Moore failed to deal with a cross from the left and winger Dragan Džajić fired his team into the lead. No equaliser was forthcoming, but Mullery managed to make history by becoming the first player to be sent off in a full England international, kicking out in retaliation after yet another assault from behind from Trivic.

'It was nasty,' Mullery remembers. 'They were the dirtiest side I had ever played against. Other than the goalkeeper, they had 10 players who wanted to kick you. As the final whistle was approaching, this fellow did me down the back of my calf. I thought he had a nail sticking out of his studs the way the blood was pumping. So I turned round and kicked him in the cobblers.'

Ramsey told Mullery, 'If you hadn't done it, I would have,' demonstrating an empathy that Ball would experience in similar circumstances a few years later. 'Alf even paid my fine,' Mullery adds. 'He said, "I am glad somebody did something," and sent me a cheque for 50 quid.'

Ramsey was no sentimentalist, though, and by the time the 1968–69 season neared its conclusion, Hunt and Greaves were gone for good and a run of mediocre results in friendlies had been banished by a 5–0 Wembley thrashing of France in which Lee had scored his first England goal. 'Alan was a very good player to play with,' Lee explains. 'He got it and gave it to you, simply, quickly and efficiently, which is what you want as a striker. He let me get the ball into my feet as soon as possible and get on with it. And although he wasn't the quickest in the world, he could read the game like the *Beano*.'

Television viewers were now preparing for a veritable orgy of live football, with the entire Home International tournament played within a week, kick-off times staggered so that all the games could be broadcast. That meant more live matches in eight days than the country was used to seeing in two years. Ball's participation, according to some observers, could not be taken for granted. He'd looked tired and off the pace late in the season, they said. Typically, he responded with an outstanding series, culminating in the 4–1 win against Scotland at Wembley. He was involved in the move that created the first goal for Peters, had a shot parried to help set up a Hurst penalty for the third, and slipped a return pass to Peters for the final goal. He even pulled out his favourite party trick, knocking a rabona down the right flank for Tommy Wright to create another chance.

Starved of competitive football because of automatic qualification for the World Cup, England had treated the British championships as proper tournament play, but an even more relevant test was offered by their tour of Mexico, Uruguay and Brazil. After a goalless draw in the Azteca Stadium, the venue for the following year's final, and a 2–1 win in Uruguay, Ball was in confident mood before the much-anticipated visit to Rio's Maracanã Stadium. Asked for an assessment of the great Pelé, he dead-panned, 'I've looked at him a bit hard and I didn't see any wings. He can be stopped all right.' Pelé, meanwhile, would describe Ball later in the year as 'one of the greatest midfield players in the world'.

The way England led for most of the match through Bell's strike, before conceding twice in the final 11 minutes, meant Ramsey's men flew home feeling they had nothing to fear when they returned to that part of the world a year hence. A season of uninspiring friendlies and Home Internationals did little to dampen confidence. A 3–1 win in Belgium, in which Ball scored twice, had shown exactly what England were capable of. The *Daily Mirror* said of Ball after that game that 'his enthusiasm always seems to act like a massive dose of adrenalin on England', while Ball himself said of the team move that had set up his first, 'If Brazil had scored a goal like that we would not have heard the last of it.'

England's squad departed for Mexico a full four weeks before the action began in order to become accustomed to the high altitude, by which time they had recorded a No1 single, *Back Home*, been equipped with aertex shirts and slow-dissolving salt tablets to combat the heat and packed enough fish fingers to last the entire tournament. The steak they took was not allowed into the country, but two weeks of conditioning in Mexico, followed by wins in warm-up games in Colombia – where Ball scored again – and Ecuador increased their hunger for the real action.[1]

The mood of tranquillity was demolished during a stopover in Colombia's capital city Bogotá, as the squad returned to Mexico. Killing time at the Hotel Tequendama, where they had stayed a few days earlier, skipper Bobby Moore was pulled out of a showing of the movie *Shenandoah* and arrested for allegedly stealing a bracelet from one of the hotel stores. Accusations had originally been made shortly after Moore and Bobby Charlton had visited the shop several days before, but had been dismissed as ridiculous and filed away as one of those bizarre occurrences that befall European visitors in exotic parts of the world. But now, amid claims of new eyewitness evidence, Moore was taken to court and placed under house arrest at the home of the head of the Colombian Football Federation while his team-mates flew back to Mexico. Unaware until take-off what was going on, England's players mixed incredulity with a deep concern that even the formality of dismissing the charges could take so long that their leader would miss some, or all, of the tournament.

Conceding that England were unpopular visitors to that part of the world, partly because of their status as champions yet also because of their perceived distrust of all things Latin American, Ball knew that the accusations were preposterous. 'There would never, ever conceivably be any chance that Bobby could have done that,' he said, suggesting it was part of a plot to destabilise the team.

No one was more worried than Ramsey. When Moore finally turned up in Mexico four days later, still wearing the same clothes, his

1 Journalist Kevin Moseley recalled an incident in Ecuador, where Ball had been having trouble sleeping and had headed to the bar in the hotel discotheque for a drink at 3am – wearing only his underpants.

manager greeted him at the airport with the closest to a show of emotion that anyone could remember. Moore, meanwhile, remained unflappable, having broken down the accusers' inconsistent and flawed testimony as though he was dealing with a lower division centre-forward. He apologised for his dishevelled appearance and got back to the business of retaining the World Cup.

That quest, which was enthralling the folks back home far more than Labour prime minister Harold Wilson's impending attempt to win a third general election against Edward Heath's Tory challenge, began against Romania in Guadalajara's Jalisco Stadium. Moore showed no sign of his ordeal and Hurst picked up where he left off four years earlier by scoring the only goal of the game, a scruffy finish resulting from Ball's chip into the box. The result, though, was more important than aesthetics. 'We were a little bit cautious,' Ball conceded. 'But we knew we couldn't get beaten.'

With Keith Newton having been hacked out of the game by the Romanians, the inclusion of Everton right-back Wright was the only change for the match that many expected to be the defining moment of the tournament. England's players emerged from a largely sleepless night, courtesy of mischievous Mexican fans besieging their city centre hotel, rubbed their eyes and prepared for a high-noon showdown against Brazil.

With the players casting virtually no shadow as the sun reached its full height, England appeared to be struggling to contain their natural instincts to play the kind of high-tempo game that would be suicidal in such heat. It meant, though, that they enjoyed early ascendancy; at least until the moment when Jairzinho burst past Terry Cooper and crossed to the head of the leaping Pelé, whose fierce downward header appeared bound for the net until Banks jerked across goal to pull off arguably the most famous save in football history.

Even as the game gradually slowed, Ball, typically, looked keen to inject some pace, but was obstructed by Pelé when he set off on one run from the half-way line. He often dropped deep to set attacks in motion, leaving Lee to occupy the right flank, but Lee was back in a central position after 33 minutes to connect with the diving header that Felix parried.

Meanwhile, evoking memories of Nobby Stiles against Eusebio four years earlier, Mullery shadowed Pelé. He even reduced him to diving in search of free-kicks, prompting Hugh Johns to remind ITV viewers among the combined 25 million watching on Britain's two rival broadcasters that the great man had done some professional acting in Brazil. At the back, Moore exhibited cool control, often emerging with the ball from frantic scuffles around the box like a commuter calmly stepping out of a crowded train carriage. His second-half tackle on Jairzinho, winning the ball with what appeared to be the wrong foot after backing off and biding his time, has been immortalised in song, but an earlier, more orthodox, dispossession of Tostão was almost as good.

It was clearly going to take something special to beat England's defence. It was Tostão who provided it after an hour, although Ball felt the Brazilian had elbowed him out of his path before weaving his way across the edge of the penalty area and swivelling to drop the ball at the feet of Pelé. Seeing the overlap outside him, Pelé rolled the ball for Jairzinho to fire past Banks.

Bell replaced Charlton, but it was the introduction of Jeff Astle for Lee that signalled England's new approach to breaching a defence that commentators took delight in describing as slow and ill-disciplined. The tactic of launching long balls into the box might have seemed a crude response, but immediately after Moore's most famous tackle, the Brazilian defence made a hash of dealing with one such delivery and the ball fell for Astle to shoot wide with the goal at his mercy.

With 12 minutes to play, the ball fell in the left corner of the box at the feet of Ball, whose attempt clipped the bar. 'My shot was always going away from Felix in goal, but I knew that it would hit the bar,' he said. 'I prayed that it would dip an inch or so.' He then had another attempt that looped over the top. By the end of the game, both teams looked likely to add to the score, but neither did and England were destined to finish second in their group. Hardly a disaster, especially given the general view that they had proved themselves a match for Brazil. 'In the mere matter of chances, [England] might well have won and certainly drawn,' *The Times* reported.

'Tostão had fantastic luck in his run to set up the goal,' was Ball's verdict. 'We could have done with a little of that good fortune in the last half hour when we did enough to have won. I'm sure we would have won if we had met again. Their defence was weak, especially the goalkeeper.'

In the build-up to the final group game against Czechoslovakia, Ball lightened the mood by allowing himself to be positioned as the 'Barber of Guadalajara', pictured by press photographers cutting Hurst's hair. Meanwhile, Mullery recalls that the squad were frequently entertained by the antics of Ball and Astle, who he describes as 'like Morecambe and Wise'. He explains, 'Bally took the piss out of Jeff something rotten. At one stage they were playing cards with me and Geoff Hurst, and Bally said quietly, "Let's wind Jeff up. I will raise £200." Jeff couldn't believe it and said, "Did you say 200 quid?" Bally said, "Well, I am on a thousand quid a week at Everton." This was 1970 so no way was he on that; he was on about £200. Geoff saw him for £400 and Bally had nothing in his hand. "Why did you bet all that money?" Jeff asked, and added, "When I get back I am going to ask my manager for £1,000 a week." Literally, a week after he was back we heard he was asking for a transfer because he was not getting £1,000 a week. That was Bally's doing.'

For the Czechoslovakia match, Ball was left on the bench for some rest as England – in a light blue kit thought to be kinder in the heat than the usual change strip of red – required debutant Allan Clarke's penalty to complete the formalities of reaching the quarter-finals. Ball came on after 65 minutes, hitting the bar again, and England headed east for Leon, where West Germany had won their group.

The colours in which the England and West Germany players took the field for a Sunday midday kick-off mirrored their meeting at Wembley four years earlier, Ramsey having decided that the poor visibility of pastel blue made it less desirable than the vivid, historically significant, scarlet. Approximately half the characters were the same as in 1966, although the stocky Bayern Munich poacher, Gerd Müller, was a notable newcomer. He had scored seven goals in Mexico already, including consecutive hat-tricks. Meanwhile, England's yellow goalkeeping jersey was worn by Bonetti, thrown into the biggest game of his life after Banks was taken ill with a severe stomach upset; an ironic – and, some maintain, suspicious – blow given the great lengths England, with all their fish fingers, had gone to in order to guard against such an occurrence.

By half-time it didn't look like making much difference. England gave a composed performance and went in a goal up, scored after 32 minutes. Newton advanced on the German area and played a diagonal ball towards the near post, finding Mullery to run in and sweep the ball into goal from six yards.

Ball was prominent on the right wing in the early stages of the second half, but it was from a deeper, more central position that he played the pass forward to Hurst that ended with an overlapping Newton crossing to the far post. 'Hurst!' shouted ITV's Hugh Johns as Peters converted England's second goal, although that was a better effort than the Mexican TV producer who put 'Newton' up on the screen. Whatever, England were two goals up and seemingly heading to the semi-finals.

Ball would say later that England had never played better during his international career than in those first 50-odd minutes. 'Goodnight. God bless. See you in Munich,' he squeaked excitedly in the ears of his opponents as the game restarted. 'He probably lost us the game,' Mullery laughs when reminded of Ball's boasting. 'But that was the way he played and the way he was as a person.' It was unthinkable that Ball might be caught out by his conceit, but, with hindsight, he admitted that his over-confidence should have been seen as a warning sign. 'Being in complete control can be dangerous. A team can see too much of the ball. That is what happened in Leon. We started to think, "This is it. We're through."'

Charlton's angry reaction to being asked to run into space after a pass from Ball suggested that the Manchester United man's 32-year-old legs were ready to be rested for the next challenge, as they had been in each preceding game. In fact, it was Germany who made the decisive substitution, sending on Jürgen Grabowski to patrol the right wing against Terry Cooper, growing tired from the amount of over-lapping required of Ramsey's wingless pattern of play. Charlton had one more raid in him after being released by Ball, but Bell was already stationed on the sidelines ready to replace him when, with just over 20 minutes remaining, Beckenbauer shot across goal from the right corner of the box and the ball bounced under Bonetti's arms. 'Müller' offered the hapless caption operator. Ramsey, of course, knew better and immediately sent on Bell to take over the job of shadowing West

Germany's scorer. 'I could feel the game slowly slipping away from us,' Ball admitted. 'Suddenly West Germany were back in the game. Beckenbauer's goal was like giving the team oxygen masks.'

With 10 minutes to go, Norman Hunter was sent on for Peters. 'Stop them playing and help TC,' Ramsey instructed him. Within a minute, a speculative long ball into the England area had evaded Mullery, plopped on to the back of Uwe Seeler's head and arced over Bonetti in no-man's land. West Germany were rampant and Ramsey's substitutions would be the subject of debate for years to come. 'They were fabulous substitutions at the time,' said Ball. 'Colin Bell and Norman Hunter were two great lads in the middle of the park; great runners, great lungs.' He told author Jeff Dawson, 'I would have made exactly the same decision.'

Hurst's effort was ruled out for a dubious offside and then Lee looked like he had been brought down in the box late in the first period of extra time. Argentinian referee Norberto Angel Coerezza disagreed, just as he had tended to favour the Germans in most decisions. Ball, his rolled-down socks reminiscent of four years earlier, fired in a cross that just evaded Hurst's head early in the second period, while commentators began explaining the potential process of drawing lots to decide the winner. They need not have bothered. Grabowski turned Cooper this way and that and crossed to the far post, Johannes Löhr headed across goal and an unmarked Müller jumped to volley past Bonetti. Eleven minutes later, England were no longer world champions.

'I still can't believe we lost,' says Lee. 'Germany had four or five world-class players and we made them look like selling-platers. Alf made a mistake when he picked Peter Bonetti. I think he should have picked Alex Stepney, who was more of a big-time player and had played really well in the European Cup final. We were all devastated, but Alan would openly show it.'

Ball, who had fired a half-volley high and wide with his left foot late in the game, was in tears in the dressing room. He had never been subjected to such misery by the game he loved so much. 'It was disbelief,' he told Dawson for *Back Home*. 'A bizarre, bizarre game. I never ever witnessed again going through the emotions and how it was towards the end of that game.'

Mullery adds, 'When we lost you couldn't find anyone who was sicker than him. For two days before we could go home it was a very quiet place, which was very unusual for Alan.'

While West Germany looked forward to what would be one of the World Cup's greatest games – a 4–3 defeat by Italy after extra-time – England's media began the business of questioning Ramsey's continued suitability for his job. Ball was one of those asked if the manager should resign. 'No chance of that,' he snapped. 'Who would take his place?' And he would write in *Shoot!*, 'Alf wasn't to blame for the defeat. We were – the players. He did all he could. We blew it.'

Handed a meaningless medal for reaching the last eight, Ball shaped to throw it out of the window of the bus as they left the stadium. Team physician Dr Neil Phillips asked if he could have it as a souvenir for his children instead. Ball happily handed it over. He needed nothing to remind him of this day. The pain of losing would remain to do that.

7

WHITE FEET, BLUE HEART

'All farewells should be sudden, when forever'

– Lord Byron

WITH England's World Cup defence ended prematurely, Alan Ball returned home to prepare for Everton's bid to retain their League Championship and an assault on the European Cup. First, there was the relatively mundane matter of the FA Charity Shield. What went into the record books as a routine 2–1 win against FA Cup holders Chelsea at Stamford Bridge turned out to be a significant moment in Ball's career and football history. Thanks to his footwear.

The chain of events leading to Ball running out for the curtain-raiser to the 1970–71 season in eye-catching white boots began with a young executive called Brian Hewitt being appointed to drive UK marketing for sportswear company Hummel, then based in Germany but later to move to Denmark. 'Trying to get into a market dominated by Adidas and Puma was daunting, to say the least,' he explains. 'People I got to take sales were those I knew in the industry, so I was selling a small amount of boots on the back of favours. We sold bugger all to nothing. About March, I said to Hummel, "You'll not last long unless we do something different." I came up with an idea that had not been done before – white boots. And the reason why I said white was because hockey players at that time wore white boots.'

Hewitt realised that with George Best hawking his Stylo Matchmakers – laces on the side – Bobby Charlton having his own range of boots and Eusebio being one of the faces of Puma, Hummel's new brand would need a star endorsement. 'We spoke to Bally and he bought into the idea. It was not a lot of money,' continues Hewitt, who, when reminded that Ball himself recalled his contract being worth £2,000 a year, adds, 'That sounds about right. They wouldn't put their laces in for that now, would they?

'We put his name on the side and we made these, basically, plastic boots. We had a good model coming in from Germany, which was basically a hockey boot, and we had two places making them in the UK; a co-operative in Heckmondwike in Yorkshire, and the people who used to make the Tuf shoes. But when we took the white boots to the market, people said, "Do you sell handbags with them?" They thought girls played in coloured boots. Calling in a few favours again, I managed to sell-in three to five thousand before the start of the season.'

Ball's appearance in the Charity Shield in front of the BBC cameras offered a great opportunity for promotion, but, as Hewitt recalls, 'He didn't have any white boots he could play in. This was days before the game. I said, "We are going to have to do something because he is going out in white boots." We got a pair of his Adidas boots and I took them off to Heckmondwike and said, "Spray those beggars white so it stays on and put chevrons on them." God knows how many times they sprayed them. They were absolutely gleaming. We got them out of the factory, put them on a Red Star train down to King's Cross on Saturday morning, got one of my guys to pick them up and Bally got them about an hour before kick-off. It was that close.'

It proved well worth the effort as the cameras inevitably homed in on Ball's revolutionary footwear. 'All through the game,' Hewitt recalls, 'the camera goes down on his feet and Kenneth Wolstenholme is calling him things like "twinkle toes". They had never seen this before. And then it went berserk. On Monday morning we sold 12,000 pairs over the telephone. It was astronomical. The Liverpool shops were snapping them up like crazy.'

Opposing fans inevitably seized upon Ball's boots as an additional reason to give him abuse when he visited their grounds. But, one month into the season, he insisted in his *Shoot!* column, 'Come what may, I'm sticking with my new white playing shoes. Okay, I've heard some of the comments from the terraces, but if I took notice of all that I'd probably never turn out in another game. Anyway, they're my own sponsored make, called Fireball. Most important is that they are damn comfortable and that's what matters most of all.' Which was complete tosh, of course.

Interviewed in 1999, Ball voiced his real feelings. 'They were the worst boots you could ever wish to wear. I remember them bringing them to me and thinking, "Oh no", but the monetary gains were huge, about two grand a year. I thought I would give them a try. Anyway, they brought these boots to me and they were shocking.' Ball continued, 'I wore them for a period of time but then I took my Adidas boots and painted them white. They were better boots to play in. I got away with it until it rained one day.'

Ball's claim that Hummel were furious at a deception that was revealed only by bad weather is another piece of artistic licence, something else he played up to get a laugh in his after-dinner routine. As Hewitt's Charity Shield story indicates, it was an approved idea to paint Ball's preferred boots white, a practice Ball insisted on continuing until Hummel could finally manufacture a shoe to his liking. Take a close-up look of pictures of Ball at that time and you can frequently see the black creeping up from the sole of the boot as the moisture of the grass, or mud, eats away at the white coating.

Painting duties appear to have been shared around. Gary Imlach, son of Everton coach Stewart – recalling that Ball usually wore 'a pair of Adidas 2000s with a fresh coat of Dulux' – says, 'The story was that he didn't like the new ones so Dad painted his old ones up for him. We had the Hummel boots as evidence, although sadly there was a fire at the place where my brother kept all the memorabilia and they went up in flames. We also had some of his Adidas 2000s because they used to tap the squad numbers in tiny little tacks into the sole of the boots, presumably for identification when they were hanging up in the boot room. His squad number was 21 and that is how you knew you had Alan Ball's boots, proof that they were historical relics.'

Hewitt continues, 'In the end, Germany turned out some of the real things and he wore them in later days.' Yet, despite the powerful image of Ball in white boots that endures in the minds of football fans of a certain age, he was back in black after only two seasons. Hewitt guesses that around 50,000 pairs of Alan Ball-endorsed white boots were sold in that period and, despite the initial wave of alternative footwear dying out by the middle of the 1970s, the palette had been established for a new multi-coloured millennium and a significant milestone created in the cultural history of the sport. So much so that when Jeff Dawson summarised the changing face of football between 1970 and 1974 in *Back Home*, his book about the Mexico World Cup, he highlighted two things: that England no longer ruled the world and 'Alan Ball had started wearing white boots'.

It was not just the look of Ball's feet that was changing for the new season. So was his role within his club. Having helped to lift the League Championship trophy as understudy to Brian Labone, he was now given the Everton captaincy on a permanent basis because of his teammate's ongoing injury problems. To call it a disaster would be an overstatement, although not by much.

'I took my responsibilities very seriously – some people thought too seriously,' he admitted in his fourth *International Soccer Annual*. 'By the end of the season I was being accepted as the skipper of the team, so far as the fans were concerned. They had come to recognise that I would make mistakes and that I would take a little time to adjust.'

The qualification 'so far as the fans were concerned' suggests that Ball was sufficiently self-aware to know that all was not well within the dressing room. 'If he was having a bit of a bad game himself he would come in and would be fuming at players, especially Howard Kendall,' says John Hurst. 'He used to get frustrated and ended up having a go at players when there was no need to.'

Joe Royle continues, 'He changed a bit as captain, his attitude. He was never a good loser anyway, but after losses he could be a little bit critical and probably fell out with one or two senior players because of that.'

In light of Ball's self-confessed love of betting and his subsequent admission of the financial problems he was having by the end of his time at Arsenal, Royle's next comment is intriguing. 'I don't know, has anybody mentioned things off the pitch with his gambling? That was always a theory among the team; that he had a problem because he loved a gamble.' Yet Royle doesn't necessarily believe that such pressure, if indeed it existed, would have been a significant factor in his approach to his new role. 'I wouldn't say that was something that would have changed his attitude. He just took the captaincy a little too seriously. He was a captain without being a captain anyway. He led by inspiration every week.'

Jimmy Husband adds, 'Alan had enough say when he wasn't captain, but when Brian was no longer captain it made Alan more boisterous, I suppose. Vociferous. I can remember the players rebelling against him.'

Harry Catterick admitted to author John Roberts that Ball's promotion might not have been his smartest move, explaining that he 'he felt so much responsibility that he wanted to do more and maybe that affected his game a bit'.

Under the new leadership of Ball, Everton failed to win any of the first six games in defence of their title. It took only until the third game of that sequence, another battle against Leeds United at Elland Road, for Ball's frustration to spill over. With Everton defending a 2–1 lead, England full-back Keith Newton headed across his own area to the feet of Billy Bremner, who fired in an equaliser. Ball's autobiography recalls that he was so incensed that he struck Newton on the pitch and continued their argument in the dressing room after Leeds had added a winning goal.

In the book *Everton Greats: Where Are They Now?* Newton said that by the time of Ball's departure from Everton he had 'driven us mad with his incessant moaning'. Recalling the Elland Road incident – although making no mention of a punch – he said, 'Bally came racing back to have a right go at the defence. We just felt it was totally uncalled for and that he'd be better occupied getting back up the pitch and doing his own job. With all due respect to him, Alan Ball wasn't very good for team morale.'

Four days later, during a 2–2 draw at Chelsea, referee John Gow was forced to step between Ball and Kendall as they began shoving each other during an argument over who should take a free-kick. 'I remember at Chelsea he had Howard in tears,' says Roger Kenyon. 'He shouted at him that much that Howard broke down and started crying. Bally could be very verbal, but the effect really depends on your personality. Certain players, like Howard, could take it really personally and it affected them. Bally often used to have a go at Howard, who I think needed a bit of a kick up the arse. It was proved that it worked, though, because Howard went on to great things.'

Kendall would reveal years later his increasing sense of frustration at the changes he saw in Ball after the 1970 title victory; an evolution not necessarily related to his acquisition of the captaincy. He reckoned that Ball senior had advised him to look to the future and, for the sake of longevity, cut down on the miles he was covering every season. Remembering Ball getting into the opponents' penalty area less frequently and instead 'dropping back and taking the ball off Tommy Wright', Kendall would be forced to tell him to 'clear off'.

Ball's outbursts sparked a debate in the newspapers about the nature of captaincy and, in particular, his own suitability for the role. 'I try to learn from all the great captains,' Ball commented, citing the statesmanlike Moore and adding, 'I also want to get the enthusiasm of Dave Mackay into my game.'

Ball received support from loyal allies. Moore, a close friend who would become 'Uncle Bobby' to his children, insisted, 'Alan is a natural for captaincy. He gets himself totally involved in every game and can lift his teammates.' And Sir Alf Ramsey offered a practical endorsement by naming Ball to lead his Football League XI against the Irish League.

In 1974 Ball would reveal his disappointment that support from within the Everton team had been less forthcoming than he'd hoped. 'I was captain of Everton for a while, but as a tempestuous player I never had the backing I needed. Whenever I did something wrong, nobody jumped to my defence.'

Everton's results, however, did little to support the cause of Ball's leadership. Failure to win more than seven games by the turn of the year meant their title defence never progressed beyond the theoretical stage. Catterick made much of the fact that Ball, Labone, Wright and Newton had suffered from their exertions in Mexico – even, nonsensically, claiming there had been some kind of conspiracy to hamper his club. John Hurst supports the fatigue theory by saying, 'We'd had a long season, then several players went to Mexico and we just didn't set off right the next year. It was disappointing. It was tiredness.' All of which is fair enough to a point, but the 1969–70 season had actually been shortened to allow for Mexico and there had still been seven weeks between England's exit and Everton's engagement in the Charity Shield, a length of time that must seem exceedingly generous to modern managers. Leeds had seen just as many of their men go to Mexico after one of the most gruelling seasons ever undertaken by any club and were in the thick of another Championship race and on their way to winning the European Fairs Cup.

Catterick's response had been to buy Nottingham Forest midfielder Henry Newton, whom he struggled to fit into the team. He had been beaten to the signature of Preston North End's Archie Gemmill by the persistence of Brian Clough, who refused to leave the Scotsman's house until he agreed to join Derby County. Seeking an explanation for Everton's woes in one of his *Shoot!* columns, Ball suggested, 'Footballers lose confidence more quickly than people in any other walk of life.'

In March, Everton experienced what Royle describes as 'the week a team died'. Progress to the quarter-finals of the European Cup had begun with the comfortable 9–2 aggregate dismantling of Keflavik. These were still the days when no Icelandic team could hope to compete with a group of full-time professional footballers and Ball helped himself to a hat-trick in a 6–2 home win.

A truer test presented itself in the second round, the last 16, where Borussia Moenchengladbach were the opposition. Following a 1–1 draw in Germany, Everton took a home lead after only one minute when Johnny Morrissey's cross bounced into the net, but the only further goal was Borussia's equaliser. After a scoreless extra-time, Everton made history by becoming the first English team to participate in a penalty shoot-out in European competition. Until now, UEFA had used replays and the eventual toss of a coin to determine tied contests. After Royle's opening effort was saved, Ball was the first Everton scorer. A German miss and Andy Rankin's diving stop from Ludwig Müller saw Everton prevail 4–3, although so unused to this situation were television producers at the time that ITV added the penalties to the second-leg scoreline and captioned the result: Everton 5, Moenchengladbach 4. Broadcasters would soon get the hang of it, as, sadly for future English sides, would the Germans.

After such a struggle, a quarter-final draw that paired Everton with Panathinaikos was greeted with quiet satisfaction. Even the management of the great Hungarian Ferenc Puskás failed to convince many observers that the Greek champions offered much threat. Ball was already saying, 'Somehow it seems only right that we should win the European Cup – because of the facilities we have got. Everything that happens here is for the betterment of football. The grandstand, the pitch, the attitude to the game.'

The Greek team went into the tie on the back of a warning from their sports minister Constantinos Aslanidis to play within the rules. 'The legs of Everton players such as Alan Ball cost fortunes,' he said. 'It is not good doing them damage just to get a good football result.' They got their result anyway, only a last-minute goal at Goodison Park from 19-year-old David Johnson allowing Everton to head to Athens for the second leg with a 1–1 draw. Unusually for someone who loved football as much as he did, Ball admitted that 'I can't say I'm looking forward to the [return] match with any great enthusiasm', citing reports he'd heard about primitive stadium facilities. Even more frustrating than 'dingy' changing rooms, though, was a goalless draw and defeat on away goals, ending Everton's hopes of reaching the final at Wembley.

Everton had less than three days – which they spent at the Lymm Hotel in Warrington – to get over their disappointment before facing Liverpool at Old Trafford in the semi-finals of the FA Cup. Their place in the last four had been secured by a 5–0 thrashing of Colchester United, the Fourth Division team that had shocked Leeds United 3–2 in the fifth round, and now they found themselves as many people's favourites against a Liverpool side that Bill Shankly was in the process of overhauling for future triumphs. After 10 minutes, Alan Whittle headed across the Stretford End goal for Ball to score with a half-volley, but the course of the match changed when Labone was forced off with a leg injury after 51 minutes. Full-back Sandy Brown came off the bench and, rather than any kind of tactical reshuffle, stepped straight into Labone's territory. With Catterick absent because of a bad case of flu, Wilf Dixon made the decision yet, according to one report, 'Brown's positional sense was lacking at critical times.'

'It was a funny old game,' says Royle, although he doesn't sound much like laughing about it. 'Until Brian got injured we were back to our best, we really were. It was just like the good old days. And then I felt there was a tactical mistake by Wilf, putting Sandy Brown on at centre-half. He just couldn't handle the size of John Toshack. Looking back, I think I would have handled the aerial threat better, and I am equally certain that if Harry had been there that is what he would have done.' Once the requisite period of supporting his right-hand man had elapsed, Catterick would end up saying exactly that.

Within minutes of the substitution, the blond figure of Alun Evans drove through the heart of Everton's defence to equalise. With 17 minutes remaining, Toshack won a high ball in the face of a dual challenge by Keith Newton and Rankin and it fell for Brian Hall to score the winning goal. 'The team died that week, losing to Panathinaikos and Liverpool,' says Royle. The frustration of those disappointments was considered by reporters to be responsible for Ball losing his cool in Everton's next match against West Ham United, throttling Billy Bonds and having to be restrained by teammates after a tangle in midfield.

Having finished 14th one year after winning the title, Everton fared no better over the first half of the 1971–72 season, winning only six games before New Year. With Harvey playing intermittently because of an arthritic hip, Ball was absent for six weeks with a pelvic injury. He put his relatively poor form since the World Cup down to the deep-rooted effects of that ailment more than basic fatigue. But, as bad as things looked at Goodison Park, no one was expecting the remedy that Catterick prescribed shortly before Christmas.

To say that the sale of Alan Ball to Arsenal took football by surprise would be an understatement, although with comedian Benny Hill sitting at No.1 in the UK charts with a song about a milkman this was clearly the season of the surreal. Not a single newspaper had offered any speculation about a transfer that was about to leave its subject as bemused as anyone.

Catterick simply summoned Ball to his office three days after a home defeat against Derby County, explained his intention to drop him from the team and added that he was prepared to sell him. There was already a big club – the champions and FA Cup holders, no less – ready to pay the £220,000 that Everton were demanding. And their manager Bertie Mee was down the corridor waiting to talk him into signing.

Ball knew he had played badly against Derby, but in mitigation could point out that Lesley had given birth to their second daughter,

Keely, the night before the match. Even without meeting Mee, Ball left Catterick's office suspecting that he would be signing for Arsenal. 'I'd already decided that I would never play for Everton again,' he recalled. 'I'd given everything to the club, but my pride had been hurt, my faith destroyed. Arsenal were willing to pay a record fee for me, yet I wasn't good enough for Everton.'

In his autobiography, Kendall recalled the moment when, in his opinion, Catterick had decided to sell the increasingly frustrated and disruptive Ball. Dixon had suddenly stopped a training session one day and asked, 'Alan, what's wrong with you?'

'You could see Bally wasn't interested,' said Kendall. 'He was sulking or having a strop. He put his hands out and said, "How can I play with this lot?" Most of the players he'd not long ago won the League title with were standing there looking on.'

In the weeks after the deal, Catterick would insist that 'team spirit has risen 200 per cent' since Ball's departure. When he went in front of the cameras on the day of the transfer he argued that 'Alan Ball had ceased to be the player he was'. Insisting that Ball was showing no sign of regaining form and that 'it was good business to part with him', he added, 'I don't think it was so much of a shock to the players.'

Which is not how many of them recall events. 'We couldn't believe it,' says Hurst. 'We were training and the physio Norman Borrowdale came out and shouted for Bally to come in. Next thing we knew he was getting his jacket and telling us he was going to Arsenal. We all thought he was taking the mickey.'

Inevitably, the memories of how people heard the news betray some basic inconsistencies, but the general recollection of astonishment is universal. 'We used to go to the café for lunch,' says Kenyon. 'We were saying, "Where is Bally?" He came along half an hour later, crying his eyes out. That is when he told us Catterick was selling him; that he'd had his best days out of him and he was going to cash in.'

Royle continues, 'We always thought he was Harry's favourite. It made us all the more surprised when he came out of Harry's office and declared he was going to move. We always thought Harry would build a new team around Bally. There were all kinds of rumours that Alan had wanted to move, that there were financial problems and this, that and the other. But we were all surprised when he went.'

Rumours began circulating around Merseyside that evening and Everton commercial director David Exall was soon fielding calls from agitated journalists. The club offered no comment, but the next day's newspapers anticipated the second record transfer of Ball's career. When he and his father arrived at Watford Gap to rendezvous with Arsenal officials, there were plenty of photographers waiting for them. At the White House Hotel in Regent's Park, Ball reached final agreement with Mee on the personal terms of his move before heading to Highbury to complete his medical and talk to reporters. 'I am sure I will fit in quickly at Arsenal,' he said, although his assessment of the team for which he was leaving the School of Science was not exactly effusive. 'They are a workmanlike side who play for each other and that will suit me fine.'

Ball's national profile was such that his transfer was the page one lead story in the *Daily Mirror* – partly because they had immediately signed him up to be a columnist – and considered important enough for various other front pages, with Lesley and new daughter Keely the focus of the photos and headlines. 'This is the only member of the family not bothered by all the excitement,' Lesley offered while holding her five-day-old daughter. Meanwhile, Ball, with a £10,000 cut of the transfer fee heading for his bank account, responded, 'They say the streets of London are paved with gold and now I believe it. I am going to give my wife and two little girls the Christmas of a lifetime.'

Even Ball's mother, Val, was asked for comment, admitting that she had shed some tears at the thought of her son moving so far from home. 'I knew this was a selfish attitude to take,' she said. 'You have to put sentiment to one side. There was no sentiment in Everton's decision to sell him. But we'll miss him terribly.'

Mee, not a manager known for extravagance with his employers' cash, beamed liked a pools winner and declared, 'There is no doubt in my mind that it is money well invested. I have had a short-list of world-class players in my mind for several years and Alan Ball's name has always been prominent on it.' Explaining that he had been routinely phoning Catterick every few months to check on Ball's availability, he continued, 'I did not think I would ever get the chance to buy him. Alan has this terrible habit of wanting to win everything. I was surprised that he did not want to fight me for the lunch bill.'

Meanwhile, Ball announced, 'I don't know whether I am on my head or my elbow. Believe me, it's not easy to leave Merseyside. There's something special about that place – the people and the atmosphere.' And, in his customary style of slipping into the third person, he added, 'A lot of people are saying that Alan Ball has lost his old fire and flair' – by whom he presumably meant Catterick and his staff. 'A lot of people are going to be proved wrong.'

Back in Liverpool, where they were still struggling to fathom why The Beatles had found it impossible to work together for the past two years, people had another mystery to ponder, although the red half of the city could not have been happier. Kevin Keegan, a young forward becoming an important part of the Anfield first team, laughs, 'On the Everton side they were distraught, but we just looked at it and thought, "Right, that will make it a bit easier when we play them." We were shocked, but we were quite pleased because he was such a great player.'

Offering a blue perspective, Kenyon insists, 'Harry broke the team up too early. Apart from maybe Labby, Sandy Brown, Westy and Johnny Morrissey, all the rest of the lads were in their early 20s. You would have thought we could go on for another three or four years at the top.'

Royle believes Catterick over-reacted to the disappointing year suffered by both Ball and Everton immediately after the club's title triumph. 'We had a bad season, but probably before making rash moves like selling Alan, Harry might have given it another season because it was a young enough side and had prospects coming through. To this day, I don't think anyone knows why Alan went from being Harry's favourite player to a saleable asset. But Harry was a very shrewd man. He was aware that he had bought him for a record fee and could sell him for twice that.'

Even Kendall, despite his unflattering depiction of Ball's final year or so at the club, would conclude, 'Alan's departure left a huge void in the Everton team.'

Perhaps the person happiest that Ball was leaving Merseyside was Bill Shankly. Legend has it that the Liverpool manager left him a message saying, 'You signed for Arsenal at 3.30, didn't you? How do I know? Because I felt like a big thorn had been pulled out of my side.'

Of more practical assistance was Shankly's support of Ball at yet another FA disciplinary commission hearing shortly after his transfer. Appealing, successfully, against a booking he received in his final Merseyside derby, Ball did so without representation from his former club and instead relied on the evidence of Shankly and Liverpool full-back Chris Lawler. 'It is unbelievable that Everton should have left Ball stranded,' said Shankly, happy to have a dig at the arch-enemy. 'I think the FA should have ordered them to be there. Arsenal were in the dark and asked me to help.'

As I share a pre-performance drink with Kenny O'Connell and Bobby Parry in the Lowther Pavilion in Lytham St Annes, a short hop along the coast from Ball's first football home in Blackpool, it is obvious that he was irreplaceable in the hearts of many Evertonians.

O'Connell, nervously awaiting the curtain to go up on the latest performance of his play, *Ball of Fire*, explains, 'I was 15 years old when he helped us win the title and he was my hero. They have always loved him at Everton. I think it is because when he came, even though we weren't struggling, we couldn't beat Liverpool. As soon as he came, we beat them practically every time and we seemed to get better and better. When he got his white boots he was like a real star. Manchester United had George Best, but we'd never had one.'

The fourth play that O'Connell has written, *Ball of Fire* depicts the key scenes of Ball's life, illustrated by videos and linked by a poetic narration written by Parry and read by former Everton midfielder Ronny Goodlass. One of the youth players who formed part of Stewart Imlach's boot-painting detail, Goodlass has been scurrying around the theatre, helping to set up the stall that sells merchandise for his charity and stopping for a chat before rushing off to get changed for the show.

Parry, a long-time Goodison Park season-ticket holder, can barely believe he is involved in such a project. 'It started off when I wrote a poem and entered a competition to win an evening with Ronny and the Everton hierarchy,' he says. 'To cut a long story short, they approached me and asked if I minded them using my poem. It happened almost by accident, but the way it works is unbelievable.

My era was the late Seventies and I only heard Alan Ball playing for Everton on the radio, but he was always there in the background. My dad and older brother were massive fans and I ended up falling in love with him. Why do Evertonians love him so much? It is just how down to earth he was. He felt like he was one of us. He was one of the boys.'

O'Connell continues, 'He was in tune with the fans in every way. He didn't come across as someone who was apart from the fans. You look at someone like Ronaldo now, you could never feel like part of his life, but with Alan Ball you could. The way he went to Eddie Cavanagh's son's christening and became his godfather; things like that mean a lot to the fans.'[1]

The anniversary of Ball's arrival at Everton half a century earlier has been celebrated by the staging of a special exhibition by the Everton FC Heritage Society, while the audience in Blackpool, not as partisan and raucous as those who have seen O'Connell's play in Liverpool, contains more blue shirts than tangerine. Clearly, there is a significant constituency of Everton fans eager to memorialise Ball's contribution to the club.

'There are still enough people around who remember him to keep his name alive,' says Royle. 'And everyone in that team would say the same; he was the best player we played with. He was a very special player. He wasn't just a talent; he worked for the team. He would certainly get in any modern-day team.'

Kenyon agrees that Ball ranks as 'probably the best player I have played with and without doubt the most committed professional,' although adding with a chuckle, 'He could also be a nasty little bastard and turn on you.' According to Husband, 'His enthusiasm was unbelievable. He used to lose his temper with players on the field; he wanted to win so much. So the crowd loved him.'

John Hurst insists, 'He is one of the best players that England ever had. Parents have said to their children, "You should have seen Alan Ball." He has been passed down. He was tremendously loved.'

---

1 Cavanagh, who had been on the Goodison Park books as a player, was the Everton fan who came to the nation's attention by racing on to the Wembley pitch during the 1966 FA Cup final, evading the tackle of a policeman who was left sprawling on the turf with Cavanagh's jacket in hand as the invader raced off into the distance.

The love was reciprocated. Even though Ball's career still had more than a decade to run and would continue to be something about which he was passionate to his core, club football would never be quite the same again. Even his new Arsenal teammates would recognise it. 'Everton were always his number one team,' says Peter Storey. 'It broke his heart a little bit when he was frozen out of Goodison Park.' And Kenny Swain, one of his future players at Portsmouth, adds, 'Even when he finished playing, the real love of his career was not Arsenal or Southampton or even England. It was Everton.'

Ball himself concluded, 'That goodbye to Goodison really turned me over. It wasn't easy. In a way it was hell. I'd always had in my mind that when I left Everton they would have to push me out in a wheelchair.'

Son Jimmy, who, like his siblings, grew up an Everton fan even though he was born after Ball had departed Merseyside, can understand that devotion to the club more easily than he can articulate it. 'Everton Football Club is something in itself,' he says, 'something you can't quite put into words. The supporters, and how unique and incredible and passionate they are; it's just special. If you don't understand, then you don't understand; if you do understand, then you get it. That is the mystique of it.

'Dad used to say, "I loved playing in front of them, loved that patch of grass." He wanted his ashes scattered on the pitch in front of the Gwaldys Street End, but all we could do was lay a wreath and hope he was happy with that. It was a special in time in his wonderful career; he was in his pomp. People who were there say no one will ever compare. People younger than me tell me he was their dad's hero. They talk about him like he was a god. It is very humbling and very emotional.'

8
STUCK IN THE MIDDLE

'If a square peg doesn't fit a round hole, neither the peg nor the hole is to blame'

– writer Jeffrey Bryant

I N one of those quirks of fate that football routinely manufactures, the first time Alan Ball ran out at Highbury as an Arsenal player, on New Year's Day, he looked across the half-way line and saw his old teammates. It was bad enough for the Everton fans that their hero no longer patrolled their midfield, but to encounter him in direct opposition while the scars of his departure were still raw and bleeding seemed too cruel.

'I couldn't believe it on the news,' says playwright Kenny O'Connell. 'Why? You never really sold players for money back then. You wouldn't have dreamed of Liverpool selling Tommy Smith or Ian Callaghan. The Liverpool fans were made up. I remember one coming round knocking on my door, saying "He's gone, hasn't he?"'

'It seemed like a mistake,' says Gary Imlach, son of Everton coach Stewart. 'You just kept waiting for the correction. I couldn't quite process it. You are not part of the grown up world of transfer deals at that age, even though I knew my dad had bounced around everywhere. Bally was an Everton player playing for Arsenal. It seemed like he was making some odd guest appearance in a red kit that didn't suit him. It was completely wrong. I never fully came to terms with him being an Arsenal player and I didn't believe he really thought he was an Arsenal player.'

Ball admitted in his *Daily Mirror* column that it was hardly the introduction to his new home that he would have wished. 'I'm not just playing against my old teammates,' he said. 'I'll also be battling with my emotions.'

Ball had discussed the Highbury clash – which would end up as a 1–1 draw – in the first *Shoot!* issue of 1972. But he'd done so from an Everton perspective, Christmas having meant the deadline for his article was before his transfer. 'I'm glad manager Bertie Mee hasn't splashed out thousands of pounds in the transfer market,' he wrote, unaware of the impending irony of the comment. 'After winning the Double, it was fair to give the players who achieved this a chance.' And, without realising it, he'd hit the nail that defined the early part of his Arsenal career squarely on the head.

The Gunners had adopted a fashion of football that fitted snugly around the shape of the players they had. Now they faced a choice: tailor their game to place Ball's midfield skills at the centre of their design, or make Ball squeeze into the off-the-peg direct methods that had won them the League and FA Cup. On the face of it, a group of players used to delivering the ball quickly to two formidable forwards in John Radford and Ray Kennedy appeared to have little use for someone accustomed to linking the different units of his team.

It meant that, for the most part, Ball spent the early part of his Highbury career learning to adapt and attempting to keep his frustration under control. And by the time a change of approach and coaching staff found more of the game being filtered through him, he simply didn't have the quality of personnel around him to keep Arsenal challenging for honours. Within three years of the Double, key figures such as Bob Wilson, Frank McLintock, George Graham and Kennedy were gone; the game-changing Charlie George was mostly injured or falling out with management; and the effectiveness of others was waning with age.

'I would have sold the North Bank before I sold Ray Kennedy,' says McNab of the shock £200,000 transfer that materialised in July 1974, Bill Shankly's last act as Liverpool manager. 'I and a few others had become extremely concerned about the sale of players who had achieved so much. Ray had put on weight and was causing discipline problems, but I would not have sold him. I felt the same when they sold Charlie. You just do not get players of that quality.'

Yet Graham, sold to Manchester United a year after Ball's arrival, acknowledges, 'Sometimes you need new blood and you think you see it early. Sometimes you can keep people for too long. As a manager, you should never sit on the fence and Bertie didn't. All the great managers are tough; they make hard decisions about letting players go.' Ball knew that only too well, having been the first clear manifestation of Harry Catterick's intent to overhaul his Everton side.

Mee's makeover at Highbury meant that where Ball had once been flanked by Harvey and Kendall at Everton, he would end up sharing the Gunners' midfield with journeymen John Matthews or Trevor Ross and promising, but still developing, talent such as Liam Brady. Meanwhile, a defence that had once provided the foundation of Arsenal's success was entrusted to unspectacular pros like Richie Powling and Terry Mancini. The team Ball found himself skippering in 1974 was a far cry from the English champions for whom he made his debut in a 1–1 draw at Nottingham Forest in December 1971.

Seventeen barren years at Highbury had ended on a memorable April night in 1970 when Arsenal completed a 4–3 aggregate victory over Anderlecht of Belgium to win the European Fairs Cup, their first trophy since winning the League in 1953. Under the management of former physiotherapist Mee and a master technician in coach Don Howe, the club had used their European success as a springboard to domestic dominance – for a season anyway. As Christmas 1971 approached, Arsenal's First Division crown had slipped irreversibly. Howe had gone at the start of the season, offered the chance to manage West Bromwich Albion. Steve Burtenshaw stepped up from the reserves to replace the man Mee had just described in the latest *Arsenal Football Book* as 'the best coach in the business'.

The early months of 1971–72 had seen a George Best-inspired Manchester United reprising, for a few months, the flair and ability everyone thought they had left behind in the Sixties. It was also the time of a sudden clampdown on foul play, the result of a memorandum received in the post by referees on the Monday morning after Arsenal had opened the season by beating Chelsea 3–0 at Highbury. Dubbed 'The Refs' Revolution', the measures saw the number of bookings soar to unrecognisable levels for the era, with the eradication of the tackle from behind the most significant of the new directives. Such was the prevalence of that particular tactic that Ball's new colleague John Radford had begun wearing shin pads on the back of his legs, while Joe Royle recalls the lengths Ball was forced to go to protect himself. 'I remember seeing him before a game padding himself up with a lot of cotton wool around his feet and his shins. I said to him, "It is taking a bit to get you on the pitch now." He just laughed and said, "Whatever it takes." He had obviously been targeted and it was the days when the tackle from behind was not legal, but was ignored at times.'

The endeavours to clean up the game contributed to an exhilarating title race won by Brian Clough's stylish Derby County ahead of close challengers Liverpool, Leeds and Manchester City. Arsenal would finish fifth without ever being serious contenders. Meanwhile, George Eastham, packed off to Stoke City five years earlier by Arsenal and thought to be too lightweight for the robust modern game, became the symbol of the season's reinvention by returning to the Potteries from South Africa to score the winning goal in the League Cup final against Chelsea. ·

Teams such as Arsenal, for whom organisation and resilience were a greater part of their DNA than flair and individualism, were always likely to benefit less from the new wave washing over the First Division. 'I feel we were affected in those early matches by the referees' crackdown,' says skipper McLintock. 'It probably made us less challenging.'

As Christmas approached, though, the start of another FA Cup run was arriving and the quarter-finals of the European Cup had been reached with comfort. What little was wrong, Mee believed, could be solved with fresh impetus, someone who could snap the club out of its hangover. Arsenal had reached the top without a household name; maybe a bit of star power could keep them there – although McLintock recalls such an approach as 'flawed thinking'. So it was that Mee came to be at Goodison Park, poised for the biggest signing of his career.

Yet Mee had achieved success by allowing his coaching staff to construct an effective framework and helping them to slot the right-shaped pieces into it. It was an approach Alf Ramsey would have recognised. Ball might well have been enjoying greater freedom and protection under the new rules as an individual, but whether he fitted into the weave of Arsenal's traditional cloth was debatable.

'He was used to setting the tempo for his teams and having the ball going through him,' says McLintock, while McNab argues, 'Our greatest quality was that we were predictable to one another. Our two central strikers were the best in the business, so why would you not play that way? The season after the Double, teams did start sitting central midfield players in front of Raddy and Ray, which killed the space in front of these two and prevented long early balls into feet. Now we needed to develop attacks through the midfield, so in came Bally.'

Ball found the club easy to fall in love with; from the overpowering scent of history in the marble halls, to the club blazers and the way in which nothing was overlooked when it came to ensuring the comfort of players. 'Bertie was very proud of Arsenal and what they stood for,' he told me in 2005. 'All you had to do was play football. Everything else was looked after and there were never any strains or stress. Everything from schooling to housing, accountancy, solicitors and hospitals was looked after. I was treated like a king at Arsenal.'

Yet that could not disguise his dissatisfaction on the field. There was no instant revolution; no sudden revision of tactics to accommodate a player used to prompting and probing on his own terms rather than chasing knock-downs from long balls. He argued with teammates and, unsuccessfully, demanded change. 'When I signed, I was in a team that had been successful playing a certain way and quite understandably they weren't going to change right away. It was hard because at other teams everything had been played through me. Arsenal were a terrific side and there were times early on when I scratched my head as to why they had bought me.'

Ball admitted that his efforts to force change that better suited his own methods made him appear like 'an upstart who had come in for a record transfer fee and was trying to single-handedly change their world'. McLintock recalls, 'Things weren't working out for him at the start. We were used to hitting balls from back to front and Bally liked it played to his feet. He was very frustrated and thought it was making him look bad. I said to him, "Look, we have been doing this for seven years. You will have to be patient."'

If the arrival of Ball created tactical ambiguity at Highbury, then it was accompanied by considerable financial animosity. While not aimed directly at Britain's most expensive footballer, it was Ball's wages that added a further ingredient to a cauldron of resentment that had barely stopped bubbling, even during the triumphant 1970–71 season.

Arsenal might have been one of the biggest, most revered clubs in English football, but they had not exactly been throwing money at their employees since threatened strike action by the Professional Footballers' Association in 1961 forced the abolition of the £20 per week maximum wage. Large parts of their players' salaries were made up of loyalty bonuses; an arrangement with the potential to leave regular first-teamers disgruntled at an annual package worth less than longer-serving reserves. The likes of McLintock, Armstrong and the departed Jon Sammels and Ian Ure were among those who had, at various times, demanded that Mee pay them more or let them go, while McNab's threat to quit Highbury early in the Double season brought to light grievances over a pay structure that appeared to favour experience over current value to the team.

Arsenal's top basic weekly wage during the Double season was £90 per week, which was supplemented by win bonuses. An additional 12.5 per cent of bonus money was paid for every completed year at Highbury. 'It was a very irritating situation,' says McNab. 'It is a good idea to reward loyalty, but when reserves are getting more than someone who is in England squads and is playing every game, there must be something wrong.'

George and Eddie Kelly would be the next ones banging on Mee's office door, early in the season that followed Ball's transfer. Scorer of the FA Cup-winning goal at Wembley, George argued, 'We feel there is an unfair gap between us and the older players when it comes to money. We are all in the same team and it can't be right that we should be so far behind them because we are younger.'

Ball's arrival had added to the unrest, his annual salary initially reported as £10,000 – although recalled by him as £12,500 – and untethered to the loyalty lottery, which upset both young and old. Ball was honest enough to share the details of his contract with his new teammates and could do nothing but remind them that 'it is there for you to attain'.

'It soon got through to us that Bally was getting paid more money,' says goalkeeper Geoff Barnett, who'd also been a teammate at Everton. 'My big buddy John Radford's attitude was, "Who is this guy

coming in and being paid all this money?" In the end we had a players' meeting about it. We met in the room down the tunnel and had a
right old ding dong. Bally said, "Don't blame me." '

Mancini, who would join Arsenal in 1974, recalls Ball making
mischief from his status as the club's highest-paid player. 'Bally loved
to wind people up,' he says. 'You used to get your pay slip in a brown
envelope on a Friday and he would open his up, stand in the middle
of the dressing room and read it and then leave it on the table for
everyone to see. He didn't mean any harm by it, but people like John
Radford, Peter Simpson and others would go fucking berserk. He was
on £250 a week after tax, plus bonuses, and it drove a wedge between
him and the other players.'

Radford continues, 'Bringing in Bally caused a lot of aggro. I
remember going to see Bertie for a rise and was told there was no
more money. I said, "Well, what about Alan Ball?" I was told, "He is
a superstar." Once you start getting older and start finding out what
other players are being paid, you fight your corner.'

McNab was one of those unconcerned about Ball's wage packet. 'I
had always felt that Arsenal would not attract the world's best to come
and play for the same money as me,' he says. 'I recall comments from
quite a number of players that we were the ones who won the Double,
but Bally had come in and got the reward. I just thought Bally would
make us a better team, win more games, get more win bonuses and
help create the dynasty I thought we could become.'

Retaining the FA Cup would be a first step towards that goal.
Arsenal had made it to Wembley in 1971 after being drawn away in
every round and the pattern was to be repeated a year later, beginning
with a third-round trip to Swindon Town, where Ball scored his first
Gunners goal in a 2–0 win. Victory at Reading meant a fifth-round tie
against Derby County, a 2–2 draw at the Baseball Ground being
followed by a 0–0 stalemate at Highbury in a match played on a
midweek afternoon because of the miners' strike that had left Britain's
power stations low on coal supplies. Kennedy settled the second replay
at Leicester City's Filbert Street; then Ball struck the single goal that
won the quarter-final tie at Second Division Orient.

Meanwhile, Arsenal's European Cup assault would not continue
beyond the last eight. Two seasons earlier they had swept past Ajax in

the Fairs Cup semi-finals, since when the Dutch team had won the European Cup and were building a three-year dynasty in that competition. Ball, not signed in time to be eligible to play, watched as Arsenal lost 2–1 in Amsterdam, a respectable enough result. But their fate was sealed by a 1–0 loss at Highbury, where Graham headed a heartbreaking own goal.

Stoke were Arsenal's FA Cup semi-final opponents for the second successive year and once again a replay was required, although in less dramatic circumstances than the last-minute Peter Storey penalty that had rescued the Gunners at Hillsborough 12 months earlier. This time, George Armstrong drove Arsenal into the lead from the edge of the Villa Park penalty area, but they were forced to stick Radford in goal with 15 minutes remaining after Wilson ruptured a knee cartilage. By that time, however, the goalkeeper had already struggled on for five minutes, during which time Simpson, over-compensating for his stricken colleague, turned an attempted interception into his own net. Radford held firm and the tie went to a replay at Goodison Park.

Jimmy Greenhoff scored first, with a penalty, before George replied with Arsenal's own spot-kick 10 minutes after half-time. The Gunners' winning goal is disputed to this day, Radford scoring after George had looked suspiciously offside before delivering his cross. The truth, so Stoke fans will tell you, is that referee Keith Walker and linesman Bob Mathewson mistook the white coat of a programme seller for a white-shirted defender. 'There is conjecture on this claim, however,' stated an article in the *Stoke Sentinel* in 2014. 'The bloke in the white coat might have been selling peanuts or ice cream.'

And so, for the second time in his career, Ball looked forward to an FA Cup final, this time against Leeds United. Unlike 1968, he was playing for the underdogs, not a situation Ball would allow to pass without mention. 'It is true that someone at Elland Road has succeeded in performing a masterly piece of public brain-washing on behalf of their sound, but hardly super, set-up,' he wrote of Arsenal's opponents. 'I detect a deficiency in the character of Leeds. They've lost too many of the big ones.'

Arsenal and Leeds had besmirched the hallowed Wembley turf four years previously in a bad-tempered League Cup final that Leeds had won via a disputed Terry Cooper goal. Arsenal's desire to prevent their

rivals taking the FA Cup from them and completing the first part of a
potential Double meant that this contest was never likely to be for the
faint-hearted. Bonhomie was out of the window the instant partici-
pants in the pre-game celebrations of the tournament's centenary had
cleared the pitch. The ball had not even left the centre circle when Ball
fell victim to the first foul of the match, inflicted by Allan Clarke.
McNab responded by slicing Peter Lorimer in half to earn the first
booking of the contest after 45 seconds. When BBC commentator
David Coleman had informed viewers that 'there were some people
who expected this game to produce a lot of goals', no one could figure
out who he was referring to. More prescient was the view of *Goal* writer
Eric Nicholls, who greeted the prospect of an Arsenal–Leeds final
with, 'I think I'll go the pictures. Anything must be better than that.'

Storey and George made clear very quickly, and very emphatically,
an intention not to allow Eddie Gray the freedom that had earned
him man-of-the-match honours at Wembley two years earlier. In
return, Ball was victimised by Hunter, booked for a hack just before
half-time, while Clarke was caught by the television cameras yanking
back George's head by his long hair as he stood in a defensive wall.
George was booked for arguing, but escaped further punishment after
issuing retribution on Clarke. Then Ball hacked through Bremner's
legs as he shielded the ball and attempted to drag his opponent from
the grass as he lay apparently injured. It was hardly entertainment fit
for the watching Queen.

Arsenal had taken the field with the following line-up, Ball's
displacement of Kennedy being the one outfield change from the
winning team against Liverpool a year earlier:

Barnett

Rice   McLintock   Simpson   McNab

Storey   Ball   Graham   Armstrong

George   Radford

Substitute: Kennedy

Ball, in his white boots, had stood alongside George, in red footwear, to kick off the game – a colourful Wembley first – and had

instantly begun darting here and there as Arsenal moved the ball
around in the opening exchanges. It was he who almost broke through
after 32 minutes when Armstrong's left-wing corner floated to the
edge of the penalty area. Ball met it with a fierce low volley and Paul
Reaney made one of those clearances by the post that had become a
career trademark. 'I don't think I've ever hit a better shot in my life,'
Ball revealed. 'I was already half-way into my joy dance as Reaney
stuck a foot out and deflected the whole destiny of the Cup.'

A Lorimer shot, parried away by Barnett, was the closest to a Leeds
goal that the first half could offer and the second period was not
exactly filling reporters' notebooks with incident. Mick Jones capital-
ised on a slip by McNab to cross for Clarke to score with a diving
header after 54 minutes and that was it as far as goals were concerned.
George hit the bar from 15 yards after Ball's low shot from outside the
box struck a defender, and Ball was soon hearing the final whistle
sound on a second FA Cup final defeat.

As much as it had hurt Arsenal to lose at Wembley, the greater wound,
it appeared, had been inflicted by the words of Ajax coach Ştefan
Kovács after winning at Highbury on the way to retaining the
European Cup. 'I was a little surprised that Arsenal seemed to have so
few ideas,' he said damningly. 'All they did was concentrate on the
long ball down the middle.'

The contrast to Ajax's flexible and fluid Total Football, a style where
players interchanged positions at will and attacks originated from
anywhere on the field, was stark. Mee, as someone who constantly urged
his players to 'remember who you are and what you represent' felt that
Arsenal, having returned to the pinnacle of the English game, had a
responsibility now to uphold loftier values than simply lumping the ball
downfield. No Arsenal team should be the subject of derision. He had
suggested a desire to employ more aesthetic methods in his acquisition
of Ball; now, as the 1972–73 season kicked off, he was to go for the full
Dutch. 'A wind of change is blowing through the game,' he said. 'Ajax
and West Germany have proved you can entertain and get results.'

Instead of letting his coaches devise Arsenal's approach, Mee was
prepared to dictate to Steve Burtenshaw. 'Bertie wanted a more Total

Football type of team,' says Burtenshaw. 'I was not 100 per cent in agreement. Bertie wanted to think about building for three or four or years ahead, but I was more interested in the next few games. He felt that Arsenal should be innovative. He thought that we'd done well with what we had, but now he wanted a more attractive style. To do that, we had to change our philosophy and change players. I warned him it would not come quickly or easily.

'That is why he had been keen to bring in Ball, one of the best touch footballers in the country. You have got to start somewhere and it began with Alan Ball. One way to change is to work with the players you have. But if they have been successful with a different system, you have to try to change slowly – not overnight. Or you can change players. That was going to take time as well.'

Had he been able to eavesdrop on Mee's conversations, it would have been music to Ball's ears. He scored the only goal of an opening-day win at Leicester City and then purred around the field as Arsenal stuck five past Wolverhampton Wanderers at Highbury. After they had made it three straight wins by beating Stoke City, Peter Batt wrote in the *Sun*, 'I saw enough here to convince me that these new-style Gunners really can lead English soccer out of the dark age.'

Ball was suddenly a far happier figure. His feet might have abandoned the white-boot experiment that had achieved an impact and longevity far beyond its two years, but now there was more substance to his play, if a little less sartorial style. 'I preached the need to play the ball through me, through the middle, from where I could prompt more initiatives,' Ball recalled, citing the support he received from McLintock – 'the best, most forceful captain I have ever played under'.

Four wins and three draws from seven games were justifying the new methods, with the *Daily Express* reporting, 'The best thing about the start of the new season was the return to peak form of Alan Ball. Arsenal's "all-in" football system revolved around him and it was precise passes and intelligent positional play that kept everything flowing.'

Burtenshaw, though, could still see warning signs. 'Getting the players Bertie wanted took longer than he hoped. He had specific players in mind, but it was difficult to get them. I often heard him say, "I am not paying that." He wasn't worried about paying it for Alan Ball but there were others for whom he would not pay that money.'

George was in favour, despite his pay dispute, and even the fragile skills of Peter Marinello, a somewhat forgotten figure since his £100,000 signing from Hibernian three years earlier, were given a chance to flourish in the new system, ahead of the honest endeavour of Armstrong. Yet Ball, it became apparent as results began to falter, was being asked to carry too much creative responsibility on his own – and even he was absent for three games after being sent off in a defeat at Sheffield United. When a new player did arrive, it was Coventry City centre-back Jeff Blockley, a £200,000 acquisition whose signing began the premature phasing out of McLintock.

At the end of November, the Gunners were knocked out of the League Cup 3–0 by Norwich City at Highbury. Four days later they shipped five goals to Derby County in the Baseball Ground mud. According to McLintock, 'Abandoning our pressing game allowed Alan to shine, but the team as whole went downhill.' Total Football had not been a total disaster, but with his team still challenging for another title, Mee went back to the tried and tested before it was too late. Marinello and George were dropped; the Radford–Kennedy partnership was restored; and Ball would once again spend periods looking up in the sky as Arsenal returned to their direct methods. 'So ended Arsenal's four-month flirtation with a more flowing style,' wrote Ken Jones in *Goal*. 'It had not been entirely unconvincing. But something had gone from Arsenal's game.'

By way of vindication, what followed was a 15-game unbeaten run that propelled Arsenal into a two-horse race with Liverpool and into the latter stages of the FA Cup once more. Despite the change of emphasis, Ball continued to play a significant role, his temporary installation as the focal point of the team appearing to lift his mood, form and confidence, a state of affairs that outlasted the Dutch flirtation. Throughout his five years at Highbury, it was the period when his own performance and that of the team were in closest harmony.

Ball continued his personal record of success at Anfield when the two contenders met in February, giving Arsenal the lead with a low, well-placed penalty before Radford settled a 2-0 win with a fine individual effort. 'I was determined to show Merseyside what a mistake

Everton made in selling me,' he said, that chip weighing as heavy as ever on his shoulder. In the end, a run of five games with only one win and one goal allowed Liverpool to stretch away to a three-point title victory; a dip in form that immediately followed two draining games against Chelsea to earn a place in the FA Cup semi-finals. Despite a crop of injuries, Arsenal had drawn 2–2 at Stamford Bridge, where a rare Ball headed goal wiped out an early Chelsea lead. Chelsea then scored first at Highbury, only for referee Norman Burtenshaw to rule – after consulting his linesman under pressure from angry Arsenal players – that Armstrong had been inside the area when brought down by Steve Kember. Ball stuck away the penalty and Kennedy headed a second-half winner.

Ball was by now considered one of the outstanding players of the season and was pictured by renowned celebrity photographer Terry O'Neill in bowler hat and braces above a headline that read, 'Clockwork touch from Alan Ball'. Given the controversy over Stanley Kubrick's recent movie version of the Anthony Burgess novel *A Clockwork Orange* – withdrawn from cinemas and its 'ultraviolence' condemned as a potential template for football fans – Ball might have thought twice about adopting the sartorial style of the movie's anti-hero, but the accompanying story worked hard to justify it. 'Clockwork Orange? Well, he never stops running and he has that mop of fiery red hair,' read the article's clumsy prose. Bobby Moore was recruited to add, 'It seems you just have to wind him up like a clockwork toy and he runs all day.' Ball rounded off the piece himself by saying, 'The only time I feel tired is when the wife asks me to wash up.' The Seventies truly were another country.

Ball was one of a collection of football figures who had teamed up with O'Neill over the previous year under the collective name of 'The Clan' and were frequently pictured modelling clothing, plugging restaurants, appearing on Christmas editions of *The Big Match* and generally aiming to cross the drawbridge between sport and celebrity that had been lowered by George Best. The group, which included Alan Hudson, Geoff Hurst, Terry Venables, Rodney Marsh, Malcolm Allison, Gordon Banks, Martin Buchan, Francis Lee, Martin Chivers, Terry Mancini and Phil Beal, didn't exactly become millionaires from their endeavours. In fact, Mancini struggles to recall much about the whole episode other than to explain, 'We would go out for lunch and stay all night. With no paparazzi around, no one taking pictures with a mobile phone, you could go out and have a good time. In our era many players would still have been under the influence at three o'clock on Saturday.'

Only Second Division Sunderland now stood between Arsenal and what, it transpired, would have been a Wembley rematch with Leeds. Blockley, although scarcely fit himself, was forced back into the team when McLintock, who had been deputising for him, was injured a week before the semi-final. Nineteen minutes into the game, Blockley left Wilson stranded with a poor backpass and Vic Halom gave Sunderland the lead. Billy Hughes scored in the second half and George's late goal was scant consolation; nor was Sunderland's subsequent upset of Leeds in the final.

Ball would never get as close again to winning a trophy at Highbury.

9

IN THE RED

'The lights were going out all over Britain, and no one was quite sure if we'd see them lit again'

— Alwyn W. Turner, *Crisis? What Crisis? Britain in the 1970s*

EVENTS in Britain in the early 1970s were setting the tone for a troublesome decade ahead; in government, in economic matters and in the results of the England football team. Few would have predicted when the final whistle sounded on the Mexico World Cup that it would be twelve years before England qualified again for the finals. And, just as the post-1970 period saw the erosion of Sir Alf Ramsey's fortunes, so Prime Minister Edward Heath, who had swept to power four days after West Germany brought England's reign to an end, began his losing battle against the relentless force of industrial disputes, economic decline, social unrest and sectarian violence in Northern Ireland. No wonder that when young Lennie Godber, in the first episode of BBC sitcom *Porridge* in 1974, voices doubts about his ability to survive in prison, Ronnie Barker's Fletcher responds, 'Cheer up, could be worse. State this country's in you could be free, stuck outside with no work and a crumbling economy.' The Swinging Sixties, had they ever really existed for ordinary folk, had quickly become history.

Heath's predecessor, Harold Wilson, had long believed his fate to be mystically linked to that of Ramsey. The highs and lows of 1966 and 1970 – general elections mirroring World Cups – had given form to his superstition. If Heath had possessed an inkling of interest in foot-ball he would have been duly warned, unable to ignore the parallel paths of prime minister and England manager.

Chronicling the period, historian Dominic Sandbrook says in *State of Emergency* that the early 1970s 'represented something of a reckoning for a country and a consensus that had been living on borrowed time'. He might have been referring to English football, so blinded by flashes of club success in Europe that it failed to spot the manhole of international competition down which it was about to plummet.

While Heath turned to Europe, and entry into the Common Market, as a potential route to salvation, Ramsey expected the 1972 European Championship to prove that his side remained a global power and likely to challenge robustly for the 1974 World Cup in West Germany. When they qualified, functionally rather than spectacularly, for the quarter-finals it was West Germany who were again put in their path. The Germans had been building on their semi-final achievement in Mexico with a team that was embracing much of the same Total Football philosophy of Holland's European Cup holders, Ajax. England didn't know what was about to hit them.

They had encountered nothing too testing in a qualifying campaign against Greece, Malta and Switzerland, during which they dropped only one point. Their first match, a 1–0 win in Malta, came while Bobby Moore was out of favour at West Ham United and excluded from Ramsey's squad, a turn of events that brought Alan Ball into the debate about who should fill in as captain. His rival was Tottenham Hotspur's Alan Mullery and, conveniently for the newspapers, the First Division fixture list pitted the two men against each other four days before the international. 'We will no doubt be in touch verbally and physically,' said Mullery. 'Bally and I are the same type of skipper. We go through a game continually chatting, whether it's encouraging a colleague or having a moan.' That the honour eventually went to Mullery was seen as a sign that Ball's record of ill-discipline would prevent him ever leading his country.

The game, played on a sandy pitch in Valetta, saw the England debuts of Derby County defender Roy McFarland, Everton colleagues Colin Harvey and Joe Royle and Spurs centre-forward Martin Chivers, who all took their places alongside the core of Ramsey's established troopers. It is to the credit of the England manager and men such as Ball that Chivers recalls, 'It was the easiest team I ever went into because it was full of great players. Bally was the bubbly one; the one who got everyone excited and wound everyone up, not always for the better. He was always very friendly and terrific company. It was just a comfortable England team to go into.'

'It was very homely,' says McFarland. 'I was in awe of the players who had won the World Cup, but they made you feel welcome and part of the family. Bally was brilliant with me. I will never forget that. He loved a laugh and if we were having a team meeting and Alf got his words mixed up, as he did quite often, Alan would dive in and put him right. I could sense that Alf enjoyed it as well and there was a rapport between them.'

Mick Channon, whose England debut would come a year later, adds, 'If you knew Alan, you didn't want to slip up verbally. He would be all over you. Alf talked with that plum in his mouth and a few of the senior boys became confident that they could have some fun. Alf wasn't daft; you could see that little grin just enough to say that he was enjoying the banter. I don't know if Alf was ever close to anyone, but you knew there was that loyalty from him. It was bloody hard to get into the squad, but if you did what he wanted you became one of his men and it was a damn sight harder to get out of it.'

McFarland continues, 'Alf had a love for those older players because of what they had done for him. Maybe in the long term he did hang on a little bit too long to some, but certainly not in the case of Alan Ball.'

Increasingly, Ramsey's critics came to suggest that such loyalty was a sign of complacency. Certainly, England were unprepared for what happened when the Germans arrived at Wembley. Even though he was 27 and had made his international debut in 1965, Günter Netzer's exclusion from World Cup action in 1966 and 1970 meant that few had anticipated his performance. 'We hadn't been told a thing about him,' Moore would lament.

The impact Netzer was about to make on English football was as profound as the effect Donny Osmond and his brothers would be having on schoolgirls across the country when they arrived in Britain a couple of weeks later: lots of weak-kneed swooning – and that was just the England defence. All long blond hair and broad-shouldered arrogance, Netzer strutted around Wembley, surrounded by team-mates who rotated and interchanged with practised ease. Ball conceded that Netzer had given 'one of the most complete midfield displays ever seen at the stadium'. An attack-orientated midfield three of Ball, Bell and Peters were overwhelmed, lacking the enforcer who might have made it harder for Netzer and his pals to pass their way through them. England looked archaic by comparison. 'I sensed during the first 10 minutes that we could be in trouble because of the way we were being caught coming forward,' Ball admitted. Meanwhile, Moore, playing in the unaccustomed position of right central defender, had the poorest game anyone could remember. 'On reflection, both decisions were mistakes,' Moore would say of the midfield and the defensive selections.

'Netzer had the game of his life,' says Chivers. 'But he was never the same again as he was on that night. They took us to the cleaners.' Francis Lee equalised the Germans' first-half goal and Gordon Banks was unlucky not to keep out a Netzer penalty, but the final score of 3–1 did not flatter the visitors. Ramsey's response in the return leg in Berlin was to reinforce the midfield with Storey and Hunter. A strong-armed goalless draw was an honourable enough result in isolation, but worthless in the context of the tie and many felt Ramsey had missed the chance to offer experience to some new faces.

Daily Express writer Desmond Hackett reported a tense altercation between him and Ball as they travelled home, an incident he used as evidence that Ramsey's senior players were being overplayed to the point of exhaustion:

> How else could you account for the anger of that amiable little red-head Alan Ball? On Sunday, he told manager Ramsey he did not wish to play anymore. But Ramsey calmed him down and he promised he would be on parade for the work-out on Thursday before the first of the Home Internationals against Wales on Saturday. Manager Ramsey was not the only one to suffer the wrath of wearied Ball. At the Berlin airport, he threatened to punch me on the nose for not being too complimentary about his recent performances. In his own words: 'I am fed up of you slagging me every time I play.' Sorry, Alan. I still rate you one of the greatest, but more of a victim of being compelled to play too many vital games. This emphasises my insistence that younger players should have been drafted to get the atmosphere of full internationals.

Ball found the ideal energiser in the form of the contest against Scotland at Hampden Park a couple of weeks later. 'It's pretty common knowledge that Alf did not like the Scots,' recalled Malcolm Macdonald, 'but his dislike was nothing compared to Bally's hatred of them.'

Chivers explains, 'When you arrived at those games, the coach started rocking because Bally was signalling to all the Scotland supporters what he thought of them. We used to scream at him to sit down.' And Mullery adds, 'He would go out and upset 50,000 Scotsmen before the game. When we got out there to take an early look at the pitch we would be booed and Bally was winding them up, giving them the finger signs.'

On this occasion, Ball quickly had 120,000 baying for his blood when he crudely chopped down Billy Bremner from behind, much as he had done in the FA Cup final a few weeks earlier, before turning to see the referee showing him a yellow card. 'Bally and Bremner were the culprits,' says Chivers. 'The two smallest players, they used to wind each other up in the press during the week. We were all fighting a battle up there, but they were having their own private war.'

The feud had its roots in all those crucial Everton–Leeds contests in the late 1960s, not to mention the Scots' win at Wembley in 1967, when Bremner had trailed Ball around telling him he was 'a poof and a softie' and laughing as Denis Law and Jim Baxter kept calling him 'Jimmy Clitheroe'.[1] Bremner also took exception to comparisons between him and his rival. 'For heaven's sake, he was English and couldn't possibly have the heart of a Scot,' he said, only half-jokingly. 'He was a good little player, though, and a right handful whenever I faced him.'

The Scots fans had further reason to turn on Ball after 28 minutes. Intercepting a pass, he instigated a move with Chivers and Bell that ended with him advancing into the Scotland area and receiving the ball again from his centre-forward. The finish was scruffy, but Ball's celebration made it clear how much it meant to him. Chivers

1 Clitheroe was a diminutive northern comedian, best known for his long-running radio show, *The Clitheroe Kid*, in which he played an 11-year-old schoolboy with a high-pitched voice.

continues, 'Bally was such a good player to play with. He would keep at you all the time and was full of encouragement. He would never just play his own game; he would help other people in theirs. If I missed a chance he would say, "Come on, big fella. You will get one next time."'

Ball was not finished yet. With time running out, he sat on the ball and directed a V-sign at the terraces. 'We'll never get out of here alive,' Chivers warned his colleagues. And then he took the ball to the corner and wiped his nose on the flag. Far from admonishing him, Ramsey greeted him with a broad grin and told him, 'You really are a naughty boy.'

In truth, Ball had become something of a pantomime villain to the Scots. When he sat on the ball, he knew they loved that he willingly turned himself into a target. That relationship was summarised in the obituary that would be published in one of Scotland's leading newspapers, the *Glasgow Herald*:

> The raucous roars of derision that Ball attracted from Scottish fans were, of course, the most noisy, if strangely sincere, strain of backhanded compliments. He should have been one of us. Red-haired, crabbit, never beaten and able to pass off either foot, Ball seemed to have been separated from his footballing twin, Billy Bremner, at birth . . . he was always at his most animated against Scotland. He was inspired rather than destroyed by adversity. He was a great footballer. And we Scots appreciated that, though we had a funny way of showing it.

England's 1972–73 international season would conclude with a European tour that might hold the key to qualification for the World Cup finals. In a three-team group, England began with two games against Wales – a narrow win in Cardiff followed by a disappointing 1–1 draw at Wembley, where only 62,273 turned up to watch opposition they could see any old year.

In the first of the Welsh contests, it had been Kevin Keegan's turn to make his debut and experience the dressing-room force that was Alan Ball, launching an enduring friendship. 'He was a dominant character on and off the field, larger than life, great company and great fun to be around,' Keegan relates. 'He was one of the ones you really looked up to, having played in a World Cup-winning side when he was so young. Bobby Moore was very much the leader but Alf treated him and Bally the same as everyone and was quite strict with them. If he had favourites – and I am sure Alan would have been one of them – he didn't show it.'

Scotland provided England with a pick-me-up once more, February's 5–0 thumping of Willie Ormond's team ruining the Scottish FA's centenary celebrations and proving the efficacy of a new three-man strike force of Channon, Allan Clarke and Chivers, firmly established as England's leading number nine after a couple of brilliant seasons for Tottenham. Chivers scored three more in a clean sweep of the Home Internationals, during which Ball was involved in a bizarre incident at Wembley. After a Scotland fan raced on to the field and threw a punch at him, Ball claimed he bore no grudge against his assailant. 'That man would be welcome in my house for a drink,' he announced. 'He caught me with a glancing blow. That did not hurt, but it did hurt me to see the way the police dragged him away.' Not exactly the message the authorities would have desired as they fought their exhausting battle against football hooliganism.

After a draw in Czechoslovakia, England resumed World Cup duty against Poland, the recent Olympic champions. In the Slaski Stadium in Chorzow, near the forbidding mining city of Katowice, Ramsey abandoned his triple strike force for the first time since the dropped point against Wales, picking Storey instead of Channon and opting for his tried and trusted formation:

Shilton

Madeley   McFarland   Moore   Hughes

Storey

Bell   Ball   Peters

Chivers   Clarke

Ball admitted that he 'didn't feel the old confidence' as the team took the field in unfamiliar yellow shirts. He would explain, 'The squad did not have the all-round strength of either the '66 or '70 squads. The new boys were leaning heavily on the older players, whereas it was time the older players should have been able to lean on the new boys a bit.'

Poland took the lead within seven minutes, Jan Banas losing Moore at the near post and appearing to get the final touch on Robert Gadocha's free-kick, although historical records vary in crediting the goal to Banas, Gadocha or Moore. Peter Shilton blamed Ball for allowing the delivery to get as far as it did, telling him he should have been the third man in the wall rather than picking up a man to mark. During a half-time disagreement, Ball reminded his goalkeeper that such actions had led to conceding a goal in Czechoslovakia. Worse was on its way a minute into the second half, when Moore was caught in possession by Wlodzimierz Lubański, who advanced into the area and fired past Shilton. McFarland recalls the shock of such an occurrence. 'Bobby never made mistakes,' he says. Chivers adds, 'After such a magnificent career, Bobby had a bad game. For all the great games that he had, that was one of his worst.'

England offered little in response and a frustrated Ball, sporting unfamiliar stubble, bristled to the point where he got himself sent off with 11 minutes left. Having initially fouled Leslaw Ćmikiewicz, Ball marched towards the Polish midfielder, believing that he had tried to put his boot in the face of Martin Peters as they ended up tangled on the floor. Ball grabbed his opponent by the throat and raised his knee in the direction of his red shorts. During the inevitable kerfuffle that followed the brandishing of the red card, Ball looked like he was about to thump defender Krzysztof Rzesný. He was eventually led away by England trainer Harold Shepherdson. Ramsey would claim reflexively that Ball had been struck in the face first, but even Ball knew that being 'frustrated because we were not playing well' was no excuse for actions that rubber-stamped the inevitable England defeat.

As disappointed and angry as they knew Ramsey was, roommates Ball and Moore were hardly expecting to be visited in their hotel room that night by their manager – unless it was for a rollicking. Instead, Ramsey showed his compassion to Moore, his trusted lieutenant, and Ball, a man who described the wearing of an England shirt as 'the greatest honour that any footballer with real English blood in his veins can obtain'. Both, Ramsey knew, were struggling with the guilt of having let down the team. With a selection of teammates already in their room, Ramsey arrived at 11pm and, according to Ball, was still there at 4am. 'He sat up half the night with me. He realised how distraught I was. He knew how I felt and he did something to ease it.'

As often with Ball's recall, the sentiment might have been more accurate than the detail. McFarland remembers, 'The only thing you could drink out there was beer so we ordered a couple of crates. We were all disappointed and sat in Bally and Bobby's room talking about how poorly we had performed. There was a knock and Alf came in and said, "Can I join you boys?" and then said, "It was my fault. We didn't get that near post sorted out." The Poles wanted to take the free-kick quickly so Colin Bell stayed out there to stop them and Moore took his place trying to cover the front post. It was Colin's job to do that. We should have reorganised ourselves, but Alf insisted it was his fault. He drank his beer, persuaded everyone he was to blame and walked out.'

Ball's gloom at his dismissal deepened a month later when FIFA suspended him for England's next two World Cup games, the second of which was still expected to be the opening game of the 1974 finals. 'This could end my international career,' he groaned. 'I was expecting to be banned for the next match against Poland, but this two-match suspension has come as a real shock.'

In October, England faced the final match of the qualification group. Viewers tuning in to watch live on ITV as their team sought the victory needed to send them to the finals were reassured to hear Brian Clough predict a comfortable victory. Suspended and, as it turned out, nursing a knee injury anyway, Ball was invited by Ramsey to sit behind the England bench. He watched Polish goalkeeper Jan Tomaszewski, dismissed by Clough as a 'clown', pull off a series of amazing saves and England, who had stuck seven goals past Austria a few weeks earlier, suffer a string of near-misses. And then, not far in front of him, he saw Norman Hunter, preferred to Moore, lose the ball on the touchline, allowing a break that ended with Jan Domarski scoring with a shot that slipped under Shilton's body. When Clarke equalised from the spot, there was still plenty of time for the winner. Yet fortune and a goalkeeper having the game of his life conspired against them. Ramsey's team were out. 'We created so many chances but couldn't put the ball in the net,' sighs Chivers, sounding no less

incredulous four decades later than he looked as he left the field with
Ball, flared trousers flapping below a long double-breasted overcoat.

With predictable loyalty, Ball wrote, 'In no way is Sir Alf Ramsey to
blame for our failure to qualify, even though he was criticised for his
team selection – as usual.' More controversially, he used his magazine
column to place some of the blame for England's failure on an
apathetic football public, whose increasing desertion of League games
had been adding to the pervading mood of crisis in the national game:

> While the ultimate blame must lie with the players, the England fans
> have a lot to answer for. It was a disgrace to see only 60,000 turn up for
> the World Cup tie against Wales . . . perhaps with the sort of backing
> Scotland or Poland have had we'd have won – and made qualification
> much easier. Oh yes, the fans turned out when we played Poland, but
> we needed them more against Wales. The English public don't deserve
> a successful national team and if they haven't got one at present, it's
> only fitting.

While England were proving how far they had fallen behind other
European footballing nations, Bertie Mee had decided that Arsenal
weren't cut out to be Ajax, despite the previous season's continental
pastiche. Ball, meanwhile, limited his 1973–74 forecasts to declaring
that Arsenal would finish above Derby County after Brian Clough
had angered him by predicting a poor Gunners campaign. Ball was
no great admirer of someone who was the antithesis of men such as
Ramsey, Catterick and Mee. 'In my book Clough is a dictator,' was his
assessment. 'He wants to rule football and have everybody doing as he
says. What he does, he does for himself.' On another occasion he
called Clough 'self-opinionated to the point of boredom'. Lawrie
McMenemy would suggest that his antipathy towards one of England's
most successful managers stemmed from a disagreement during a
chance holiday meeting in Torremolinos.

Yet Clough was right on this occasion, and Ball would have to
console himself with the mess that Clough got himself into with the
Derby directors, quitting the club and ending up at Third Division
Brighton and Hove Albion. There were changes afoot at Highbury,
too. Early in the 1973–74 season, Mee's players decided that a new

coach was needed. It produced the arrival of a man with whom Ball would form a close relationship.

A 3–0 home victory against Manchester United on the opening day of the season was the perfect indicator of what was to come for the former European champions, who would end up being relegated. For the Gunners, the bright sunshine of the day created a mirage. Before long they were being thrashed 5–0 at Sheffield United, where Ball had to suffer Tony Currie performing his own favourite trick of sitting on the ball.

It was only a few weeks into the campaign before senior players were urging new club captain Bob McNab to tell Mee that they wanted a change on the training pitch. A friend and neighbour of coach Steve Burtenshaw, McNab reluctantly agreed that he, Bob Wilson, George Armstrong and Ball should present the players' views. 'There was growing discontent in the dressing room,' recalls Wilson, although he admits that Burtenshaw was in an almost impossible situation. 'Following Don Howe was like following the Messiah'.

According to McNab, 'There were strong feelings against the club for allowing Don to leave, and Steve probably bore the brunt of that. Some players started taking advantage.'

Storey recalls Ball as being a 'terrible moaner', who did not rate Burtenshaw as a coach, but adds, 'None of the lads feared [Steve] and several of them knew he'd never give them a hard time if they slacked or put on a few pounds.'

Mee responded with pragmatism, realising that the players' belief that they could no longer work effectively with Burtenshaw would be self-fulfilling. 'Bertie knew that if you lost the players you could be making all the right noises but would be wasting your time,' says club physiotherapist Fred Street. Burtenshaw, who describes the story of the players forcing him out as 'a load of crap' and puts his departure down to a basic philosophical difference with Mee, was quickly on his way out. Ball remembered Mee being 'upset that it had to happen', but believed, 'Steve had reached the point where the players would not respond to him.'

No one responded more than Ball to Burtenshaw's replacement, Bobby Campbell, an abrasive Liverpudlian who had helped manager Gordon Jago to steer Queens Park Rangers back into the First

Division. 'I don't think Arsenal got the best out of me in my first couple of seasons there,' Ball admitted. 'But then along came young players like Liam Brady and we turned our style around slightly. Bobby Campbell wanted the ball to be played through midfield and consequently that suited me a little more. I liked Bobby's style of coaching and my play benefited.'

Campbell's manner was not for everyone, however. At his first training session he intimated to the players that they had been spoiled by success and appeared to deliberately create confrontation with McNab. 'It was a bravado thing by Bobby,' says Wilson.

Results failed to match that bravado. Third Division Tranmere Rovers dumped Arsenal out of the League Cup at Highbury in the third round; Second Division Aston Villa did the same in the FA Cup in a fourth-round replay. 'My biggest disappointment was our totally inept displays against Aston Villa,' Ball said, admitting that he had given probably the worst performance of his career. By the time Arsenal had finished tenth in the First Division, Wilson had announced his intention to retire to the BBC studios and Ball had suffered a broken leg in a tackle with QPR's Terry Venables in the final match.

Ball's spell at Arsenal is by far the toughest part of his playing career to accurately characterise. At Blackpool, he was the youngster preparing for great things; at Everton he was in his prime, the team revolving around him; at Southampton, he would provide veteran leadership for an emerging side. Yet at Highbury, things were never clear-cut; from the confusion about his role and a sometimes strained relationship with certain teammates – McNab even recalled them coming to blows after one dressing-room row – to the frustration of being stuck in a declining team that failed to play in the manner he desired. Or when it tried to, couldn't get it right.

'Our biggest problem,' Ball said during 1973–74, 'can be narrowed down to the fact that we tried to play entertaining football. We decided on an attacking policy, but this has left us exposed at the back too often.'

He loved so much about Arsenal, yet no other period of his career created such ambivalence. Another of his weekly magazine columns

showed a level of introspection and world-weary maturity that
suggested that the Farnsworth lad who lived only for football might be
gone forever:

> I used to play with a smile on my face, which is more than I do now.
> This is because I'm more aware of how much winning and losing
> means. No longer am I the new boy who hasn't really grasped the
> professional game. I know exactly what winning can mean to my club,
> now Arsenal, how important it is to all concerned. Also the penalties of
> losing – loss of support, income and respect.

And in the background was a far from settled and sedate period in
his home life. His Arsenal career had begun just days after the birth of
his second daughter, Keely. Yet his family suffered cruel misfortune
before they'd barely had time to get settled, when their Labrador,
Tosca, was snatched from outside their rented family house in Palmers
Green while he was being looked after by neighbours. Tosca was
eventually found with injuries that led to his death. And while the
family were still in the process of selling their previous home in
Worsley, the house was broken into and Ball's League Championship
and FA Cup runner-up medals stolen.

A year later, Ball had to endure the torment of seeing Lesley taken
seriously ill with a staggering total of 196 gallstones. At the same time
she miscarried the baby boy she had been carrying. Such was the
agony she endured that often she could do no more than crawl on
hands and knees. Even after surgery she became weaker, until tests
revealed the collapse of her stomach wall, a condition rectified successfully by another operation. There would be more drama to come a
few weeks after Lesley had given birth to their son Jimmy Alan on 4
September 1975, when Mandy, their daughter, fell through a plate
glass window and severed the artery in her left arm.

The fluctuations of his time at Highbury were reflected in the
contradictions in the manner in which he recalled it in future years.
'My first two years at Arsenal were the hardest of my life,' he would
write in his 2004 autobiography, yet a few pages later he would recall
the social life in the latter part of that period as 'the best times of our
lives'.

Eventually earning what he recalled at different times as either £12,500 or £15,000 per year, Ball had ensured that life was enjoyed to the full, whatever the challenges he faced on the field. Not for him the simple ambition of many of his contemporaries of owning their own suburban home by the end of their career – despite his dressing-room boast to that effect in previous years. Nights out in the West End with George Graham, Frank McLintock and their families; the best clothes, jewellery, cars and holidays – they were the items that featured in the Ball budget, one that managed to end up in the red even on his salary. 'We had an overdraft, but no one worried, not even the bank managers,' he recalled. He remembered ending the night of the England victory over West Germany in 1975 footing the bill for a table that included Mel Brooks, Telly Savalas, Marty Feldman, Bobby Moore and various teammates and opponents.

'I started to live life off the pitch probably too fast for my own good,' he admitted. 'I have no idea what I was searching for, but my drinking increased and I started to stay out.' And, in an admission that relates back to the observations of Joe Royle, he confessed, 'Gambling took a hold.' He even revealed that 'we were not far from being skint'. When he went to Royal Ascot, his bets were funded by telling Lesley that he needed money for the hire of his morning suit, which, unknown to his wife, he had already bought outright from previous winnings and was kept at the house of one of his football friends.

Typically, training would be followed by a long lunch and then an evening in the Arsenal players' local, the White Hart in Southgate, before he arrived home in time for *News at Ten*. Horse racing had always been a hobby – he had co-owned a 'useless' horse called Daxal with Alex Young at Everton – and now he, Peter Marinello, Charlie George and Stan Flashman, the infamous London ticket tout and later chairman of Barnet, took up joint ownership of a colt called Go Go Gunner. A descendant of the most famous of all stallions, Northern Dancer, Go Go Gunner gave his owners a decent run for their money, winning four races.

Ball missed the first eight games of the 1974–75 season, re-fracturing his leg in a friendly in Holland, but on his return was appointed captain. Only a couple of weeks earlier he had written, 'I've no ambitions to be captain again. I'm content to help in any way I can, but someone else can lead out the team.' Mee clearly hadn't read *Shoot!* or heard any of the Everton players discussing the problems they'd had with Ball as skipper. 'I've put myself on trial over the last 12 months and this is my reward, the captaincy of Arsenal,' was Ball's response to his appointment. 'I've done petty, silly things in the past, but I believe I have come through that; I believe I have grown up.'

After a run of ten games without a win, Ball found his team bottom of the First Division. 'I doubt the Manchester United players thought they'd go down, but if United can be relegated anybody can,' he warned. Jeff Blockley was shipped out to Leicester City, the unhappy Charlie George appeared permanently on the verge of a transfer and the man purchased to solve the problems was the bald Queens Park Rangers centre-back Terry Mancini, who cost a princely £20,000. A 32-year-old of modest talents, he appeared to have arrived mostly to help Ball to lift morale, his final act for QPR having been to drop his shorts in front of the directors' box.

'I had been pushed out at QPR because they had signed David Webb,' Mancini explains. 'Bobby Campbell had been my coach there and he suggested, "Get Mancini because he will do us a job." I wasn't an Arsenal-type player and I wasn't going to win anything, but I was going to pull the dressing room together and organise. And I could defend. I would pull and push and bollock players around me. I didn't give a fuck who they were.'

McNab, whom Mancini describes as a 'cantankerous bastard who it wasn't difficult to pick a fight with', recalls, 'I was told Terry would be great for the dressing room. I just remember thinking, "Why didn't we get Freddie Starr?"' And, according to Liam Brady, 'Most of the players did not find him funny at the time. They had too much on their minds – and it left no room for being light-hearted.'

Brady's recollection of 'disputes and personality clashes which were evident from the start of the season and got worse as the months went by' says little for Ball's ability to unite the dressing room and much about Mee's increasing detachment from his players. There was little luck going Arsenal's way, either, with winger Alex Cropley breaking his leg soon after a £150,000 move from Hibernian. Ball's two goals in yet another Anfield victory in November and a repeat performance when Liverpool were beaten at Highbury in February were rare highlights in the season.

With discontent growing among the Highbury fans, Ball spoke out. 'We can do without them. If they think they are being robbed they can send their tickets to me. How any of them can possibly doubt the ambition of the club is beyond me when we have introduced four new signings into the side this season.' Salvation lay in the two most successful of those signings, goalkeeper Jimmy Rimmer and striker Brian Kidd, who had arrived in pre-season from Manchester United. Their form at either end of the field and the prospect of an FA Cup sixth-round tie at home to West Ham United were all that kept Arsenal fans sane.

Yet by the time that biggest game of the season arrived, Ball was seething at Mee and the Arsenal directors. When the Gunners had travelled to Derby, referee John Yates sent off Ball after only 15 minutes for arguing about a booking. 'Bally lost the plot,' is how Storey remembers it. 'He was booked for lashing out at Kevin Hector while he was on the ground. Instead of keeping his trap shut, Bally continued to argue.' When Yates dismissed McNab for a similar offence in the second half, it made Arsenal only the second team to have two players sent off in a League game since the Second World War. They had also been the first, when McLintock and Storey were dismissed against Burnley seven years previously.

What made Ball's dismissal even more embarrassing was that it came only two weeks after his *Shoot!* column had carried the headline, 'Why I no longer show dissent,' and had seen him declare, 'I'm now captain of Arsenal and more concerned with stopping my teammates from arguing with the ref than doing it myself.'

Ball and McNab chose to appeal against their dismissals, but were shocked to find that the club would not back them, chairman Denis Hill-Wood insisting that he was 'upholding the image of Arsenal' and Mee pointing out that players should learn not to argue. Ball could hardly take issue with that point, having just made it himself in print, although he stated his case by arguing, 'I was not sent off for dissent. I told the ref he hadn't protected me from the rough stuff and he was weak to book me for something he had previously allowed.'

In an apparent dig at Mee, the former physiotherapist, he continued, 'Would it have been better to keep quiet? Only somebody who has never played professional football would ask a question like that. Someone who doesn't know the pressures and tensions involved in the game at the top level.' Questioned about Mee's stance, he replied, 'It's a kick in the guts. Arsenal and I can never be the same again.' And, in truth, they weren't.

The players' appeals were duly lost, as was the quarter-final against West Ham. Both Ball and McNab, before their suspensions, played in the deep mud that layered Highbury, but neither could prevent a day of unrelenting misery and a 2–0 defeat as a lightweight 21-year-old striker called Alan Taylor made his name by scoring both goals. One report described an unadventurous Gunners side as 'dinosaurs', while West Ham's Trevor Brooking recalled that 'it was obvious Arsenal were not mentally prepared for the match'. The dog-end of a relegation fight was all that was left in this ashtray of a season, with safety finally secured by Kidd's winner against fellow-strugglers Tottenham Hotspur in the penultimate game.

10

CAPTAIN CONDEMNED

'We have to distrust each other. It is our only defence against betrayal'

— Tennessee Williams

ALAN Ball stood in his Essex home and stared at the letter that had shattered his world. Don Revie, the man who had given him the greatest individual recognition of his career only five months earlier, had not even bothered to sign it.

It was dated 19 August 1975, only four days after the back page of the *Daily Mirror* had carried a happy photograph of him, as England's football captain, on Brighton beach with Tony Greig, the leader of the nation's cricket team. And it had arrived after his wife Lesley had fielded a call from a reporter looking for a reaction to the FA's declaration that Ball, after a run of six unbeaten games as Revie's skipper, was not even in the squad for the first international of the new season.

Revie had not telephoned, made no attempt to offer advance warning. He had simply dispatched a letter that he'd got his secretary to sign for him. He even acknowledged that it was probable that his message would arrive too late. It read:

> Dear Alan,
>
> I hope you receive this letter before you read the morning papers, as I would like to thank you for all you have done for the Football Association and me personally over the last season.
>
> I have not selected you for the Squad for the Switzerland match, and I will be making Gerry Francis captain. I have not discarded you completely, and I only hope that you will, if recalled for any special match, play for me. I know this must come as a terrible blow, but I am letting you know first the complete position.

I hope that you soon get all your difficulties sorted out. If I can help in any way I will only be too pleased to do so, as you know.

Good luck in the future.

Yours sincerely,

Team Manager

Dictated by Mr Revie, signed in his absence

The 'difficulties' referred to in the letter were that summer's dispute with Arsenal – of which more later – but Revie's claim that he was 'letting you know first' had Ball fuming. To him the letter would become 'a constant reminder that in this game there are very few people you can really trust'. At a loss to know why he had been dropped after leading England to a 5–1 win over Scotland in their most recent international, Ball would spend the next few weeks expecting some kind of further explanation. Revie died before such a conversation could take place.

Ball's initial response to the appointment of Revie as England manager in the summer of 1974 had been one of nervousness. He had originally been omitted from the squad for what turned out to be Sir Alf Ramsey's final England game, saying, 'I suspect I am a victim of the rebuilding programme'. Then, after getting a late call-up and coming on as substitute in the 0–0 draw in Portugal, he was part of the last squad named by Ramsey. 'I am sure Alf will see my role as helping the younger players establish themselves,' he said. Ball's broken leg eventually prevented him from joining the squad, and then Ramsey was fired before the players ever met up. Ball's reaction to that news was hardly one of a man with an eye on ensuring that he would be part of future England plans. He wrote in his *Shoot!* column:

His departure left me cold, I was shocked. I'll have to watch what I write otherwise I will be in trouble with the authorities. I must confess I have lost a little faith in the men who rule our football after the handling of Alf. Surely after all he's done for the country he deserved better treatment?

After Joe Mercer took charge for the summer matches, the permanent successor to Ramsey was named and Ball wondered what his international future held after his previous snub of Revie while he was manager at Leeds. Yet, in the end, Revie made him captain of his country; an honour that had Ball 'walking on air' and feeling as though 'the little lad from Farnworth had finally hit the jackpot'.

That Ball featured somewhere in the new manager's plans was evident when he was among more than 80 players summoned to Revie's initial get-together, even though he was still injured. Ball's first impression was hardly favourable, though, coming away with the feeling that Revie believed a pay rise from £100 to £200 per game was all that was needed to give England's players the impetus they needed to make up the ground they'd lost in world football. An unused squad member for the promising 3–0 win over Czechoslovakia in the first game of a new era and on the bench for the next two matches, Ball was desperately hoping to be back in the team when West Germany returned to Wembley in March 1975. By now he was the only survivor of the World Cup final in the England set-up.

Still feeling down over Arsenal's FA Cup quarter-final exit to West Ham United the previous day, Ball could barely believe his ears when Revie approached him on reporting to the England camp with the news that 'I want you to captain the side'. A press conference was called and Ball, who had impressed with his club form in a struggling side, was introduced as his country's new skipper.

Knowing that Ball's disciplinary record would be brought up by many and that Colin Todd had been seen as the safer option, Revie insisted, 'I expect him to set an example to his colleagues, to the game, to all those watching on TV, and in particular to schoolboys throughout the country. Alan Ball doesn't like losing. He has tremendous ability. He's a brilliant reader of the game, understands what's going on and very few players have got his ability.'

Ball suggested that Ramsey's concern over his behaviour had prevented him being considered for the role before. 'Alf always gave me the job of helping out on the pitch,' he explained, 'but he never gave me the captaincy because I think he was always a man of caution and was worried about the inconsistency of my character. I've always been prone to silly mistakes.'

Asked what kind of captain he would be, Ball responded, 'Bobby Moore was a great skipper. He lacked the devil within himself to make people do things, but did it by example. I learned a lot from him. The best captain I ever played under was Frank McLintock. He was much tougher, and I shall try to merge myself into a combination of the two.'

Not everyone was in accord with Revie's appointment. Walter Johnson, the MP for Derby South, complained to the sports minister that such an honour had gone to a man who had been reprimanded so frequently by the FA for his behaviour and who had been sent off on his most recent start for England almost two years earlier. In the midst of the country's crippling industrial disputes, IRA terrorism and an economic crisis that would soon see Britain going cap in hand to the International Monetary Fund, it was incongruously reassuring to see that Alan Ball's disciplinary record could create ripples of concern in the House of Commons. 'Popularity, or lack of it, is something I've lived with for some time,' was Ball's philosophical reaction. 'I treated this remark with the contempt it deserved.'

In a warning sign for Ball, his old Blackpool housemate Emlyn Hughes wasn't too thrilled about developments either. He'd been discarded as captain via a letter from Revie. To make matters worse, Hughes would be called to Revie's hotel room a few weeks later on the eve of a game against Wales and told, 'I'm not picking you for tomorrow's game and I will not be needing you in the future.' As proof of Revie's contrary nature, however, Hughes would be back a little more than a year later, and would go on to skipper his country again.

Ball couldn't have been happier that his national boss had placed such faith in him for a big game against the world champions. A friendly in name only, England had a point to prove after missing the World Cup finals. His first task was to discover what he could about new teammates, phoning Terry Mancini for a character assessment of his former Queens Park Rangers colleague Ian Gillard, who would be England's left-back. Then he had to calm the mood of Newcastle United centre-forward Malcolm Macdonald, who had been greeted by Revie with the warning that he had only been picked because of media pressure and that 'if you don't score I'll never pick you again'.

Before the on-field test, there was a battle simply to get to Wembley Stadium. 'We used to have a motor cycle out-rider because as you got near to Wembley the traffic could be quite heavy,' recalls England physiotherapist Fred Street. 'We left the hotel and he took us through some little private estate. It was a bloody great bus, one of the first that had a kitchen and chefs on it. We were going down this little country road that was getting narrower and narrower. Don Revie was having a baby! Eventually the driver had to try to turn round and he backs into a ditch and gets stuck there. It was surreal. We were due at Wembley in the next half-hour and I am going round to houses, knocking on the doors and asking if anyone has old blankets or buckets we can use. We were putting things under the back wheels trying to get out the ditch. We were about to give up when a police jeep came along and gave us a little tow and we were on our way. We were going like the clappers down the North Circular. It was a bit tight and we had a hell of a night.'

On a rainy London evening, Ball walked out at the head of his team, the first time he had taken the field in the red and blue trimmed Admiral kit that was a new feature of Revie's reign. As the players lined up for national anthems, the cameras settled on Ball and ITV commentator Brian Moore declared, 'Whatever people may say about his record – sent off five times – I believe England could have no finer captain tonight.'

Even though he points out that 'being captain in football is not like being a cricket captain', Mick Channon states, 'Bally was inspirational, so full of enthusiasm.' And Ball could have asked for no finer performance from his men. Playing in what was almost an old-fashioned right-half position, he could see the shape of the game ahead of him and it was England who created the more pleasing patterns. Colin Bell had already come close from long range before he turned home a 27th-minute free-kick from Alan Hudson, who, according to Ball, 'had as good an international debut as I have ever seen'.

England's dominance grew after half-time, Hudson spending more time probing on the right, Kevin Keegan darting around on the left and Macdonald firing in some decent efforts from long range. 'Bally did his best to get me a goal,' Macdonald recalled and, after 66 minutes, Ball received a quickly-taken free-kick and crossed from near the right-hand corner flag for Macdonald to head home at the far post. Before the final whistle, Ball was orchestrating a series of passes among his teammates that had the crowd cheering, ending with

Keegan clipping the crossbar with the last kick of the match. 'Ball prowled and probed, challenged and chased non-stop, justifying completely his selection as skipper,' the *Daily Mirror* concluded.

Having hugged every teammate as they left the field, Ball was in the mood to celebrate and quickly organised a night out for players from both teams. 'They held him in utter reverence,' noted Macdonald of the Germans, happy to be among the group who partied at La Valbonne near Regent Street. Ball collected £50 a head from his England colleagues, made up any shortfall himself and refused to let their opponents, and various other visitors to their table, pay for a single drink.

'After that West Germany match I felt more convinced than ever that we were really on our way,' Ball said. 'I think it was as good a side as England had produced since the 1970 World Cup finals.' He felt that the players had responded 'without question' to his captaincy. 'I loved every second of it,' he continued. 'Urging people on, making them do things they didn't think they were capable of and, I like to think, setting them an example worth following.'

Next up were Cyprus in a European Championship qualifier at Wembley. Macdonald had again been given a score-or-else message by Revie, and once more Ball had told him not to worry. On the day of the game, Ball called Macdonald to him, along with Channon and Bell, and reminded the group that the record number of goals in a single game by an England player was five. 'Tonight, this man is going to break that record and score six,' he said, before pointing to Channon and Bell and continuing, 'and you, you and me are going to make those goals for him.' Ball instructed the man known to fans as Supermac to 'keep making your runs and leave the rest to us'.

'From the downer of Don Revie, what Alan Ball said made me feel 12 feet tall,' recalls Macdonald, who duly responded with all five goals in a 5–0 win, Ball combining with substitute Dave Thomas to set up the final two. A record-breaking sixth goal was disallowed.

A single-goal win in the return game in Cyprus was followed by draws against Northern Ireland and Wales in the Home Internationals. Whether or not England would fulfil the fixture in Belfast had been the subject of much conjecture, amid concerns over the players' safety during the ongoing Troubles in Northern Ireland. Originally canvassed by the press for his views, Ball said he would 'go anywhere to play for England', but when the FA announced a month before the trip that the game would definitely go ahead, the England captain was more circumspect. 'I have to make a big decision. My wife Lesley is not pleased at all.' With the players having been told that a refusal to travel would not be held against them, Ball continued, 'However good the security arrangements are, there are bound to be problems. There is a lot to be considered, especially for a family man.'

In the end, Ball and his colleagues all went and the real story of the early part of the British championships was Keegan's walk-out after being omitted from the game against Wales. Keegan was back in the fold – and the starting line-up – for the visit of Scotland to Wembley. 'I don't think Bally said much to me,' he recalls. 'He probably took the mickey and said, "Welcome back, we didn't miss you!"'

As you watch a recording of the match, Ball emerges first, chest pumped out with pride, but the way he knocks a ball from foot to foot during the walk towards the Royal Box shows a confidence, even nonchalance, that speaks of a man who has been here numerous times; who knows that this is where he belongs. The idea that this might be the final England game of his career appears remote, even though Brian Moore cautions, 'His form has wavered over the last few England games and there has been a lot of criticism of him.' Ball is shown in close-up during the national anthem. He doesn't sing, but the deep breaths he takes at the appropriate points in the song suggest he is humming along.

Which is exactly what England did; two up inside the first six minutes through a long shot on the run by Francis and a looping header by Kevin Beattie. Ball was involved three times in the build-up for the second goal; an interception, a cushioned header back to Francis and a first-time flick down the right wing to set up Keegan's cross to the goalscorer.

For the remainder of the match, Ball – his engine perhaps not what it once was – still managed to scoot across the width of the midfield, allowing Bell and Francis to take up the more advanced positions. Those two players added the third and fourth goals with further shots from outside the area, either side of a Scotland penalty just before half-time, before Ipswich Town's David Johnson completed the 5–1 scoreline. The final whistle brought Scotland fans racing on to the field – although not with the quantity or the intent of two years later – and the final camera shots of Ball's international career are a somewhat undignified race to the tunnel; no opportunity to savour the achievements of the afternoon.

After a hot summer during which his Arsenal future became increasingly hazy and he was removed from the club captaincy, Ball approached the season saying, 'I talked it over with Don Revie when I went on the [transfer] list and he told me I would carry on until he thought otherwise.' But, after he was left out of Arsenal's opening game at Burnley and told by Bertie Mee that he couldn't play for the reserves because of the risk of injury, Revie's letter arrived.

It was the manner in which he had been discarded that hurt more than the dismissal itself. After all, he had sat and listened to Revie saying of his original appointment, 'Ball can do a job for me; perhaps not for 1978, but certainly for the next two or three matches, putting things right out on the pitch where I am unable to be in touch with the players.' If that was how Revie saw it, fine. Ball knew he was still viewed as a Ramsey man and that the performances of Gerry Francis marked him out as the player around whom Revie wanted to construct a new team. But at least have the courtesy to tell him. Revie's casual remark that both of his discarded captains, Ball and Hughes, would understand his position once they became managers did nothing to ease the hurt.

Ball wondered whether he was paying the price for breaking an evening curfew with a group of teammates at England's headquarters at West Lodge Park hotel in Cockfosters. Whatever the truth, Gordon Hill, about to break into Revie's squad after a move from Millwall to Manchester United, argued, 'There's no doubt Bally was discarded too soon. He could have continued to do a tremendous job for his country, bringing class and stability to a side struggling to find its feet.'

Even wife Lesley felt angry enough to create headlines of her own by saying, 'It's disgraceful to treat Alan like this after what he has done for English football in the past 10 years.' She continued, 'Alan himself did not seem unduly surprised at the news. He has had so many kicks in the teeth lately that nothing that happens now seems to shock him.'

And, acknowledging the industrial relations environment of the times, she concluded, 'It just does not make sense. If he was working in any other job he would have the unions behind him, screaming victimisation. After all, what has he done wrong?'

New skipper Francis, who had made his England debut in Revie's first game and had still played only four times for his country, would have welcomed the continued presence of Ball in the side. 'I think Alan was one of the people who actually helped me get into the team,' he recalls. 'We drew a game 2–2 at Arsenal and Alan was telling people how well I had played. Playing alongside him in the England team was fantastic for me. He was a hero to me anyway, but his ability, his enthusiasm, his one-touch football was outstanding. As an opponent you would try to get close to him, but he was so quick in getting rid of the ball, knowing who he was going to pass to before he got it. Playing with him, he played balls to you quickly and early and was obviously a very confident, experienced international. I don't think people realise the pressure on you when you play for England, so somebody like Alan was really important because he had been there, seen it, done it and won the World Cup. He was very helpful and instrumental in helping people settle down, certainly me.

'We had a good unbeaten run going, culminating in that win against Scotland, and he was an excellent captain. To be honest, when I spoke to Don when I was made captain, I wasn't happy about Alan not being in the team. If Don wanted to make me captain, that was fine, but I was still happy that Alan could have been there helping me. Age is not a barrier in football; it is about whether you can perform. And the balance of experience with youth is vitally important. I was quite disappointed when I learned Alan was not being kept in the squad.'

With international football now part of his history, Ball set about resolving the mess that his club career had become. Even before he'd learned that his decade as an England player was being brought to end, Ball had made up his mind that he no longer wanted to be an Arsenal man. Disillusioned by the team's struggles and the club's lack of support in his disciplinary hearing in the spring, he had been further dismayed to read in the press that Arsenal were prepared to listen to offers for him. 'Why is it that the only way I can find out about things is reading the newspapers?' he asked, although manager Bertie Mee insisted it had been mere media speculation. Ball treated it as the last straw and asked for a transfer.

'I was becoming more restless and disillusioned,' he would explain. 'I could see things needed to be done to improve the team but nothing was happening. I didn't want to take over but I thought my ideas were worth listening to. I thought my request would shake Mee into action.'

In a sense, it did. Mee finally sold Charlie George – to Derby County for £90,000 – dropped Ball for the start of the 1975–76 season, made Eddie Kelly the leader on the field and appointed Mancini club captain. Ball returned for the fourth game, scoring from the penalty spot in a win against Norwich City, and would eventually withdraw his transfer request in November, after reported interest from Stoke City, Manchester City and Hull City. 'Bobby Campbell was perhaps the only one at the time who knew how I felt and it was he who finally persuaded me to stay at Highbury. I knew I could work well with Bobby.' Ball wrote to the board and informed them of his decision. 'I've never been too proud to admit a mistake,' he explained.

Yet Ball's eventual reinstatement as team captain caused further issues, at least for Kelly, who had already sensed that it was Ball towards whom young players like Liam Brady, Frank Stapleton and David O'Leary looked for leadership. Kelly saw Ball named captain when he was forced to miss five games with pneumonia, but was shocked when the former skipper continued to lead out the team when he was healthy again. 'The only thing I was ever upset about at Arsenal was the way they took the captaincy away from me,' Kelly states. 'I still don't know why they did it. No one ever told me.' After his England experience, Ball was at least able to empathise with Kelly's hurt.

Ball's closeness to Campbell had become the subject of whispers of unrest among some teammates, with suggestions that the pair were taking over from Mee as the power brokers in the club. Peter Storey felt that Ball was being 'indulged' and 'had a lot of influence in the picking of the team'. John Radford argues, 'I didn't like Bobby Campbell as a coach and, as much as I liked Alan Ball, the two were running the place.'

Mee, who had never been a tracksuit manager, was having less and less contact with his players. 'Bertie did not seem quite as strong or sure of himself,' says Bob McNab, who left for Wolves in the summer of 1975. 'The dressing room had gone from a very positive atmosphere to one of backbiting. There were rumours that Bobby Campbell wanted the manager's job, with Bally as first-team coach. They were very close.'

Ball dismissed talk of trying to exert unwanted influence at the club as 'nonsense'. Full-back Sammy Nelson supports Ball's rebuttal. 'Bobby was the coach, so he obviously was going to have a lot of input,' he notes. 'Bally was the senior player and he always wanted to voice his opinion. But they didn't make any decisions – that was down to the board.'

Interviewed for my biography of Bertie Mee, Ball said, 'I don't agree that Bobby and I started to run the place. There were still a lot of good players and strong characters there. And I don't think Bertie was losing interest; he was still as passionate about the club up until the day he left.'

That day was looming. Late in a season that brought another flirtation with relegation and an eventual finishing position of 17th, Mee announced that it would be his final campaign. But there was still time to deliver one last rousing speech to his players as the relegation battle intensified; a piece of oratory that stunned those players who had come to believe that their manager no longer cared. Speaking with passion, as well as carefully chosen words, Mee told his players that Arsenal was his life, and that his ideal departure would be to drop down dead on the Highbury pitch. Brady would write, 'By the time he finished countering our accusation of neglect he had earned genuine applause from the players.' Arsenal went out and thrashed West Ham United 6-1 in their next game.

Ball, who scored two of his nine League goals in that match, played all 39 remaining First Division games once his early-season exile had been ended, but could do nothing to change the fortunes of the man he had come to admire. In *Bertie Mee: Arsenal's Officer and Gentleman*, I wrote:

Alan Ball's was probably the signing about which Mee was questioned most often in later years. Quite simply, he never managed to harness Ball's ability to the collective benefit of the team. Even Ball himself concedes that he was discontent with his personal play during the earlier seasons of his Arsenal career, when the club was still challenging for honours. Yet, as the team's fortunes waned, so Ball's own game flourished. How much more rewarding might Mee's final seasons at Highbury have been had he and his coaches been able to solve the conundrum of why the form of the team and its most renowned player appeared to be mutually exclusive?

Ball reflected, for the same book, that 'I loved my time at Arsenal and the one thing that galls me to this day is that we did not win a trophy, even though we were often knocking on the door.' He concluded, 'I was desperate to help them to win something, not just for me but for Bertie Mee, who had spent so much money on me. We had a good crop of kids coming through who went on to great success and at times we played great football. Overall, the club was in a healthy state, but on the field it was frustrating that we couldn't quite win anything.'

When Mee's replacement, the Tottenham Hotspur manager and former Arsenal captain Terry Neill, arrived at Highbury, it did not take Ball long to realise that if Neill was to take the club back towards the top of the English game – which he would – then he would probably not be around to see it. Given that he had been among those rooting for Campbell to get the job, he was never likely to welcome an alternative candidate with open arms and his memory that 'Neill had none of [Campbell's] qualities' and that 'he quickly fell out with many of the playing staff' should be viewed through that lens. Nor was Neill likely to be throwing man-hugs in the direction of someone he knew was opposed to his appointment. He knew Ball carried influence and 'realised there would be some opposition'.

Ball's position became even more deeply entrenched when Neill moved quickly to replace Campbell. To make things even worse, the man Ball admired was exchanged for former Blackpool and Everton coach Wilf Dixon, for whom he had little respect. 'I realised straightaway he was not my kind of person,' was how Ball recorded his reaction to Neill. He believed that Neill would aim to win over the dressing room by removing the most powerful voice inside it.

Neill, meanwhile, described Ball as 'one of the most difficult players with whom I have had to work' adding the assertion that 'Bally hadn't been all that popular with his Arsenal teammates, most of whom were glad to get some peace and quiet after he had left.' The final remark contains echoes of Keith Newton talking about Ball's departure from Everton, but any comment by either Ball or Neill about the other is indicative of – and shaped by – the non-relationship that existed between them.

An incident before a pre-season game against Grasshoppers in Zurich was significant enough for Ball to relate it in detail in two auto-biographies, recalling that Neill not only used toy soldiers and cowboys to make a tactical point on a model pitch, but attracted sniggers from his players for referring to different sections of his team in military terms. Neill, too, considered it important enough to address in his own book, *Revelations of a Football Manager*. He felt that Ball told the story 'to ridicule me', which was undoubtedly true, and argued that he 'was doing the same as any other manager or coach might do in simi-lar circumstances with chessmen, sauce bottles, tea cups or whatever is available' – although quite why Neill happened to have a bag of toy figures to hand on an overseas trip is not explained.

Ball noted his contempt at a training routine that involved the ball being thrown from behind the goal for players to tap into an empty net from inside the penalty area. Again, Neill would respond in print, noting that Ball 'never offered anything constructive as an alternative'.

Typical of Ball's playing career, however, was that even those with whom he didn't get along – and he would admit that there were plenty in that group – had no hesitation in acknowledging his contribution on the field. 'Whatever faults Bally may have had or whatever the differences between us, there was no denying his great ability and his enthusiasm for the game,' Neill stated. 'He was also an inspirational captain,' he said, although adding, in a somewhat contradictory tone, that 'some players complained that he ranted and raved too much'.

Neill's first few months as Arsenal manager were memorable for a storybook hat-trick by Macdonald, signed for £333,333, against his former Newcastle United teammates at Highbury early in December in Ball's final game for the club. The die had been irrevocably cast three days earlier when Ball ignored Neill's instruction that Trevor

Ross should mark Queens Park Rangers midfielder Don Masson in a League Cup quarter-final at Loftus Road and took on the role himself. Arsenal lost 2–1 and Ball made it clear that he believed Neill's half-time insistence on reverting to his original plan was responsible for the result.

Ball had long since warned Lesley that they might soon find themselves on the move. 'I don't like this guy and he doesn't like me,' he'd said. With Neill negotiating with Stoke City to bring in Alan Hudson to fill the number eight shirt and his relationship with Ball now at breaking point, that time had come. Financially, as it turned out, not a moment too soon.

The Balls' bank account had continued to take a battering, even after drinking buddies like Frank McLintock and George Graham moved away. A few games in the summer of 1976 for Hellenic in South Africa were supposed to help to bolster the family coffers, only for phone calls home from his hotel room to wipe out much of what he was earning and for the club to inform him that he was restricted in how much money he could take out of the country in any case. His finances were about to be rescued, however, by a man who would hold Ball's trust until the day he died.

The football grapevine worked quickly. And in the days before puppeteer agents pulled the strings on both sides of a deal, transfers could be conjured up and concluded with equal speed. Lawrie McMenemy had heard that Ball was unhappy at Highbury and that his club might be persuaded to sell. 'When you are in the game, you are part of a family and the whispers come around,' McMenemy explains.

A couple of phone calls later, Ball was arriving at The Dell, home of the FA Cup winners, but a club stuck in the Second Division. It was late afternoon, with few others around, as he climbed the stairs to the manager's office. 'He came towards me with his arm out and I stood up and I walked round him,' McMenemy recalls. 'I went and locked the door. He said, "What did you do that for?" 'I said, "I am not letting you out until you sign."'

McMenemy began his sales pitch. 'Cards on the table, Alan. It is a good club. I want you here. You know what we are and what we can do, but I want you here for one job; to get us promoted.'

The former Coldstream guardsman towered over the diminutive Ball. The World Cup winner was not one to be intimidated, even by such an imposing figure, but he took little time to buy into McMenemy's masterplan. He would run things from midfield, inspire those around him and lift the team to promotion out of the Second Division. The affable Geordie, who had never amounted to much as a player but had won Fourth Division titles as a manager at Doncaster Rovers and Grimsby Town, was an easy man to believe in. Especially when he had at his disposal talented and experienced players who had beaten Manchester United to win the FA Cup at Wembley.

As early as 1971, Ball had demonstrated a soft spot for Southampton when he wrote, 'It's a really friendly little ground – and the Hampshire crowd is very appreciative of good, skilful football.' Now, thanks to his meeting with the manager, he 'had a belief that we would do well'.

'He more or less agreed straight away,' continues McMenemy, whose next task was to persuade Ball of the wisdom of his financial advice. Having made some discreet enquiries, Ball's prospective boss knew the former England captain had debts to pay, little money to spare and would quickly spend whatever he got. Local journalist Pat Symes even recalls, 'The rumour was that Southampton agreed to pay off his betting debts. I don't know if that was true, but it was said his debts were £30,000.'

McMenemy's memory endorses that general picture, if not the exact detail. 'Money meant very little to Alan. If he had a fiver he would spend a tenner. He got the agreed basic, the same bonuses that everybody got for wins and draws and a promotion bonus was written in. But when he joined he could get a signing-on fee. I said, "Right, that will be your signing-on fee, but I am not giving it to you. You haven't got a house, have you?" In those days, if you were a top player you had a club house. He had one at Arsenal and I said, "Alan, with due respect, you are not going to have many more moves. You need to get on the housing list." He shrugged his shoulders and we shook hands and off he went.'

McMenemy now had to persuade Arsenal to sell Ball to him. He offered them 60,000 reasons to do so. The Gunners' public acceptance of Southampton's fee was somewhat unexpected given that only a week earlier chairman Denis Hill-Wood had dismissed Blackpool's attempt to take Ball back to his first club by saying, 'Their manager must be joking if he thinks Ball will be leaving us for £50,000. Alan is one of the best midfield players in the world and certainly the best man we've got. He won't be leaving Highbury for that amount.' An extra £10,000 was apparently all the upgrade it needed to meet the Gunners' valuation of world class, especially when Neill was perfectly happy to part company with a player with whom he had a fractious relationship.

McMenemy, meanwhile, had not heard the last of the issue of the signing-on bonus. 'A few days later, there is a bang on the door and in comes Lesley saying, "Where is my husband's bloody signing-on fee?" I sat her down and I told her the same as I'd told Alan. She wasn't happy, but they started looking for a house. We would take them round and show them areas. He finished up with a house and I still pass it regularly and say, "God bless you, Bally." They thanked me because they realised they had done the right thing.'

Another member of the family was about to weigh in. Ball senior tried to talk his son out of dropping out of the First Division, believing it represented settling for 'second best'. But a decade after his first thought had to been to call his dad after being offered a deal by Everton, Ball confessed he had 'become almost immune' to criticism and disagreement from his father and ignored his objections. When news of the transfer was confirmed, Southampton's new recruit spoke excitedly about the challenge he had accepted.

'He's my sort of man,' he said of McMenemy, 'a true professional with no humbug' – making it impossible not to wonder whether that was a jibe at his most recent boss. 'It's been a bit hectic lately and for me a bit of a riddle. My manager at Arsenal, Terry Neill, made a sudden decision to part with my services and this came right out of the blue. Maybe I've grown a bit cynical about the soccer scene and it was the type of man I was dealing with that was most important to me. Many shrewd judges of the game reckon I'm playing as well as ever. I know that I'm as fit as ever and that English football today is crying out for ball players.'

Promising that his style of play would bring out the best in former England teammate Mick Channon, he continued, 'With the Saints I might not get to heaven, but we might make the First Division before

I hang up my boots. There is a lot of talent in the Southampton team. Perhaps they need a coordinator, a key man. Perhaps I can be that key.'

As for Arsenal, Ball insisted, 'I still love them,' but he didn't sound sorry to be leaving the club. 'When one of my greatest mates, John Radford, left for West Ham last week, I knew it was the final break-up of the great side I joined. For some obscure reason somebody thought Alan Hudson and I would be too much in the same side. That could be one of the greatest soccer mistakes of all time.'

Ball also had a thought for another of his old teams, over whom he had chosen Southampton. 'I am more than a little sad about Blackpool. Obviously I have a real soft spot for the club.' Yet Bloomfield Road had not seen the last of its 1966 hero.

11

THE BEAUTIFUL SOUTH

'A man does not have to be an angel in order to be a saint'

– Nobel Peace Prize winner Albert Schweitzer

THE desk from which Mick Channon plans his assaults on racing's top prizes sits at one end of a modern, wooden-floored space that serves both as the administration hub of West Ilsley Stables and a visitors' reception. On the book shelves in the waiting area, stallion guides share space with vintage football books and a selection of biographies. Trophies and photographs adorn window ledges and furniture tops, while a flat-screen television shows Sky Sports News. At the business end, the far wall is dominated by a single mounted black and white photograph. Not of Channon in top hat and tails celebrating a Royal Ascot victory, nor of any of the Group One winners that he has produced during his post-football career as one of Britain's leading trainers. It is of two men, wearing Southampton shirts, laughing together on the football field. As Channon studies bloodstock sales reports and plots the training programmes and racing schedules of the 120 horses in his charge on the west Berkshire downs, it is Alan Ball who smiles down upon him.

'I miss him,' says Channon, glancing up at the image of him and his friend while he waits for a group of two-year-olds to return from the gallops. 'He still makes me smile. Things happen and you realise that he would have cracked a joke or taken the piss. Little things crop up every day and you think, "Bally would have made something of that." He loved life, loved a drink and loved a bet. I can't speak highly enough of him. You could be down, and he would come in and tell you a story or tell you a joke to brighten you up. He was a breath of fresh air.'

Ball's transfer to Southampton in December 1976 was an opportunity to cement a friendship that had been forged in the England dressing room and had developed over a mutual interest in horses and nights out. 'What you saw was what you got with Alan; he was lively and bubbly,' continues Channon, who was unsurprised to see Ball dropping down a division to join him at The Dell. 'It didn't matter to Alan. All he ever wanted to do was play football. He didn't give a shit if he was playing in a red shirt, blue shirt or green shirt. He wanted to play, or coach or train kids. I saw him when he was mobile and active and a top player – great touch, great vision, almost a complete player. But Southampton was perfect for him at his age. He'd lost half a yard of pace, but he had a quick brain and got even sharper and cuter when he got older. The first yard was in his head.'

For the third time in his career, Ball had been signed by the FA Cup holders. As at Arsenal, he had missed the deadline for the European quarter-finals and would have to watch as his new team went down narrowly over two legs to holders Anderlecht in the Cup Winners' Cup. It was promotion, however, for which he had been acquired, although when he made his debut at Plymouth Argyle, as captain, the Saints were in 15th place and closer to relegation.

'Lawrie McMenemy brought in some players you would never have thought you would see there,' says David Peach, left-back in the victorious Wembley team. 'The First Division was our target. We'd got relegated and the Cup put a shine on it so the hurt wasn't so bad, but Alan was what we needed. He was a great leader.'

Covering the team for national newspapers, local journalist Pat Symes says, 'Bally brought a little bit of extra class. Lawrie's team was a strange concoction of nasty Scots and journeymen, but he tried to improve the quality.' And he added newsworthiness invaluable to an agency man working on the south coast. 'Bally was very helpful. I am not sure I enjoyed the greatest of relationships with him, but he would jump up and down and then be your pal. There was always that fiery part about him and a few minutes later he would be all right.'

Even with Ball in the team, Southampton would fall a further three places during his first few weeks, but a 3–0 win in an FA Cup replay at Chelsea had offered promise of improvement to come and they leapt up to 12th with a 6–0 win at Carlisle United, the kind of scoreline that one might have expected more frequently with an all-star front three of Channon, Ted MacDougall and Peter Osgood. It marked the beginning of a run of 11 League games in which they were beaten only once, helping them towards a final placing of ninth and inspiring optimism about the following season.

Ball had scored his first Southampton goal in a 3–3 draw against Nottingham Forest in the FA Cup, but only one strike in 23 League games indicated the deeper role he was taking on the field. Even though he had continued to achieve double figures pretty much every season while at Arsenal, goals were not what he had been signed for. Enjoying the 'carte blanche to run the middle of the park', Ball had also been instructed by McMenemy to seize control of a dressing room that featured what Ball described as a collection of 'footballers, mimics, know-alls and whimsies'. McMenemy admitted that the likes of Osgood, Jim McCalliog and Jim Steele enjoyed socialising and, even though Ball matched their love of a night out, the manager felt he could rely on his new leader to demonstrate when it was time to go to work.

'There were some good names there that he knew and then there were some young 'uns,' McMenemy continues. 'He was an inspiration to the youngsters, he settled straight in and the crowd loved him. As I got to know Alan, he was the most likeable fellow; he loved life, he loved football and he was a big family man. He liked a night out – he was of that era – and one day Bally looked at Lew Chatterley, our trainer, and said, "Lew, Wimpey's couldn't lift me today." But the minute his feet touched the grass he lit up. That was him all over. If you have a World Cup winner of his age doing it, then nobody in the club can give you less than 100 per cent.'

McMenemy turned the signing of experienced internationals into something of a trademark in the late 1970s and early 1980s. Names such as Charlie George, Kevin Keegan, Frank Worthington, Dave Watson, Peter Shilton and Mick Mills would all succumb to the manager's charm. 'In the lower divisions you are 90 per cent a coach and 10 per cent a manager, because you don't have the players,' he explains. 'Higher up, you had the players and you also had all those internationals, most of whom I got cheap because they were on their last legs. The common denominator with all of them, I would say – without insulting them – is that they were rascals. They had been around the world and played international football, but they needed managing. I loved that. They didn't need coaching, so now I was 90 per cent a manager.'

Ball quickly recognised that McMenemy was intuitive enough to discern which players among that 'mix of youngsters and strong-willed veterans' needed a firm hand and which were better off given greater rein to their personalities. Training at Southampton was conducted on public common land by the county cricket ground rather than the purpose-built complexes Ball had been used to at Everton and Arsenal. If the balls were lost, the players would run back down the road to The Dell. Older players such as Ball, Osgood and MacDougall were given leeway to take days off.

'Pressure was on us because Lawrie had to prove that signing these players wasn't just for fun,' says Peach. 'But he was a great man manager and he got respect from those players. Players like Osgood and Ball came, a bit of devilment in them, and they just needed a little bit of slack that they probably didn't get in other places. He gave them that and they would cross rivers for him.'

McMenemy continues, 'Alan fitted into that category of players who needed managing. One morning, the trainer warned me they'd all brought their suits and ties. I told him to get me a paper and I looked in it and saw Newbury's first race was 1.45. They were all waiting for me at the training ground so I said, "What a wonderful day. The weather is fantastic. Aren't we lucky to be out here instead of at the docks or down the mines? It makes you want to be out here all day." Bally and his pals are looking at each other. "Unless we have a good session," I said. Well, Brazil couldn't have beaten us that morning. They kept running by the trainer and saying, "What time is it?" Eventually I said, "Well done. In you go," and they were in like a flash. Within minutes Channon, Ossie and Bally drove out with their suits on. I put my hand up and they put the window down and I said to Bally, "Put us a tenner on the first race, will you?" That is what it was all about. They knew I knew. If they ever crossed the line I would bring them up to my office quietly. Some people need a cuddle, some need a kick up the backside. I would have a rascal if he could play, but I wouldn't have a villain if he was the best player in the world.

'All teams are made up of road sweepers and violinists. Every now and again a road sweeper thinks he is a violinist, so you have got to point out that he isn't. And, once in a while you have to remind a violinist that without the road sweepers he wouldn't have the bloody ball. The art of management is getting the balance.'

Ball, who had been one of Alf Ramsey's road sweepers in 1966, was now what McMenemy called his 'master violinist'. He continues, 'I remember one day as he went out I said, "Let's have some one-touch today, Bally." He looked over and said, "Half a touch, do you?" He could do that; he had peripheral vision. He wanted the ball all the time. You would look at some teams and you would see that a player was not interested, but Alan loved pulling the strings. He loved setting things up.'

A maestro thrives on the big stage, of course, and in among the visits to football and geographical outposts such as Plymouth, Carlisle United and Hereford United during his early weeks at Southampton, Ball relished a return to one of the game's great theatres when the fifth round of the FA Cup threw up a rematch of the previous season's final against Manchester United. Ball was eager to help his new colleagues prove that their surprise victory at Wembley, courtesy of a late Bobby Stokes goal, had been no fluke. Southampton were even bigger underdogs at Old Trafford than 10 months earlier, but they earned a replay before Jimmy Greenhoff's double gave United a 2–1 victory at The Dell.

As much as Ball was relishing his new challenge, it turned out that Alan Ball senior had not been the only person concerned about him stepping down a division. The editors of *Shoot!* decided that their readers wanted to hear from the likes of England captain Gerry Francis, United's Gordon Hill and Aston Villa centre-forward Andy Gray rather than a former England player stuck in the Second Division. His ghostwriter, Christopher Davies, was the one to tell him he was longer required. 'Editors only sign contracts,' he laughs. 'They leave it to the workers to pass on the bad news. I don't recall how much notice we gave him, maybe a month or so, and he was really pissed off about it. His attitude towards me really changed, but you can't keep a column going indefinitely.'

Ball was quickly on target as the 1977–78 campaign kicked off with a home draw against Brighton and Hove Albion. When Southampton followed up by losing at Stoke City, they were hardly making a case for people to tip them to go up. But then a couple of three-game winning streaks meant that they spent the autumn just outside the promotion places.

A return to Arsenal presented itself in the third round of the League Cup, although Ball insisted, 'I've nothing to prove and it's great to be going back, but our bid for promotion overshadows everything.' A 2–0 defeat ended Southampton's interest in the competition, while an early FA Cup exit at Bristol Rovers left them to concentrate on the season's prime objective. Six wins in seven games either side of New Year aided that cause, Ball scoring in Christmas wins against Cardiff City and Charlton Athletic.

Channon had taken the chance to sign for Manchester City for £300,000 in the summer and Osgood was soon heading to the United States. But McMenemy had brought in Phil Boyer to resume a striking partnership with MacDougall that had previously thrived at York City, Bournemouth and Norwich City. When Boyer scored twice in a 3–1 Easter win at Bristol Rovers late in March it meant Southampton had lost only once in 15 games and showed no sign of relinquishing their grip on promotion.

Signings such as centre-half Chris Nicholl from Aston Villa had added stability at the back and only twice during that run had Saints conceded more than a single goal. Steve Moran, an apprentice on his way to becoming a prolific scorer for the club in the 1980s, recalls Ball's admiration for the Northern Ireland stopper. 'Chris was not one for drinking and going out and would keep himself to himself,' he explains. 'Bally used to tell him, "I hate everything you stand for. But between three o'clock and quarter to five you will do for me. I wouldn't want anyone else."'

Defeat at Cardiff City proved only a temporary setback. Blackburn Rovers were overwhelmed 5–0 and four more games without defeat meant that a draw at Orient in the penultimate game all but secured promotion – unless Brighton could overturn a big deficit in goal difference on the final day of the season. Southampton entertained Tottenham Hotspur in the last game, knowing that a win could clinch the Second Division title, with a single point enough to end any mathematical doubts about their elevation. Third-placed Spurs also needed only a draw to return to the top flight at the first attempt, but

Saints had no thought of going through the motions for a mutually beneficial result. It is hard to imagine any team with Ball in it ever following that course. Southampton, however, did appear less inclined to commit to attack than in previous games. MacDougall recalled being angry at what he felt was the casual approach of young midfielder Steve Williams and ended up throwing his tea cup at him during a half-time row. An eventual 0–0 draw confirmed Bolton Wanderers as champions and Southampton and Tottenham as the other promoted teams, leaving Brighton fans down the coast crying 'conspiracy'.

Asked to assess his contribution to promotion, Ball responded, 'I give a team a lot more balance these days. Instead of charging around all over the place I read the game better and put more thought into it.'

Peach enthuses about Ball's influence, recalling that his mere presence 'gave you a massive lift'. He adds, 'He had that desire and enthusiasm and if there was a problem Alan soon let you know. We would have meetings and it would be sorted. He had achieved everything and he was a great player and his enthusiasm never dwindled. I have sat on team coaches on the way home and – yes, we'd had a couple of drinks – but Alan would be crying as he was talking and trying to help you with your game. He was so passionate.'

Moran also recalls those journeys where 'Bally would sit in the front with Lawrie and have a few whiskies. After an hour or so he would come down the coach and, one by one, would either slaughter you or tell you he loved you. He loved kissing, and breathing whisky fumes all over you.'

MacDougall described Ball as an 'inspirational captain who at times played as if he would get us promoted single-handedly', while McMenemy, asked to identify the most important member of his squad, stated, 'Pound for pound, it has to be Alan Ball. His enthusiasm and dedication are tremendous. I pride myself on the fact that in these days of inflation I've built a First Division team that has only one six figure signing [Boyer].'

McMenemy, who had recently interviewed unsuccessfully for the England job that was awarded permanently to interim manager Ron Greenwood, was now Leeds United's preferred choice to replace the sacked Jimmy Armfield. 'If Lawrie goes, you can ring me at any hour of the day or night,' Ball told his club through the press. In the end, McMenemy chose to stay at The Dell and Ball's ambitions were delayed.

Meanwhile, Tottenham made the biggest moves of the summer, taking advantage of the European Economic Community ruling in February that a player's nationality was not a lawful reason to prevent a club signing him. Clubs were now permitted two overseas players and Spurs manager Keith Burkinshaw spent more than £700,000 on midfielders Ossie Ardiles and Ricardo Villa from Argentina's newly-crowned World Cup winners. Southampton also responded quickly, if more modestly, by paying £50,000 for Yugoslav right-back Ivan Golac.

Ball angered McMenemy by phoning him one evening, questioning the strength of the Saints squad and expressing doubts about Golac. 'He was out of order,' McMenemy noted in his diary. 'He'd had a drink or two and his tongue was loose.' Next morning, Ball marched into the manager's office, offered his hand and apologised.

McMenemy's book *The Diary of a Season* offers some fascinating snapshots of Ball as club captain; full of passion, quick to praise, motivate and support, yet often harsh of tongue on the pitch or training ground. McMenemy would recall that 'more than once I had to order him not to be so bloody cruel with those less talented than himself', but put it down to 'the no-mercy way he was brought up'.

The affection in which McMenemy holds Ball frequently jumps out of the pages of his diary, yet his fatherly indulgence never creates a threat of being undermined. McMenemy is clearly the boss and on the Monday after a defeat at Leeds United, Ball is thoughtful enough to visit his office to ensure that he is not too downhearted. One revealing passage occurs in mid-November when McMenemy describes Ball in tears, fearful that his influence is waning over younger players, such as Nick Holmes, who, McMenemy believes, think they no longer require his guidance. McMenemy ends up reminding Holmes to take advantage of Ball. 'He's still a great player who can help you,' he tells him. In December, when Ball is fined £3,000 for revealing in his autobiography the illegal payments he received from Don Revie almost 13 years earlier, McMenemy notes that 'he would struggle to find it' and offers a club loan.

While Spurs' exotic imports were making their debuts in a fanfare at Brian Clough's Nottingham Forest, surprise League champions in their first season back in the First Division, Southampton were kicking off 1978–79 with defeat at Norwich. It was an appropriate portent of a low-key League campaign in which they finished 13th. Yet the cup competitions kept Ball's team in the national spotlight.

Two goals each from Boyer and MacDougall, in one of his last games before returning to Bournemouth, marked a 5–2 win at Birmingham City to launch their League Cup campaign. Derby County and Reading were beaten to set up a quarter-final against Manchester City at The Dell. Boyer scored the first goal in a 2–1 win and Southampton prepared for a semi-final against Leeds. Nicholl suggested before the tie, 'We've improved since the opening part of the season and a lot depends on how Alan Ball plays. When he is in the right mood the whole team benefits from it. There is nobody like him for setting up goals and he has a big influence on the young players.'

McMenemy gave a half-hour team talk before the first leg at Elland Road, but saw his team fall behind to a Tony Currie goal after 25 minutes. They conceded a second to Ray Hankin shortly after half-time, but were level within 16 minutes after a Holmes header and a Steve Williams volley. Boyer was sent off nine minutes from time, but the 2–2 draw left Southampton in a strong position a week later. Winger Terry Curran's scruffy finish put them ahead before half-time of the second leg and the crowd at The Dell roared their team through to Wembley.

According to McMenemy, Ball played his best football at Southampton during the League Cup, saying that 'his legs were still carrying him like a champion and his football brain was in overdrive'. So thrilled was Ball at his unexpected return to the national stadium that he turned up at McMenemy's house the next morning without sleeping, having run up a celebration bill that his manager said was 'best described as considerable'. McMenemy continues, 'Bally called me and said the players wanted me to join them, but I told him I couldn't because I was celebrating with the staff. We ended up paying Bally's bill, though. Getting to Wembley was an unexpected bonus for him. We signed him to get us promoted and this was a lovely surprise.'

Ball was always quick to repay McMenemy via public acknowledgement of his respect for his manager. Before the final, he stated,
'I've had a few bosses, but Lawrie is the only one who makes me feel
like Alf Ramsey made me feel when I pulled on an England shirt.'

For the 32nd and final time, Ball marched out at Wembley, a couple
of places behind McMenemy, who had found Forest assistant manager
Peter Taylor on his right shoulder rather than Brian Clough.
Regardless of who led them out, and in spite of injuries to defenders
Viv Anderson and Kenny Burns, the holders and League champions
were heavy favourites against a Southampton line-up that included
only two survivors of the FA Cup triumph three years earlier:

Gennoe

Golac   Waldron   Nicholl   Peach

Curran   Williams   Ball   Holmes

Hayes   Boyer

Substitute: Sealy

Sitting on the bench with the Southampton staff was comedian
Freddie Starr, who had shown up at the team hotel, waltzed uninvited
on to the coach and simply strolled into the stadium with the players.
McMenemy, amused by his cheek, let him stay. With piles of snow
bordering the pitch – evidence of Britain's coldest winter since the
infamous freeze of 1962–63[1] – Southampton started with high-tempo
intent, again undaunted by the Wembley odds-makers, and Terry
Gennoe's save from a Garry Birtles header represented the only time
in the first half that the dangerous John Robertson was able to work
any magic on Forest's left wing.

---

1 The weather left egg on the faces of the producers of a movie called *Yesterday's
Hero*, in which Ian McShane plays an ageing footballer offered one last shot at glory.
The idea of using real clips from the League Cup final to double as the fictitious
'Saints versus Leicester Forest' FA Cup final probably seemed like a good idea until
the never-ending winter meant that cinema goers would be left wondering why a
game traditionally played in early summer sunshine had mounds of filthy-looking
snow as its backdrop.

Ball demonstrated his appetite for the contest by scuffling on the touchline with Martin O'Neill as they disputed a throw. McMenemy quietly urged Ball not to try to win the game on his own after a couple of misplaced passes, but was quickly cheering his contribution as Southampton took the lead after 16 minutes. Peach cut in from the left and shaped to attempt a shot, before squaring the ball to his right instead. Ball allowed it to run across his body, waiting for the exact moment to deliver an incisive first-time return into the path of Peach, who had continued his run into the box. He took the ball in his stride to round Peter Shilton and score into an empty goal. Ball galloped towards the bench, intent on catching the eye of Clough. His face bore 'a twisted look', according to McMenemy, who was forced to wave his arms at his skipper and yell, 'Hey, you. Settle yourself down.'

Ball was revelling in the familiar surroundings, whether it was releasing the dangerous Curran on the right, or skipping past Colin Barrett on the left to cross for Boyer to have his shot blocked. As the players left the field at half-time, ITV's cameras picked out Ball, allowing Brian Moore to state, 'The biggest contribution of all, though, coming inevitably from that man in the middle of the field, Alan Ball, who's been everywhere; cajoling and arguing with his teammates and making sure they keep on the right track. A tremendous solo performance from him.'

Yet Ball's hopes of winning a domestic final at Wembley at his third attempt were swept aside after the break by a galvanised Forest. He was lucky not to inadvertently give them an equaliser when the ball ricocheted off his leg and rolled inches wide, but Birtles made Nicholl's day a misery as he forced his team into the lead. First he stole the ball off the centre-back's feet to level the scores, then he raced away from his flailing attempt to keep up with him before sliding the ball under Gennoe. When Tony Woodcock scored the third with a first-time finish there were only eight minutes left and, even though Holmes slammed in a brilliant half-volley to make the score 3–2, the Saints' challenge was done. 'We played well first half,' says Peach. 'Second half we struggled a little bit and lost our way. Defensively, they weren't great goals they scored, but on the balance of play they were a bit better than us.'

With the League Cup's tradition of honouring the losers first, Ball was quickly up the 39 steps to the Royal Box to collect his runners-up tankard, stumbling momentarily as he began his descent. Once dressed, he told Moore that 'we came in at half-time very pleased with the way we played' but admitted that Forest's second-half performance had merited victory. Then it was off to the team's post-match dinner, where a proud McMenemy declared that he would fine anyone who was found looking miserable. Jimmy Tarbuck took the stage to ensure that Saints kept laughing in the face of defeat.

The 1978–79 'Winter of Discontent' had been one of turmoil for the country and its rulers. The unions' refusal to accept an extension of pay restrictions had led to industrial disorder, symbolised by the mounting piles of rubbish in town centres when the dustmen became the latest group of workers to go on strike. In the week after Southampton's League Cup defeat at Wembley, James Callaghan would hear Conservative leader Margaret Thatcher call for a vote of no confidence in his Labour government. The vote would pass one week later and, before the football season was over, the country would have its first female prime minister.

The national sport was in no less a state of chaos, although it was the Arctic weather more than the frosty state of industrial relations that was the problem. Postponements had been arriving like snow drifts ever since temperatures plummeted over New Year and, only two days after Wembley, Ball found himself lining up at The Dell against Arsenal in the fifth round of the FA Cup. Southampton failed to hold on to their lead and they were in action again 48 hours later in a replay at Highbury, where two Alan Sunderland goals meant that Saints' season was effectively over.

'Bally sat looking like a man of fifty, his face grey and sunken,' McMenemy recorded in his diary, describing the scene in Highbury's visitors' changing room. 'I sat next to him and put my arm round him. If a photographer had been allowed in, his picture would show as never shown before the effect defeat can have on a man like Bally.'

Building on the foundations of their first season back in the First Division, Southampton, with Channon back at the club, found themselves in the top three in February 1980 and would finish the season in eighth place. A 2–0 win against Aston Villa on 15 March was significant in that it marked, for now, the end of Ball's career at the club.

Seeking to help him out financially, McMenemy had applied to the Football League for permission to stage a testimonial game, even though regulations stated that a player had to be with a single club for 10 years in order to qualify. Ball was 'angered by the injustice of it all' when the League turned down the request. McMenemy's response was to tell Ball he could become a free agent at the end of the season and determine his own future. He didn't have to wait that long.

Having found themselves playing in the third tier for the first time, Blackpool had identified their former World Cup winner as the man to guide them back up the divisions. In February, sensing that the time was right for all parties, they came up with a £25,000 deal to take him back to Bloomfield Road, although the arrangement was complicated by a pre-existing agreement that he would be transferred by Southampton to Vancouver Whitecaps for the forthcoming summer season in North America. 'It wasn't a difficult sell,' recalls Peter Lawson, then chairman of Blackpool. 'Alan had good memories of the club, he was a Farnworth boy, just down the road, and it was easy for him to go and see his mum.'

Channon, meanwhile, saw Ball's desire to enter management as a logical step for someone for whom 'football was his life'. He explains, 'He just wanted be involved in the game. He knew nothing else. He loved every aspect of it and he would talk football for hours. We could have a night out and come in at midnight and Bally would want to sit there until four o'clock talking football. That would drive me fucking mad. He was football nuts.'

The man being replaced at Blackpool, Stan Ternent, surprised Ball by generously spending several days reintroducing him to the club and offering a full briefing on what he could expect when he embarked on a three-year contract that would not officially start until the summer. 'The whole set-up was a joke,' was how Ternent would look back on Blackpool at that time. 'There were more rats than traps behind the scenes,' was another of his remarks. Ternent's assistance was a big-hearted gesture, considering that John Sadler was arguing in the *Sun* that 'the Blackpool board have betrayed Ternent by bringing in Alan Ball behind his back'.

Ball initially remained contracted to Southampton as a player, turning out for them until he travelled to Vancouver in the middle of March. However, that did not stop him making an immediate approach to MacDougall, his former teammate at The Dell, to leave Bournemouth and join him as player-coach and to run things for him until he was clear of other commitments. Blackpool were not altogether impressed with this development, not because they disapproved of MacDougall but because, according to Lawson, 'We know nothing about it.' The chairman told reporters, 'We find it hard to believe Alan would make this public before discussing it with the board. We're not telling him who to appoint, but we would have thought he would have told us.'

Blackpool were being reminded that Ball intended to do things his way. It had been no different when a red-haired teenager with a point to prove arrived on their doorstep in 1962. Ball was given a rapturous reception at the home victory over Colchester United on the first day of March, but the knowledge that he was heading off for his third summer in the North American Soccer League meant he felt pressure to do whatever he could without delay. By the time he boarded the plane for Canada, the playing staff had been reduced from 34 to 19. 'My office door was red hot,' he said. 'I felt a bit guilty making decisions about people's livelihoods, but I had to act quickly for the club's sake.'

In truth, Ball wished he didn't have to return across the Atlantic, but he had a contract to fulfil. Besides, he was going back as defending champion.

12

MAGICAL MYSTERY TOUR

'Make your mark in New York and you are a made man'

– Mark Twain

IT is Alan Ball's equivalent of The Beatles' *Magical Mystery Tour*, largely erased from memory and regularly under-appreciated amid the career achievements that occupy a more prominent place in popular recall. Outside of the Canadian city of Vancouver, few remember that, nine years after winning the League title with Everton, Ball became a national champion once more. And he did it by galvanising a band of journeymen British professionals into overcoming some of the biggest names in world football. He even managed, by force of personality, to avert an uprising along the way. The North American Soccer League (NASL) season of 1979 remains his forgotten masterpiece.

By 1978, when Ball first ventured across the Atlantic to spend summer in the United States, the NASL bandwagon was threatening to roll right across the continent. In the end, the league's expansion to 24 teams that year prefaced a slow decline as teams spent money they didn't have striving to keep up with the New York Cosmos, the flagship franchise of American 'soccer'. Yet there was still enough buoyancy left in the NASL over the next couple of seasons to allow Ball the opportunity to add an overlooked honour to his playing résumé.

The memorable and emotional climax to the 1977 season, with Pelé winning the title for the Cosmos in his final game before retirement, had provided the impetus for the NASL Commissioner, former Wales international Phil Woosnam, to achieve his expansion ambitions. 'That was as far as we wanted to go,' he explained. 'It was a great satisfaction to me to achieve that number.' The 1975 arrival in New York of Pelé, the one player whose name transcended his sport and was familiar to an American audience, had added credibility to a league that tiptoed apologetically into life in 1967, driven largely by the interest generated by Ball and his England colleagues the previous summer. As more teams had sprung up, British players led the stampede of Europeans taking the opportunity to supplement club salaries with a few well-paid weeks on loan to NASL teams. Having to endure plastic pitches, strange variations on the rules and vast travel distances was considered a fair exchange for a fat cheque and, in most cases, a pampered lifestyle provided by their temporary employers.

NASL attendance had increased to roughly 13,000 per game in 1977, with an average of more than 29,000 for the play-offs. Crowds of 70,000 would go to see the Cosmos in big games at the new Giants Stadium in East Rutherford, New Jersey, just across the water from Manhattan, and the team's stars became regulars on the celebrity circuit, rubbing shoulders with the nightclub set at Studio 54. When Brazil's triple World Cup winner signed off by leading his team to the Soccer Bowl title in 1977, the NASL appeared healthy enough to withstand his retirement. The Cosmos still boasted the two most recent victorious World Cup captains, Brazil's Carlos Alberto and West Germany's Franz Beckenbauer, and had even tempted a current England international, Manchester City's Dennis Tueart, into a permanent transfer. Tueart concluded his debut season by scoring two goals against the Tampa Bay Rowdies as the Cosmos won a second successive title.

The seven new teams who had embarked on the 1978 season included the yellow-shirted Philadelphia Fury, whose ownership group of rock stars Rick Wakeman, Peter Frampton and Paul Simon signed a flamboyant front man in former Chelsea centre-forward Peter Osgood. He scored one goal in 22 games but, according to teammate Colin Waldron, 'had a great time socially'.

That hardly suggests the kind of environment appreciated by an arch-competitor such as Johnny Giles or his old adversary, Ball, who signed up to be the former Leeds United man's colleague in Philadelphia and scored two goals on his debut. 'It was great playing on Johnny's team for once,' Ball commented. But there was little else to give thanks for and, by the end of June, former Newcastle United manager Richard Dinnis had been sacked as the Fury's head coach.

'Richard was a former schoolteacher who had never played the game at a high level,' explains Waldron, the former Burnley centre-back. 'To go anywhere and have Ball, Osgood and Giles on your books, you would have to have great character and balls to cope with that. I felt sorry for him because he was a nice man. Those were great players, but big personalities, and it was tough for anyone to handle them.'

Ball was considered man enough to tackle such a challenge. A few years earlier he'd written that 'if I was 32 years old and I was offered a top management job I'd be terrified'. But here he was, a year older than that, being given the opportunity to take what could by no means be described as a 'top job'. He found himself in charge of a team for the first time – if you didn't count Parndon FC, the under-15 side in Harlow that he'd helped to manage while at Arsenal. 'They asked Johnny and me if we wanted the job,' he told me when interviewed for *Playing for Uncle Sam*. 'Johnny didn't, but I said I would do it to help them out. I didn't think of it as the start of a coaching career at the time. I thought I had four or five years left as a player.'

While at Arsenal, Ball had written, 'I always make a point of encouraging younger players.' Yet many would observe that Ball could too frequently deliver harsh assessments; the kind that, coming from his father, had helped to mould him into a great player. He struggled to appreciate that not everyone was wired to respond in the same posi-tive manner. A trait that witnesses would come to cite as a weakness of Ball's management style was apparent to Waldron. 'Bally was a great pro, but he was a bit hard verbally on the younger players, espe-cially the Americans,' he recalls. 'I think he used to forget what a great player he was and expected the others to live up to his standards.'

Ball owed more to the generosity of the NASL's expanded play-off system than his own team's performance in reaching a knockout game against Detroit Express, but a goal by Trevor Francis, on loan from Birmingham City, ended Philadelphia's season and allowed Ball to get back to Southampton. After his unexpected Wembley return in 1978–79, Ball flew back to the USA, where he would become the lead char-acter in the storyline of the new NASL season.

Former Blackpool colleague Tony Waiters was entering his third season as head coach of the Vancouver Whitecaps. After a 1978 campaign in which Vancouver had fallen short in the play-offs, Waiters set about strengthening a team that was already built on largely English foundations, featuring players such as Wolves goalkeeper Phil Parkes, midfielders Jon Sammels and Steve Kember, defender John Craven and forwards Derek Possee and Kevin Hector. Having appointed Ball's former Arsenal colleague Bob McNab to replace ex-England winger Alan Hinton as his number two, Waiters added former Everton stopper Roger Kenyon, Chelsea midfielder Ray Lewington and Ipswich Town forward Trevor Whymark. On the flanks he brought in Willie Johnston, the Scotland winger who had been sent home from the 1978 World Cup in Argentina for failing a drugs test, and Carl Valentine, a young flyer from Oldham Athletic.

'We were just scraping wins,' says McNab of the early part of the new season. 'We played both our wide men out as wide as possible so that we had four up front. What we weren't doing was winning second balls from dead balls and goal kicks, because teams had twice as many men in midfield. I mentioned it to Tony, but he said, "I don't want any of that Arsenal defensive stuff."'

McNab persuaded Waiters that if they could not add quantity to the midfield they could at least upgrade its quality. 'We lacked a bit of craft and confidence in midfield. My wife, Barbara, and I took Alan Ball out for dinner before we played against Philadelphia in Vancouver. Bally was magnificent in the first half of our game and I said to Tony, "I have seen the man who is going to help us – Alan Ball." Tony didn't agree with me at first, but I asked him to take a look at the tape of the game. Bally was not even fully fit, but he was unbelievable in the first half until his lack of fitness showed. I knew Bally, warts and all, from England and Arsenal and I knew he could do it for us.'

Waiters confirms that 'we signed Bally on Bob's recommendation' and adds, 'I don't think they had got on that well at Arsenal and there was even talk they'd had a fight in training one day, but Bob insisted Bally was what we needed and would be the catalyst for Soccer Bowl.'

Ball was more than happy to leave Philadelphia, where Yugoslav Marko Valok had taken on coaching duties, although he insisted he 'didn't go looking for a move'. It ended up taking several weeks for the formalities to be arranged, but Ball's impact in 15 regular-season games for the Whitecaps, including eight goals and 10 assists, was emphatic. 'I think I was the icing on the cake for them,' he said. 'They wanted a bit of experience and someone to provide leadership.'

The NASL's rule that players could only be offside within 35 yards of goal stretched the midfield areas and played to Ball's strengths. 'He absolutely had a new lease of life,' said Whitecaps general manager John Best, another Englishman 'There was space for him to use his skills and he played in a small radius instead of trying to pick out players from 30 or 40 yards.'

Ball's personality was 'the missing piece of the puzzle', according to former Millwall man Possee, while Whymark adds, 'When Alan joined it made you realise how good a player you had to be to play with guys like that in their prime and made you realise how far off top notch you really were. He had lost his legs a bit, but not upstairs.'

McNab states, 'Bally was the difference, with his class and his ability to get more out of his teammates. He was, and still is, the best one-touch footballer I have ever seen.' And Waiters took little time to accept the wisdom of his assistant's recruitment strategy. 'At Portland, Bally had given away a goal that took us to overtime. We all got together. "My fault," he said. "I have given the game away, but I will win it for you." And he scored with a header. He had such a belief in himself.'

Vancouver went on to beat Dallas Tornado in two matches in the first round of the best-of-three playoffs, before losing to Johan Cruyff's Los Angeles Aztecs in the first game of the National Conference semi-final. Before the return match, Ball went to Cruyff and warned him, 'This is our game, not yours.' The Whitecaps duly won 1–0 and the players went straight into the 30-minute mini-game decider, a unique feature of the NASL play-offs. 'We were fitter and LA were dead by the end of the game,' McNab remembers. 'Cruyff could not walk.'

Hector's decisive goal brought the Whitecaps up against the reigning champions from New York, who now had Dutchman Johan Neeskens supplying Tueart and the prolific Italian centre-forward Giorgio Chinaglia. With two four-goal wins against the Cosmos during the regular season, however, Vancouver were in no mood to play the role of underdogs. 'The Cosmos used to hate playing against us because we didn't give them any respect,' says Possee. 'Some other teams would think, "Oh, my God. We can't beat the Cosmos." We said, "Screw it. We can sort them out." '

Any inferiority complex the Whitecaps players might have harboured centred purely on salaries. According to McNab, 'Our guys were on 36,000 Canadian dollars and the New York players were on about $360,000. The Cosmos spent more on programme sellers than we did on players.'

Whymark and Johnston scored in a 2–0 home victory in the first game of the Conference final series. McNab explains, 'We fought and pressurised them everywhere. Bally was being man marked, which teams had been doing to him without success since 1966, and he bossed the midfield.'

Three days later came the kind of dramatic occasion only possible under the quirks of the NASL play-off format; more than three hours of twists and turns in steamy New Jersey heat, at the end of which 34-year-old Alan Ball was standing as tall as at any time in his career. 'It was incredible,' he said. 'We kicked off at eight o'clock and didn't finish until half past eleven.'

With the Cosmos needing to win to maintain their hopes of a third consecutive NASL title, the teams battled to a 2–2 draw after extra-time. That set up a shoot-out, during which players had to take the ball from the 35-yard line and attempt a shot against the keeper before five seconds ran out. Vancouver could only score once and the Cosmos levelled the series. For the decisive mini-game Sammels, recovered from a hamstring injury, replaced Lewington, while Possee started in place of Hector. Having endured two hours already, the players had little left to offer and it was no surprise when a bad-tempered contest ended 0–0. After various misses, including one by Beckenbauer, Ball wasted the opportunity to win the shoot-out for the Whitecaps. But the Cosmos botched their next effort and Vancouver were into the Soccer Bowl, to be played at the same Giants Stadium a week later.

But instead of preparing to face the Tampa Bay Rowdies, the Whitecaps spent most of that time harbouring animosity towards their employers. In the end, it was only Ball's intervention that ensured that Soccer Bowl '79 went ahead.

'The players felt they should have got a bigger bonus,' says Waiters. 'The attitude in the club was, "That is your contract. You signed and that's what you get." The bonus was about $5,000 or less and they wanted it doubling. I recommended to the board they found a way of doing it. In the end we tried to build in a bonus the next season but it was messy.'

NASL rules specified that all bonus money for play-off success was paid by the league, an attempt to create a more level playing field for its teams. 'A number of the owners could have paid huge bonuses if they had wanted to,' Best recalled, 'whereas a club like ours could not compete. That's why the league decided the best way was for them to control the bonuses.'

Rumours reached the Whitecaps players, however, that the Rowdies had offered their men family holidays in Hawaii as a reward for reaching the final, but this was never confirmed. 'We knew a lot of the players from Tampa Bay,' Whymark explains, 'and money came into the conversation. We formed a little committee, led by Bally and John Craven, and they went to the management. But they were told the club would not break the rules and regulations.'

As Possee puts it, 'They screwed us, basically. They wouldn't even think about it, but said they would reward us on our next contract. Then they got rid of a load of us, so we never got anything.' Talk turned to a possible boycott of the Soccer Bowl, although Possee admits, 'It was all bravado really. We wanted to play.'

A team meeting in the Giants Stadium dressing room on the eve of the match did nothing to ease the disharmony and an undercurrent of dissatisfaction continued into the ensuing training session. 'We finished the practice with a small-sided game, which turned out to be extremely physical,' McNab says. 'I think most of the players were trying to kick me.'

More than 50,000 arrived at Giants Stadium the following day, far fewer than would have been present if the Cosmos had been playing, but an encouraging showing for the NASL nevertheless. As kick-off approached, talk among the Whitecaps players focused more on finances than how to stop Ball's former England teammate Rodney Marsh, who was hoping to emulate Pelé by signing off his career with a championship. Ball decided he'd had enough.

'The money side of it was a nuisance,' he explained. 'Being a senior member of the team I decided to speak to them, away from Tony and

Bob. I said, "This is a fantastic thing you have achieved. Don't let the monetary side of things get in the way." I think the fact that it came from me made a difference. It was different to one of the management team trying to get through to them.'

'Bally was absolutely superb,' says Whymark. 'He spoke about how the cup finals he had played in had gone so fast and that he was going to enjoy every single minute of this one. He instilled that feeling in everybody and kept everybody calm.' Waiters couldn't help but notice the difference in his players by the time Ball had finished with them. 'Bally helped save the day, even though he was one of the ones stirring it up,' he admits. 'He turned the whole thing around.'

Ball's desire for victory, a need perhaps to feel once more the thrill of his glorious trophy-chasing youth, had previously been witnessed by journalist James Lawton, who had moved from the *Daily Express* to write for the *Vancouver Sun*. 'His sentimentality sometimes veered off the graph,' says Lawton, recalling one of several evenings when Ball dined at his house. 'The time I remember most vividly was when he left the table in very high spirits to visit the toilet and returned streaming tears. On his journey he had wandered into my study and seen some pictures of the old days, Shankly, Mercer et al, and one in which he figured. He said how much he pined for those days, when he was young and it seemed that all the world was before him. His mood brightened, however, when his team-mate Steve Kember played his party trick, depositing his false teeth in Lesley's wine glass. Certainly, it seemed to me that the passion Alan had for football, perhaps a little subjective at times, could never be feigned.'

In Giants Stadium, the reinvigorated Whitecaps took the lead in the 13th minute through Whymark, only for Dutchman Jan van der Veen to equalise 10 minutes later. 'We were constantly attacking,' says Whymark. 'We played very well throughout the team and bossed it. In the second half, they ran out of steam.' With almost an hour played, Ball, in his blue and white shirt with number 23 on back and front, approached the Rowdies penalty area and slipped the ball diagonally to his left. 'Bally laid the ball off to me and said, "Hit it!"' Whymark recalls. 'I whacked it and it clipped someone's heels and flew inside the near post.'

When the Rowdies took off their talisman, Marsh, with more than 10 minutes remaining, the Whitecaps sensed they were not to be denied. 'We played terrific football all the way through,' said Ball. 'We were in control of it, very comfortable and very professional. We were a good English side who were very well drilled.'

The unhappy postscript to the Whitecaps' victory lap with the gaudy silver NASL trophy was that when Ball and his teammates returned to their hotel they found their suitcases packed and their rooms occupied by new guests. McNab explains, 'The league assumed the Cosmos would win the semi-final and would not need the rooms the night of the final. We had rewritten the script but no one changed the booking. What a mess.'

The Whitecaps' financial dispute rumbled on throughout the winter of 1979–80, with some players, such as keeper Parkes, disappearing in search of fatter contracts. Former Burnley and Leeds striker Ray Hankin was among the new arrivals, but admits, 'There was a lot of bad feeling in the team because the players felt they had been promised this and that. It was very difficult to settle. The team was not doing well and the players were always talking about the bonuses. I wondered what the hell I was doing there.'

Ball, however, was too distracted to notice. Another season in the NASL was probably the last thing he needed, given the complications of his situation with Southampton and Blackpool. 'My playing career was starting to come to an end,' he explained. 'Vancouver knew what my thoughts were and I said I would play another season, but I would like to go home early. In hindsight I shouldn't have gone back at all. I was starting a brand new career and my mind was in turmoil. But I felt obliged to the club, and the fans wanted to see me and the other players back, so I decided to go.'

McNab had suggested cancelling his contract. 'There is no way anyone can give his best for any team and manage a professional club 5,000 miles away at the same time. He was spending all his time managing them by phone. As good as he had been the previous year, he became a huge negative. I had witnessed both sides of Bally at Arsenal and knew what a disruptive influence he could be if the situation was not to his benefit.'

At the end of June, Ball's departure was confirmed. 'I had to let him go,' says Waiters, 'which was tough because I had known him since he was a teenager. He was a dynamic, aggressive and assertive leader, but not only was he unhappy with the financial situation at Vancouver, he had taken the Blackpool job. His heart wasn't in it any more. I can remember vividly when I let him go. He accepted it and said, "Tony, let's just remember all the good times we had." '

13
BACK TO THE START

'It was his home now. But it could not be his home till he had gone from it and returned to it. Now he was the Prodigal Son'

— G.K. Chesterton, *Homesick at Home*

I DECIDE that it's best to check that the Peter Lawson I have found working as a solicitor in Poulton-le-Fylde is the same man who had been chairman of Blackpool when Alan Ball returned to his first professional club. 'Yes, that's me,' I'm assured, 'although I have since been declared clinically sane again.'

Elected as chairman in November 1979, Lawson had taken only a few months in the role to identify the club's World Cup winner as the man to reinvigorate a side stagnating in the Third Division. 'It was the old problem: do you spend the money available on the team — that is, the manager and players — or on the ground? People will say that if the team is good enough they will sit on orange boxes. Blackpool needed to attract people. We needed to fill the stadium. Alan was a world figure and former captain of England and he fitted the bill.'

Forward Dave Hockaday, who had seen the club heading in the wrong direction since his debut in 1976, recalls, 'It was a massive coup. It needed something because we'd had a lot of managers in not many years. Alan injected life into the club.'

Blackpool in the summer of 1980 bore little resemblance to the town in which Ball had arrived 18 years earlier. There were far fewer 'No Vacancies' signs inside the windows of the seafront hotels and plenty of empty seats at Bloomfield Road to watch a team that had spent two years competing in the Third Division. Star players such as Scottish goalkeeper George Wood and forward Mickey Walsh had left. Bob Stokoe had ended his second spell as manager after the first of those seasons in the third flight and Stan Ternent had lasted only a matter of months before Ball was recruited.

Ball had spent most of the first few months after his appointment fretting from afar as Blackpool avoided relegation to the Fourth Division on the final day of the 1979–80 season. No wonder he was desperate to escape Vancouver and begin his first full season as a Football League manager.

By the time the campaign started, several older players from the previous regime had been moved on, men such as Bobby Kerr and Dick Malone, Stokoe's FA Cup-winning skipper and right-back respectively at Sunderland. Ball told the directors he would rather search for young talent and free transfers with the hunger to prove themselves. Running a club without much money, it was exactly what Lawson wanted to hear, although he stresses that Ball's own salary was not a major factor in that policy. 'I don't remember exactly what we paid him but it wasn't a case of, "Blimey, if we sign the manager we will have to sell four players." Alan wanted to bring people in from the grassroots.'

Aged 35, Ball intended to continue playing while running the team. But whether or not he donned the tangerine jersey in matches, there was no chance of him ever turning into Harry Catterick or Bertie Mee, managers who were rarely seen in a tracksuit. 'My work's done on the training pitch,' he told reporter Malcolm Folley, who had interviewed him at his desk, observing that 'he looks like a schoolboy sentenced to an afternoon's confinement in his dad's office'. Ball warned of an uncompromising approach that had served him well as a player, but would on occasions be his downfall as a manager. 'I'll still tread on toes because I am an honest lad. If I believe someone is wrong, I will tell them so. I can't hope for all of them to like me. That's impossible.'

Hockaday was among the immediate converts. 'He and Ted MacDougall joined in the training, which raised the standard immeasurably, and there was this bubbly infectiousness that pervaded the whole club,' he says. 'His passion for the game was unrivalled. He could be one of the lads, but if you wanted to see him as manager you could have a really good chat.'

Not all of Ball's players liked him all the time, but in the games that preceded the League kick-off – some useful victories in the preliminaries of the Anglo-Scottish Cup and a two-legged win over Walsall in the League Cup – the problem appeared to be that they had too much respect for him. 'It was difficult for them at first,' Ball would admit. 'They started channelling everything through me instead of playing their own game.'

Ball had barely had time to relish the prospect of a League Cup second-round draw against Everton before rumours emerged about a possible return to Goodison Park to take over from Gordon Lee as manager. Ball ended the gossip by stating, 'I've never ducked out of a contract in my life and I don't intend to start now. I have signed for Blackpool for three years and I will see it out.'

Ball played a leading role in a win at Swindon Town on the first day of the League campaign, but saw his team achieve only a single victory in the next eight matches. Skipper and centre-back Jack Ashurst laughs at the memory of a half-time rant by Ball during a 4–2 defeat at Sheffield United. 'We didn't play well in the first half and Bally had a go at one or two of the lads in the dressing room. He said to one, "You can take your shirt off because you are not going out for the second half." Ted pulled Alan to one side and said, "We've already used the substitute." Bally went back and threw the shirt at this lad and said, "Put that back on again!" He was like that at times. But he never held a grudge. And as soon as the game was over and he'd said his piece, he was like, "Now forget it. That's it. We start again on Monday."'

The Sheffield game was also notable because it was immediately afterwards that MacDougall told him he was quitting the club because of problems in his marriage. 'Ted was Bally's buffer between the players and himself,' says Hockaday. 'When Ted had to leave, he didn't have that. Bally had great knowledge and incredible passion, but he missed Ted and needed a confidant.'

Another old ally was soon on the scene when Ball signed former Scotland, Manchester United, Burnley and Bolton Wanderers winger Willie Morgan, with whom he had shared nights out, rounds of golf, days at the races and even games of crown green bowls, but never a dressing room. 'We were in America and he convinced me it was a great idea,' Morgan laughs. 'My other choices were Leeds and Man City, but he asked if I would join him. I said, "Blackpool? You must be joking. What division are they in?" But I did it because I loved him to bits and he was one of my best friends.'

Morgan had spent years hoping that Ball would somehow end up alongside him at Old Trafford, describing him as 'the best one-touch footballer who ever played'. As they became teammates at Bloomfield Road, a sequence of three wins out of four suggested his arrival had put Blackpool back on the right track. It even triggered newspaper chatter about the vacancy that existed at Manchester City after they had once again parted company with Malcolm Allison. 'I would have to consider such an offer if it was made,' Ball remarked, contradicting his previous response to the Everton rumours. 'At the moment it is only hypothetical.' And it became even more so when a solitary win in 19 games left Ball fighting to save his own job rather than contending for another.

Morgan had seen danger signs on his first day with his new colleagues, some of whom 'couldn't pass the ball five yards'. He adds, 'It was heartbreaking for Bally sometimes. That is why so many great players of that era didn't become managers. It is difficult to sit there and look at people who are not very good.'

Another training session shocked Ball's former Everton colleague John Hurst, a Blackpool resident. 'I went over to see them train,' he explains. 'Alan was having a right go at them during a practice match. He was on about this guy not doing this, not doing that. I said to him afterwards, "Bally, they are Third Division players. They are not like the players you played with. They have ability, but they just don't see things as quick or react as quick." He couldn't grasp that. He thought everybody should be as good as he was.'

Lawson makes a similar comment. 'After Alan had been here for a while, the feedback I got from a number of spectators was, "He is too good for Blackpool." He wanted them to play one-touch football, international style, and the players we had couldn't do that.'

Hockaday adds, 'Alan had a great radar and the touch of an angel. For him, it was easy, but for the lads in the lower leagues it wasn't. It took him a while to redefine his expectations.'

One of the young players in Ball's charge was forward Wayne Harrison, who later forged a career as a youth coach in America. 'We understood Alan's frustration,' he says. 'We had good players who were good dribblers, but he had ambitions to play more like Barcelona now, which sounds crazy when talking about the Third Division. He wanted to create a team in his own style.

'I had loved him as long as I can remember. He was my inspiration. I never achieved what I wanted to as a player, but as a coach my training is based around all that he taught me. I call it the half-a-touch mentality and I teach it because of Alan Ball. In training he would say, "You only need half a touch." I liken him to Xavi in the Barcelona midfield. He would be smoking cigars in the middle until he was 40 in today's game because he could see things so quickly. I wanted to learn, but I found it difficult to change my style. He was trying to put in too much information too quickly. In purely teaching and showing you how to play he was a genius.'

The last comment is endorsed by Ashurst, already in his late 20s when Ball arrived. 'He used to say he didn't like centre-halves who just kicked the ball anywhere. He liked to see them being skilful and coming out with the ball. When I went to Carlisle and teamed up again with Bryan Robson, who I'd been with at Sunderland, he said, "You are a different player." Alan Ball made me a far better player, more skilful. I learned a lot from him.'

When Ball dropped Ashurst in December, he revealed that it had been because of a dispute over tactics. Yet even in declaring that Ashurst was being punished for stating his unhappiness with his sweeper system, Ball gave evidence of a conflicted mind when he admitted, 'It may be we will have to have a rethink.'

Ashurst explains, 'It was the only time we fell out. He wanted to play three centre-backs and, as captain, I said, "I don't think this will work." I said my piece and he said his and he said he was leaving me out. We played two games and lost them both and he called me in and was big enough to say, "You were dead right. I was wrong." He also thanked me because he'd heard through the grapevine I had said no to going on Granada TV to have a go at him. I'd told them, "No chance. I like the man too much for that."'

Even without television agitating to stir things up, the writing was already appearing on the walls of Bloomfield Road. Lawson had lost his seat on the board and Ball was left exposed to what he felt was the interference of 'a succession of know-alls'. Lawson explains, 'We had two factions. Lionel Moore was my backer, as it were, and was keen to stay in the background and let me get on with it. Then there was Cliff Sagar, who was from Taskers, the home stores, and he'd had runners going round town collecting proxy votes. When it came to the November AGM he said, "I have enough votes. I suggest you tell the AGM you are not very well and you want to retire." At the meeting, I told them I was extremely fit and that I was going to be voted off and would Mr Sagar come forward and accept my resignation. All hell broke loose after that.'

Ball's pride and lack of patience with the new men in charge were not qualities designed to survive the power politics of a football club. His father had warned him that this was a game he would have to learn to play, but he was not ready to abide by such rules. He never would be. 'I lost the boardroom,' he admitted. 'I was becoming increasingly lonely and isolated.'

Even the fans were turning against him. Not only were they enduring unsatisfactory results, but Ball had angered them in November when, after beating neighbouring non-Leaguers Fleetwood Town 4–0 in the FA Cup, he questioned whether the supporters were as ambitious and committed as he was.

A first League win in 14 games came along on 21 February when Ashurst got the only goal against Walsall, but a 2–0 defeat at Brentford a week later signalled the end of Ball's first attempt at management in England. The board members wanted him out, although they agreed that he could resign rather than being fired. His comments made clear the reality of the situation. 'It has been obvious for a while that the board didn't fancy me,' he said. 'I'm disappointed I was not allowed to do the job for which I was appointed; to rebuild the whole club.' Ball realised that taking the job 'had been a mistake' but pointed out to his employers that he had left them with some good young players. Those players would win only twice more after Ball's departure, being relegated to the Fourth Division in 23rd place.

Ball came to acknowledge that, instead of diving headlong into a player-manager's role at a struggling club, a more advisable route into management would have been via a coaching position. His old World Cup colleague Jack Charlton had tried to talk him into joining him at Sheffield Wednesday. At the very least, he should have sought to keep

Ternent, or another experienced coach. Instead, he had appointed
another rookie in MacDougall as his number two and then lost him
after a few weeks anyway. 'I was a little bit big-headed, a little head-
strong,' he admitted.

Remarkably, as Blackpool were playing at Gillingham in front of
3,434 people on the Saturday after Ball's departure, their former
manager was back in the First Division, taking on Manchester United
and helping Southampton to sixth place as England captain Kevin
Keegan scored the only goal.

'I was at the club late one day and I got a call from Bally,' Lawrie
McMenemy explains. 'He said, "I am going into a board meeting and
I think they are going to finish me." He wanted my advice, so I put
him right on the contract stuff.' Then Ball's former boss told him, 'If
it happens, get in the car and come down here. And bring your boots.'

Ball had been playing regularly and felt he was more than holding
his own physically. Within 24 hours he had joined up with his former
teammates and signed a contract. 'The players said it was like he had
never been away,' McMenemy adds. 'That was lovely. I enjoyed that.'

For Keegan, signed the previous summer from Hamburg, the next
year or so was to be eye-opening. Having played with Ball for England
and been on the receiving end of his knack of winning games at
Anfield, he was already an admirer. But now, with the Ball family
living with him while they settled back into the Southampton area, he
came to appreciate, on a daily basis, exactly how good he was.

'Alan Ball was the greatest player I have ever played with,' Keegan
states emphatically. 'I played with some great players and against some
great players, but the best I ever played with was Alan. And this was
when he was 36 years of age. It was his vision, his understanding of the
game. He was almost telepathic. He just knew what you were thinking.
He was a step ahead, different to anything else. He didn't really have
any pace, but he didn't need it because he was so clever at using the
ball, working angles and using his body. The greatest thing was his
football brain. He could see things that other players just wouldn't see.

'I didn't really know how good he was until I played with him at
club level. With England, you played a game and trained a bit, but

when you trained with him every day you thought, "Wow, heavens knows what he was like when he was 20." If I had played with him when I was younger I would have scored a lot more goals.

'He was one of those players who wouldn't go away. He might have had poor games, but he was always involved, he would never hide. He was trying to run the show all the time. We used to spend a lot of time together and I remember him telling me, "When I was young, I could run up and down the pitch. Now I run across it because it is shorter." When you watched him play that is what he did. He just moved across into little holes. His favourite saying was "feed the bear", meaning give him the ball. You could always give it to him in any situation and he would get you a free-kick or find somebody.

'If any young player wants to see what football is all about, watch Alan. He would say, "Why have two touches when you can do it with one?" It is very easy to say that to young players, but you have to have the brain. Alan knew what he was going to do with the ball before it came to him because he was so intelligent on the field. You were surprised if he gave it away.'

After victories in Ball's first four games back, Southampton were up to third place. They were able to win only two of their final six games, but a final position of sixth was enough to ensure that Ball could look forward to playing European club football for the first time since Everton's European Cup exit 11 seasons earlier.

A second-round defeat at the hands of Portugal's Sporting Lisbon, coached by Malcolm Allison, brought a quick end to Southampton's UEFA Cup run, but the League season looked like building on the promise of the previous campaign. With Chris Nicholl anchoring the back four, Mick Channon and Keegan teaming up in attack, and David Armstrong – a £680,000 signing from Middlesbrough – joining Ball and Steve Williams in midfield, Southampton went on a run from the end of October that saw them climb from midway in the table to hit top spot on the last Saturday in January with victory at Middlesbrough.

Young striker Steve Moran was also getting an opportunity to make his mark. 'Bally took me under his wing,' he recalls. 'If he thought you had a chance and liked you he was totally for you. Steve Williams was another one he nurtured. Bally used to say to Lawrie, "You have got to play the youngster; he is the legs of the team.'

Moran couldn't believe he was playing alongside 'men who had been posters on my wall' and adds, 'Bally was the best. His motto was "simplicity is genius" and he used to say the hardest pass to play is the five-yard pass because everybody wants to do something with the ball. He said that the more five-yard passes you play, the more confidence you get to play the killer ball. I was spoilt and in my latter career I probably suffered from playing with such talented players at Southampton. I just made a run and the ball would appear.'

'It was fantastic,' Armstrong concurs. 'The whole place was buzzing. We played fantastic football and had world-class players mixed with great youngsters. The Dell was a fortress and we were more or less a goal up before we went out. We expressed ourselves, scored a lot of goals and entertained. It was an electric atmosphere. Bally was the perfect example on and off the field, with his experience and one-touch play. He would help and guide players around him; defenders, attackers, he would talk to everyone. He was the marshal of the side. He enjoyed himself off the field; he liked his racing and a big sing-song and a drink. But he was a fine example to everyone about how to conduct yourself. He and Keegan were always up at the front in the long-distance running in training.

'Ball, Keegan and Channon were great friends. They enjoyed themselves and loved each other's company. They were eager and hungry to get on the training field and prepare themselves for every single game and they certainly made sure they put in a shift. Lawrie knew they liked their time off and the way they prepared was different from a lot of people, but he was the perfect man for those three. He knew that what they did wouldn't detract from what they did on the field.'

Moran adds, 'Bally loved a drink but there would be no harder worker in training the next day. If there was a cross-country run you would get pissed on the whisky fumes running behind him, but he would be up the front.' He also recalls the enjoyment Ball took from his friendly rivalry with Keegan, which manifested itself in verbal jousts, contests on the golf course, games of Scrabble and five-a-side games in the gymnasium. He comments, 'The toing and froing with Keegan was brilliant and Bally often came out on top. After five-a-sides, the winning team got to vote on the worst player on the losing team. Bally was brilliant with his one-touch stuff, but Keegan was useless – he would want too many touches. Bally would make sure Kevin got voted for because he would get really wound up at having to turn up the next day wearing a yellow bib or something. It used to do his head in and Lawrie eventually had to make sure he was on the strongest side so that his head was right.'

Reeling off his memories of Ball, Moran also recalls a close-up view of his 'professionalism' as he sat on the bench at Anfield. 'Bally had told me, "I owe Graeme Souness." He must have caught Bally with a nasty tackle in a previous game. He said, "If I don't get the opportunity in this game I will wait until the next one." After about 20 minutes, there was a bouncing ball right in front of the dug-out and Souness was going in for it. Bally could look after himself and he just left his foot in. It didn't hurt him, but was enough for Souness to look at him with respect as if to say, "OK, we are even."'

After spending the whole of February in first place, Southampton began March by beating Birmingham City 3–1 to go four points clear of Swansea City in Ball's 700th League game. 'The reason that this orange is not squeezed dry is that even at my age it is not hard work to pass the ball,' he said with his 37th birthday looming. 'I can carry on as long as there are people around me responding to my passing because the game is about movement and by playing my way you can create more attacking situations.'

Knocked off the top after a bad run of results, a televised 4–3 victory over Stoke City put Southampton back in first place for a week, but their momentum had gone and, despite Keegan's 26 League goals, they could only manage seventh place behind champions Liverpool after three wins in their final 14 games. It was against Liverpool in a 3–2 defeat at The Dell, however, that Southampton produced a wonderful goal that perfectly characterised the way they, and Ball, wanted to play. In a 15-man move, they enchanted the best team in the country by working the ball from the edge of their own box, down the left and into the Liverpool penalty area with crisp, controlled passing – eight instances of one-touch and only one of more than two touches – before Channon controlled and lashed the ball into the net.

'We had been on a real high,' Armstrong recalls. 'We felt we were a match for anyone we played. We always scored goals and created

chances but defensively we were a bit gung-ho at times, didn't quite
have the maturity to become champions.'

In the summer of 1982, while British troops were returning in triumph
from conflict in the Falklands and England's footballers were heading
off to the World Cup finals for the first time in 12 years, Ball flew
across the globe to Australia. In a brief spell with Perth-based Floreat
Athena, he scored two goals in three games and pocketed a nice-sized
cheque. He even ended up guesting for Bournemouth when they took
on the Western Australia state team.

Back in England, with Keegan having been transferred to Newcastle
United, the new season brought no rediscovery of the Saints' best
form of the previous year. Their first seven games included only one
win and featured a 6–0 thrashing at Tottenham. It was a game that
convinced Ball that his top-level playing days were coming to an end.
'Steve Perryman nutmegged Bally,' says McMenemy. 'The next morning there was a tap on my door. I kept saying "come in" and eventually I got up and went to the door and there was a pair of boots lying
there. It was Bally's way of saying "that is it". I think the Perryman
thing had made him realise. Nobody would have done that at one
time. He knew. He was an honest fella.'

Afraid that he would 'peter out' over the course of the season, Ball
asked McMenemy to release him from his contract. He played a few
more games and bowed out, poignantly, with a 3–2 win against Everton
at the end of October. Yet there was still some mileage in those boots
and McMenemy helped him to arrange a deal to play some games in
Hong Kong for Eastern Athletic, coached by Bobby Moore.

While Ball enjoyed the money, he was shocked by what he perceived
as poor facilities and the way in which the local players seemed to be
treated by the club's owners.

Moore was aware enough to coach with a light touch, as former
player Tsui Kwok-on recalled. 'I found Moore to be very serious in
training and he would work on a lot of players' techniques. If a player
didn't understand, he would go out on the field and show how something was done, He was a nice person and he was always there to
help.'

Yet, away from the field, Ball was witnessing the turmoil that Moore was going through as his marriage to Tina began to break up after he had fallen in love with his future second wife, Stephanie. He and Lesley were heartbroken after being present during one particularly vicious row between their great friends at a restaurant. 'I remember that blow-up,' recalls Ball's daughter, Mandy. 'We got to the restaurant and there was a massive argument outside. There was another time on the boat we had hired. I remember being on deck with Tina and Mum, while Dad was down below with Bobby and it was all happening.'

The chance to work with Moore had been a key factor in Ball going to Hong Kong – along with the money, of course – but a few weeks after he returned to England, it was someone he would never have described as an ally who was on the phone.

Bobby Gould, a much-travelled centre-forward whose clubs had included Coventry City, Arsenal, Wolves and West Ham United, had never been the first person Ball would seek out for a post-game handshake. So when the telephone rang, Ball was surprised to hear the voice of the man now managing Third Division Bristol Rovers.

'What are you doing?' Gould asked.

'A jigsaw with my son,' was the reply. 'Now leave me in peace, I've never liked you.'

'I hate you as well, so we're starting off even. Now how about getting your backside up here to listen to what I have got to say?'

What Gould told him was that he thought Ball's presence could help his young team in their bid to gain promotion. Ball liked what he heard enough to find himself back in training gear and explaining to television reporters his decision to return to League football. He was honest enough to admit, 'You have to feed the kids and there was no money coming in.' He also stressed that Rovers had agreed that he would be released if offered a managerial role.

According to Gould, he and Ball proceeded to 'have the time of our lives together'. But despite his happy relationship with his old enemy and the fact that he had to train only two days per week, Ball was finally finding the physical element of football a hardship. 'I need the money,' he repeated when asked to explain his motivation following a 2–1 win against Orient. 'My family is used to the best and I shall go on trying to deliver it for as long as possible. Football has always been a passion with me. I still enjoy going out there, but I have to confess it's beginning to feel as though I am just going out to work.'

Yet Ball's brain and touch remained as sharp as ever. 'We went to play in Wigan in front of two men and a dog, with the wind and rain lashing down,' Gould recalled. 'But Bally produced the finest exhibition of one-touch football I have ever seen.'

Even beyond a 21-year professional playing career that spanned more than 1,000 senior games and concluded with Rovers finishing seventh following a home draw against Cardiff City in his final game, Ball would continue to inspire admiration with his skill on the field. Journalist Pat Symes remembers seeing him turn out for the reserves while manager at Portsmouth later in the decade and noting that 'his one touch was absolutely fantastic', while McMenemy describes him taking off his tracksuit to join in a testimonial at Southampton in the mid-1990s and 'running the game' for the brief period in which he was on the field.

They represented a few additional notes to add to a scrapbook of memories and achievements that few English professional footballers could ever match. His own summary of his playing career was, 'I would like to be remembered as a friend on the football field to people who, if I played, I would help get their bonus. In terms of performances, I think I helped every single club I played for.'

And he added, 'There is no better feeling than when you are running a football match. You are conducting the orchestra, you are on the top of your form. That, to me, is the most wonderful feeling that any top sportsman can have.'

He'd known that feeling often enough. Now he would have to try to experience it vicariously through others. He was following his father into full-time coaching and management. His dad, however, was no longer there to share it with him.

14

BLOOD LINES

'The most important thing in your life is your roots, your family'

– Alan Ball

S OUTHAMPTON had beaten Leicester City in the third round of the 1981–82 FA Cup and Alan Ball set off the next day with Mick Channon and his brother, Phil, for some clay pigeon shooting in the Hampshire countryside. It was a frosty morning and Ball did little other than release the clays from the trap, but good company and a bottle of brandy made it enjoyable and there was the enticing prospect of a pint in the Malthouse. The ale and the laughter was everything Ball had anticipated. This was the life. 'He loved his Sundays,' daughter Mandy Byrne confirms. 'Even later on, when he was a manager and he had a lot weighing on his shoulders, it was his day to relax.'

The previous day, Alan Ball senior had boarded a flight for Cyprus. Aged 57, he retained his drive and passion for football, even though it had been four years since his last stint as a manager of an English club, Halifax Town. After years of managing non-League teams, it had been Halifax who had eventually given him a chance in the Football League, appointing him as manager in 1967 and being rewarded by the first promotion in their history when they went up from the Fourth Division two years later. Ball took Preston North End to the Third Division title in 1970–71, being named as that division's manager of the year, and it was one of his son's saddest moments when he had to collect him after his dad had been fired by the club in 1973. A succession of jobs, including a brief return to Halifax and several positions in Scandinavia, had followed. Ball senior's latest journey was supposed to end in a coaching position with the Cypriot club Evagoras. Instead it led to tragedy.

Lawrie McMenemy received the first call from the Foreign Office. The story they were piecing together was that Ball senior had been collected at Larnaca airport by a club official, but before they could reach their destination the car had gone off a bridge after overtaking another vehicle. It had not been a deep drop down a bank and the car had landed on four wheels, but the impact had been fatal for the passenger. Having suffered a couple of attacks during the previous two years, his heart was not strong enough to survive the trauma.

McMenemy phoned the Balls' home in Chandler's Ford. Hearing from Lesley that Alan was in the pub, McMenemy volunteered for the terrible task of breaking the news. Arriving at the Malthouse, he was greeted by Ball with, 'Come and have a drink, boss.' Instead, McMenemy asked Ball to go outside and they sat together on a bench. 'I have some bad news,' he told him. 'Your dad's died in a car crash.'

McMenemy recalls, 'He just dropped his head and I put my arm round him. We just sat there. It was one of the saddest things I have ever experienced.'

'Get me home, Lawrie,' was all Ball managed to mumble, images of his father's impact on his life playing through his mind like a movie montage. Once home, his only thought was to drive north to see his mother, a desperate journey during which every radio news bulletin told the story of his father. Ball's sister, Carol, was already at the family house in Farnworth when her brother's car pulled up. 'He was just devastated,' she remembers. 'He got out of the car and before he saw anybody he knelt down on the lawn and just howled. I had to say, "Alan, Alan! You have got to get up and come in." He was beside himself.'

Ball's immediate response to the situation was to become rude and irritable with all those who had already arrived to offer comfort. 'I wanted them out of the way,' he admitted. He eventually found his mum in her bedroom, locked in her grief. As much as Ball would miss the man who had made and mentored him, he had grown and become his own man. He would mourn, but move on. His mother, who had built her life around the movements and moods of a football man, had lost the centrepiece of her existence. The initial vagueness of the circumstances of the death merely added to her feeling of panic and helplessness.

The funeral was almost three weeks later and Ball was due to face Everton the next day, another example of how the club that was closest to his heart continually recurred at key moments in his career. McMenemy, who had first met Ball senior on FA coaching courses, told him not to think about playing, but Ball put him straight. 'If I didn't play, he would go berserk up there.'

Thereafter, it was McMenemy who became the father figure in Alan's life. 'I would like to think I was very close to him in that way,' he says, although stressing that he would stop short of offering too much managerial advice. 'I don't think any of us would say what you should or shouldn't do. I would maybe give him a tip or two or tell him if I had seen a player. I would ask how he was getting on and he might tell me if he had a problem. We had a very, very close relationship, which I was delighted about. He would often come to me about things other than football.'

While Ball had his sport to return to in the aftermath of tragedy, his mother struggled without a purpose. 'She went into herself,' says Carol. 'She started doing strange things that just weren't my mum. The doctors said she'd had a nervous breakdown. She never really spoke about it after that. She had to go into a home in Prestwich because she needed care. When she was on medication she would come out and would be fine. She used to say things like, "I can see Alan down there." When she got on medication, Alan had her for six months and I would have her for six months and she was fine. But she didn't talk about my dad a lot, and she never cried either.'

It was eight years after her husband's fatal accident that Ball's mother died, having been taken to hospital after a fall. Fate or intuition spurred Ball to drive through the night to the hospital in Barrow-in-Furness. 'It was quite bizarre,' son Jimmy recalls. 'I was asleep and he walked in fully dressed and said, "I am going to see my mum." We drove up through the Lake District, stopped and had a bacon butty on the way, and walked into her room as she looked up at us and died. It was spooky.'

Jimmy relates the story over a coffee, which he drinks wearing his Stoke City training gear. The third generation of the Ball family to take a coaching role at the club, he works with young players between the ages of 13 and 16, having accepted early in his career that coaching offered him a more sustainable pathway through football than playing. 'My dad was different with me than his dad had been with him,' he explains. 'He never coached me. He always said, "Be your own man, don't be Alan Ball's son." Maybe he didn't see the talent; rightly so, because I wasn't good enough. We had everything at our house – cricket bats, tennis rackets and whatever – but he would say, "You choose and I will be with you, but I am not going to force you."'

Family life was relatively stable during the five years Ball would spend at Portsmouth to launch his post-playing career, but Jimmy admits, 'I was a bit of tearaway. Dad would give me a telling off, but then there was that twinkle in his eye. I wasn't naughty, I just pushed the boundaries. Every time I pushed it too far I got the punishment of being sent home from school, but then the reward was being able to go to the football club with him. I was born into the industry. I used to like the characters. I would pick up on the wind-ups when they were messing with someone and I would keep the secret, so I was one of the lads.'

Even though Jimmy would play reserve games at Exeter City and Southampton when Ball was there as manager, neither he nor his father were under any illusions about his potential. 'He was always honest with me,' Jimmy explains. 'He said, "You are not going to be top level, but you might get a career out of it." I wasn't the best technically and I couldn't dribble past people. He knew I would have a scrap with someone, wouldn't let anyone boss the game, but no one was tougher on me than him. I realised I was better suited to coaching because the only time he praised me was when he saw me working with some youngsters and said, "That was really good."

'My dad and I were similar people and we got on really, really well. We never fell out, never had any of those father–son issues. As we grew older, we became mates. We used to go racing together, bet on a few horses and play golf together. We had a little box where we used to put a bit of money away ready for Royal Ascot, without telling my mum.'

At this point, Jimmy's smile gives way to an earnest expression that accompanies the declaration that 'I want to clarify something'. He continues, 'Dad wasn't a gambler. There is a perception out there that is so far from the truth. He loved a bet on the horses, but never ridiculous amounts. We are talking 20 or 30 quid at a time. He never got himself into trouble and always gambled within his means. The perception that he had gambling debts is untrue. I took care of his affairs when he died and there was nothing of that at all. It is something that irks us, an intimation that we went without because he gambled. That is rubbish.'

As we sit among the souvenirs of their father's career, barely a couple of football pitches' distance from the house where they spent most of their childhood years, Ball's daughters tell a similar story. 'We had a privileged upbringing,' says Keely Allan, in whose lounge is stored the large wooden chest that contains the memorabilia of Ball's life and death. 'Mum and Dad made us very normal and didn't send us to private schools like all the footballers do now, but we had a fantastic lifestyle and parents who were always together.'

It is impossible for Ball's children to discuss their father without acknowledging the influence of their mother, Lesley, both in organising day-to-day life and ensuring that football became something that bound the family together rather than tearing them apart. According to Jimmy, 'She enjoyed football and going to games, but I guess she had no choice. If you want to see your husband, as the wife of a footballer or manager, you go to games with him.'

Keely explains, 'She had the attitude that if you can't beat them, join them. She learned very early on that this was going to be her life. She could have decided she didn't want anything to do with football and gone shopping instead, but she went out of her way to learn the game, so it became a shared thing. She was so heavily into it that Dad would send her to Grimsby on a Tuesday night to watch a 17-year-old play. He would trust her. On a Friday night, we would all sit around the table and the discussion would be the team he was going to pick. We were part of it and that is why we didn't hate it. It wasn't all singing and dancing, though, and I remember times, like Christmas Eve, when Mum was upset because football had taken over and she hadn't been able to do stuff.'

Mandy adds, 'Christmas was always a funny time. There were games on Boxing Day so on Christmas Day they had to train until lunchtime. We had been up early, but weren't allowed to open our presents until he got back from training.'

But, far from retaining memories of a disrupted upbringing, Jimmy insists, 'We had a wonderful childhood. We travelled a lot. We all went everywhere and had those family adventures; very fond memories for all of us. I was in kindergarten in America when he was there and we all went to Hong Kong with Bobby and Tina Moore. Graham Paddon was there, too, and all the families hired a boat. We were out on the South China Sea on Christmas Day and we had the turkey rowed over to us on these little river taxis. Those times when he was with us and could shut off from football were so memorable and far outweighed the times when we never saw him.'

Through it all was the dominant force of Lesley. 'I don't think he would have done any of it without her,' Keely suggests, while Mandy states, 'She took over from his dad and he never had to grow up. He had his dad saying, "You are doing this and that," and then Mum took over and said, "Right, Alan, you have got to do this." He allowed Mum to do everything. If the phone rang and it was right here he would go, "Lesley!" But she was so proud of him. She'd been with him when he was nobody and she never jumped on a bandwagon.'

'They met so young,' Keely goes on. 'They were their only ever boyfriend and girlfriend; childhood sweethearts. They became so famous, living this amazing life, and Mum kept him real and had that mentality where she could rein him in. She could tell him he was out of order when he was wrong. She was the only one who did that and he respected and loved her for that. She was the only person he truly trusted. Mum was strong enough to back him and support him. She wanted him to do what he was good at. They were a great partnership and had a very equal relationship. She didn't always get her own way, but she definitely wore the trousers.'

Early in 1989, a few days after Ball had been sacked as Portsmouth manager, he and Lesley were asked about the key to their happy marriage by presenter Fred Dinenage on Southern TV's *Coast to Coast* programme. 'To be quite honest, Lesley has taken the brunt of it,' Ball responded. 'I have always been doing something that I love, which is playing football, travelling the world and managing, and if any credit has got to be given it is to Lesley for keeping us all together. She has brought up three lovely children.'

Asked if she had been forced to make sacrifices and would rather her husband had a nine-to-five job, Lesley replied, 'Not at all. When we met I was convinced it was going to be good and he was going to do what he said he was going to. It never entered my head that he wouldn't. The benefits of it have been great. We have lived all over the world, the kids have been to school in America and Canada . . . we have had some fabulous times. I want him to do what he wants to and what he is good at.'

Lesley had previously given an intriguing interview to the *Daily Mirror* in February 1978 in which she spoke about the fears of a football wife left at home while her husband went on the road. 'I know it happens, but Alan is kind enough not to tell me,' she said, referring to the antics of healthy, attractive young men away from the shackles of home. Her comfort in discussing such matters is indicative, however, of her trust in her own husband, about whom there are no kiss-and-tell stories in the archives. 'Footballers' wives know their husbands get offers from other women,' she continued. 'But I love having such a famous husband. I wouldn't swap it for anything.'

Lesley did admit in the article that she had been angry when Ball went to the Bahamas on a boys' holiday with his Arsenal teammates and had an airport row with him in Manchester after he turned up roaring drunk after a game in Berlin. Despite a few girls' nights out in retaliation she decided that the best way to deal with the doubts was to learn to have trust in her husband. 'As soon as you accept that not everybody is trying to get everybody else into bed, it makes life a lot easier. I've adjusted to fit in with football life.'

Admitting that her father 'wasn't an angel', Keely adds, 'I doubt that there were any other women. I think if Dad had had affairs we would have known by now; they would have come out later in life.'

If Ball had a mistress it was football. 'The family came about tenth in my order of priorities,' he wrote ruefully of his time as manager of Portsmouth. 'Football had become the all-consuming number one and I know now that this was wrong. I also knew at the time that success was all the family wanted from me.'

As Lesley's *Mirror* interviews suggests, when she fell out with her husband it was not over women; it was because, according to Keely, 'when he got his party head on you couldn't stop him'. She continues, 'They argued about drink more than anything, like if he had gone to the pub and said he would be an hour and come back five hours later pissed out of his head. Or he had brought a load of cronies back for dinner and she would have to feed everybody.'

Mandy tells of a party that went on so long that Lesley 'got out the hoover and hoovered around everyone' and an occasion when Ball had brought friends home to play records while Lesley was already in bed. 'It went on forever so she went down in her nightie and a pair of high heels, took the record off and jumped on it and shouted, "Will you all go home now!" Another time we were in Hong Kong and they went out for a New Year's meal. She came back to see if we were OK, and then she couldn't be bothered to go back. He didn't come home until late, so next morning she took us shopping and said, "Right, you can have whatever you want. Your Dad has been out, so let's go."'

But the fun outlasted the fall-outs and Ball instigated his own way of getting the family on an even keel. 'On Sundays we used to have this thing called a mad minute,' Mandy explains. 'After everybody had gone home you had to get all the frustration of the week out of your system before you started the next week. While everyone sat and watched, you could do whatever you wanted for one minute; scream, jump up and down, whatever.' Somewhat incongruously, Ball's preferred procedure was to hitch up his tracksuit trousers and pretend to be a ballet dancer, but Mandy continues, 'I can remember once I was with my boyfriend and Dad came in and said, "I fancy a mad minute," and he just stood there and laughed at my boyfriend for the whole minute.'

Keely is prompted to add, 'He was quite intimidating for boyfriends. I had one who was in the army and he stayed with us once in Exeter – downstairs obviously. Dad had had a few drinks and my boyfriend woke up with Dad at his throat, as though he had a knife, saying, "Call yourself a soldier? I could have killed you while you slept."'

As the reminiscences come thick and fast, Mandy recalls, 'If he'd had a good day at the races he come in and say, "Right, what would you do for a nifty fifty?" His toe nails were disgusting because he had lost them all playing football and they were green. He would say, "Would you kiss my big toe for a tenner?" I would never do it, but Keely would.'

Many of those interviewed for this book have remarked upon Ball's love for Lesley and his children, with Lawrie McMenemy speaking for many when he calls him 'a very, very good family man'. An example of Ball's understanding of the importance of blood ties comes from Paul Hardyman, who was part of the Portsmouth squad Ball would lead to promotion. 'To get to go on that open-top bus was something I could only have dreamed of,' he says. 'It was a day I'll never forget. I remember seeing my mum and dad in the crowd and Bally said, "Who are you waving at?" When I told him he said, "Get them in here." He managed to get them into the celebrations in the Guildhall.'

As Ball prepared to embark on his career in management, his family would be exposed to the rivalries, jealousies, passions and insecurities of the sport that he had ensured was their life. Having been a national treasure on the field, he would find that, in the dugout, being sacked was a reality of life, along with insults in his children's playgrounds and stones through the window. There would be times when Ball needed all of that family support to get him through it.

15

THE GREMLINS

'For anyone from Southampton or Portsmouth to be revered at the other club as much as Alan Ball sums him up. They had total respect and love for him'

– Lawrie McMenemy

I N the geography of English football, Lawrie McMenemy had grown up as far as it was possible to be from the club rivalries of the south coast. Hailing from the north-east and learning his managerial trade at Bishop Auckland, Doncaster Rovers and Grimsby Town, nothing had prepared him for the intensity of the ill-feeling between Southampton and the city that sits 20-odd miles down the eastbound M27: Portsmouth.

'When I first came down here I didn't realise the rivalry,' says the former Southampton manager in his Hampshire home. 'We only played occasionally and when we did it was fearsome. We played Brighton away and on the way back, passing through Portsmouth, the driver said, "Look out," and their fans were waiting on bridges, trying to drop concrete blocks on the bus.'

Anyone connected to Southampton was, according to Pompey fans, a 'scummer', which made it a bold move by manager Bobby Campbell, Alan Ball's former Arsenal coach, to summon him to Fratton Park in 1983–84 to take charge of the youth team. Campbell, a former Pompey player in the 1960s, had earned the right to have his decisions accepted by leading the club to promotion from the Third Division in his first full season, signings such as midfielder Neil Webb from Reading and striker Alan Biley from Everton helping them to top the table. Ball, undaunted by the challenge of parochialism, saw his appointment as 'a chance to learn much more about football club management' – the type of apprenticeship he had skipped at Blackpool three years earlier. Working with chief scout Derek Healey, he set about adding local talent to club resources that had been depleted by previous financial problems and a high first-team wage bill, bringing in future stars such as winger Darren Anderton.

And when Campbell paid the price for failing to direct another promotion campaign – although he ultimately accepted an out-of-court settlement for unfair dismissal – it was Ball who was asked by chairman John Deacon to take charge of the final, meaningless, home game against already-relegated Swansea City. A 5–0 win, with Biley scoring a hat-trick, might have been expected to turn Ball into an instant hero, but his background, along with the fans' affection for Campbell, meant that the terraces spent the afternoon delivering chants such as, 'You can stick your Alan Ball up your arse' and 'Alan Ball's a scummer'. Deacon was deaf to such barracking and duly confirmed Ball's appointment. 'We've given him a three-year contract and I would hope that within three years he should be able to achieve First Division status,' he announced.

Having stated that the Portsmouth job was 'all I want out of life', Ball likened the club's supporters to those with whom he'd bonded so tightly at Everton. 'They are fanatical,' he said. 'The First Division is the only place to play football and a club like this, they deserve it.'

According to midfielder Kevin Dillon, Ball's promotion was hardly a surprise in the dressing room. 'It was harsh on Bobby when he was sacked, but then we expected Bally to get the job,' he recalls, those initial terrace songs having been forgotten over the years. Instead, Dillon's memory is, 'In my mind they accepted him because of who he was and what he was. He was a World Cup winner and captain of England, so people respected him regardless of Southampton. I never felt there was any animosity.'

Alan Knight, who after 800-plus games in Portsmouth's goal knows more than most about the local rivalry, explains, 'Bally won the fans over with his passion, having his heart on his sleeve. He told players they didn't have to be the best in the world but they had to give 100 per cent. He identified with the passion of the Portsmouth supporters.'

More unexpected to Dillon than Ball's elevation had been the low profile he'd maintained at the club until then. 'With someone like

Alan Ball around, I would have thought Bobby would have used him. But maybe he saw it as a bit of competition. Alan never got involved with the first team.'

Paul Hardyman, a locally-born full-back poised to make a permanent ascent from Ball's youth team to the senior squad, already knew all about the new boss, developing an enduring admiration. 'I have a lot to thank Alan for,' he says. 'I learned so much from him. In the afternoons, he worked with the schoolboys and I helped him. We used to play games in the little gym behind the Fratton End; one- and two-touch football. His vision and ability to pass the ball was fantastic. If you gave 100 per cent he would back you, even if you had a bad game.'

Ball set about the task of making the changes he felt were necessary to challenge the top teams in the division. One transfer was enforced, however, when the chairman indicated the need to cash in on centre-forward Mark Hateley, whose elevation to the England team since arriving from Coventry City had culminated in a headed goal in the summer victory against Brazil in the Maracanâ Stadium. The £1 million the club received from AC Milan helped to buy defenders Billy Gilbert and Mick Baxter from Crystal Palace and Middlesbrough respectively; midfielder Mick Kennedy, also from Middlesbrough; and striker Scott McGarvey from Manchester United. Yet no sooner had Baxter arrived than Ball found himself having to explain to his players that their new teammate had been diagnosed with Hodgkin's lymphoma, a form of cancer. Baxter would never play professional football again and died in 1989, aged 32. Forcing himself to address practical issues, Ball signed Noel Blake from Birmingham City for £150,000 to team up with Gilbert.

'I was shocked,' says Blake. 'But it gives you a lift inside when you know someone like Bally sees something special in you. When it came to personal terms I said to him, "Can we go outside?" and I said I was unhappy with what they were offering. They were selling me short. Alan went back inside and got it changed. It showed the kind of person he was.'

Meanwhile, Kennedy effectively appointed himself skipper, sitting down in Ball's office and informing him, 'I am going to captain this club.' Kennedy, who began his career under Alan Ball senior at

Halifax, continues, 'Bally just looked at me. I thought, "Fucking say something," but he didn't say anything. First pre-season game, the ref blew his whistle for the toss and I just walked up like it was my job. I was captain for two years.'

The personality of Ball's Portsmouth was quickly established. In January 1975 he had written, 'If I am ever manager of a side that wins promotion from Division Two I'd like my team to be like the current Manchester United side. Not for me the team of grafters and hard workers. My ideal would be a bunch of players with individual skills who can also play a bit.' Faced with the reality of life at a club far less resourced than Tommy Docherty's Old Trafford side, Ball had become more pragmatic. Certainly he had players with skill, but he was building a unit designed as much for combat than complexity on the ball. The sort of team that appealed to the people of Portsmouth, steeped in the honest endeavour of the docks and the pride of the navy. 'People went to war from here,' was the reminder Ball frequently gave his men.

'None of us were shrinking violets, but that brought out the crowd's passion,' says Hardyman, who would go on to coach at the club. 'I was brought up in Portsmouth and Bally was right when he said, "These people are loyal, hard-working people. Give them everything and they will back you."'

According to Blake, 'We were Pompey through and through and a massive part of it was the manager. We played for him. We had that sort of spirit; we were all one family.'

In his autobiography, Ball would use the word 'mongrels' to describe his squad. 'Nobody liked to play against them and they had reputations that suggested they would be difficult to manage,' he said. 'But I put into practice all I had learned from Lawrie McMenemy.'

'It was all right Bally liking us,' says Kennedy, 'but we loved Bally. Nothing frightened him. It was a hostile team and there were some nutcases, but he knew that and he knew damn well he could handle us. The great thing was that whenever we went away from home it was a long trip, sometimes six or seven hours. Even if we lost and Bally had been angry, by the time we got off that bus back in Portsmouth everyone was a best mate again. If we got beat, it was done and dusted. And the bus trips were crazy. You had to get along, and if you didn't there was something wrong.'

Hardyman adds, 'Alan had values and as long as you bought into that he would like you. He loved the camaraderie that came with those lads.'

Dillon continues, 'The team we had was very competitive, as everybody knows. We had a few scallywags, but Bally loved them.' Although a Campbell signing when he joined from Birmingham, Dillon fitted that profile perfectly. 'A one-man awkward squad' was how Ball would remember him in his autobiography. 'We used to argue once a week, sometimes twice, but he liked that,' Dillon laughs, constantly referring to Ball as 'a great man'. 'We had a good relationship. I said to him once as a joke, "I am only happy when I am sad," and he used to bring that up all the time. We went to Sweden and I got a call from him about 12 o'clock at night saying, "Come to my room." I thought it was odd because he might have had a couple of drinks. He was sitting behind his desk and we spent about an hour and a half talking about his new signings. I told him what I thought of them and I don't think he liked it, but he respected my opinion because I told it like it was.

'Another time he left me out of a game on Saturday and I had to play in the reserves on Tuesday. I didn't want to play so I decided that I wasn't going to touch the ball. I don't know if you have ever tried not touching the ball in a game, but it is the hardest thing – not physically, but the most mentally stressful. I was absolutely shattered at half-time and Bally said was taking me off. He caught me afterwards and said, "That was incredible what you have just done. I did it four or five years ago" – he said he had done it while he was playing in Asia because he hadn't got paid – "I did that for a full game and I respect you for that and I am playing you on Saturday." He spotted it straight away. He was a great man manager.'

Striker Micky Quinn, a fun-loving Liverpudlian who joined the club in the spring of 1986, enjoys the memory of Ball trying to maintain control. 'That was easier said than done. I always remember his famous saying, "This is a football version of Frankenstein." If we were out of order he would say, "I created this monster and I can destroy it." The nickname we gave ourselves was The Gremlins. The off-the-field stuff, the drinking culture, was the negative side of things and wasn't funny to anyone on the outside, but in the main Alan kept things in balance.

'It was an eclectic mix and I have never known so many characters in one dressing room. It wasn't for the faint-hearted. Apprentices used to shit themselves coming in to pick up the kit. They would have a boot launched at them or a stinky slip. It was character building for them. The dressing room was a weird collection and you had to be a character to survive.'

Lee Sandford, who would work his way up into Ball's first team after being one of those terrorised apprentices, recalls that the hard men also had a softer side. 'You had to be tough. There was a big drinking culture and you had to socialise,' he explains. 'But they looked after the youngsters and showed you the ropes. At Christmas parties they would make sure the youngsters were involved and on away trips they made sure you were part of the team. But if you didn't perform on the pitch they would come down hard on you.'

Ball's collection of rogues and misfits remained unbeaten until mid-October of 1984–85 and reached Christmas in the promotion places. The game that put them second in the table, a 2–1 win over Oxford United on 22 December, has gone down in Pompey lore and become a YouTube favourite, transfer-listed Biley heading two goals at the Fratton End in the final two minutes with the crowd going crazy. A shot of Ball in the directors' box reveals a mature female fan in tears. 'There is no way surely Alan Biley will be allowed to leave Portsmouth now,' declares ITV commentator Martin Tyler. Yet Biley was soon on his way to Brighton and Hove Albion for £50,000. 'There were certain players Ball didn't get on with,' says local journalist Pat Symes. 'He sent Alan Biley to Brighton and dismantled quite a bit of Bobby Campbell's team.'

Vince Hilaire, an elegant midfielder who had won promotion as part of Crystal Palace's so-called 'Team of the Eighties' five years earlier, had been signed from Luton Town at the end of November, with Ipswich Town winger Kevin O'Callaghan arriving early in 1985. Together, they were to add a touch of culture to the chaos overseen by the tough guys.

Yet Portsmouth did not winter well. A Boxing Day draw at Brighton began a six-game run without a win and they could only draw against Fulham on New Year's Day after being 4–0 up at half-time. Even so, when they beat the London club 3–1 in the return game on 8 April they were back in second place. Again they faltered, losing to Birmingham City and Crystal Palace, meaning that they were fifth – two points adrift of the top three – when they faced promotion rivals Manchester City with four matches remaining. 'It was then that I made one of the biggest mistakes of my managerial career,' Ball stated, admitting that he should have ensured his team settled for a point rather than pressing for a winner and losing 2–1. Even when they won their final three games, they were beaten to promotion by City on goal difference.

Preparing for a second shot at promotion, Ball brought in Nottingham Forest full-back Kenny Swain, a European Cup winner at Aston Villa, and signed an old friend, Mick Channon, from Norwich City. 'I could have stayed at Forest in the First Division,' Swain explains. 'Brian Clough was the most charismatic, influential personality I have ever worked with and it was the most enjoyable period of my career. But Pompey were talking about a three-year contract and they had a fantastic opportunity to go up. On top of that, you are working for your schoolboy hero. Alan was fantastic to work for. In terms of outlook, attitude and behaviour he was a still a player, if you like. He understood players. He had a dry Lancashire humour and he could mix it with the players in terms of sharpness.'

Channon admits, 'I only went to Portsmouth because Bally wanted me there. He knew what I could do and got me to do a job for a year. It was 60 or 70 minutes and I was off. There were some rascals there. Training was more dangerous than a game.'

'Mick was terrific,' Dillon remembers. 'He told some great stories and was a great character.' On the field, Channon could still make a valuable contribution, partnering Nicky Morgan and prompting the former West Ham man to score seven goals in the first five games of the season. Again, though, Portsmouth were unable to avoid the runs of poor form that could undermine a promotion challenge. Having found themselves five points clear at the end of October and beaten Tottenham Hotspur in the League Cup for good measure, they lost four straight games from the start of November, although they still managed to lead the division from the start of the season to the middle of December.

As form fluctuated further, and with the end of the season in sight, Ball called Everton colleague Joe Royle, then manager of Oldham

Athletic, and offered £150,000 for Quinn, a no-nonsense goal-scorer.
Quinn's first impression of Ball was that 'he just seemed really genuine, infectious and passionate. I was impressed by the way he sold the
club to me and what we were going to achieve.' Portsmouth were
unbeaten in Quinn's first four games and, with seven matches left,
were seven points ahead of fourth-placed Wimbledon. But then they
lost three in a row. Confidence was shot and a 2–0 defeat at Stoke City
was effectively the end of their challenge. For the second year in a row
they finished fourth, having spent all but the final week of the season
in the promotion places. According to Kennedy, 'We knew it wasn't
Alan that fucked up, it was us as players. He can't do anything sat on
the bench.'

Once more, the realities of life prevented Ball brooding over the
misfortunes of football. In July, elder daughter Mandy collapsed at
home, bleeding heavily from the lower part of her body. Confronted
by his daughter's eyes rolling back into her head as she lost consciousness, Ball twice forced her mouth open to administer mouth-to-mouth
resuscitation. Stabilised in a hospital operating theatre, Mandy was
found to have lost half the blood in her body. Doctors discovered that
her umbilical cord had attached itself to the bowel wall and over time
had filled with corrosive fluid, causing blood vessels to break under
the pressure.

'He saved my life three times,' says Mandy, also referring to the day
when she put her arm through plate glass as a child and an occasion
when she became trapped upside down in a rubber ring in the family
swimming pool. 'He was all dressed up in his suit ready to go out to
dinner, but he just jumped in fully clothed and got me out.'

With Mandy recovering from her latest episode, the chairman's
three-season deadline began to loom large, although Deacon had no
thought of not honouring the three-year window he'd offered. 'I was
being given the time to do the job properly and that is the secret of
management,' Ball remembered.

He was also establishing his own style and methods. Not only had
he placed his faith in a disparate group of far from angelic individuals,
but he had developed a personal mantra in which he deliberately
resorted to the communication tactic he'd used in so many of those
magazine columns, referring to himself in the third person. 'If you

want to stay in an Alan Ball squad of players and if you want to stay in an Alan Ball team, Alan Ball likes people who give everything' . . . and so on.

Some cringed at the method of delivery, but most at least absorbed the message that mistakes would be tolerated, lack of application would not. 'He knew what to say, when to say it and how to say it,' Kennedy explains. 'There was no better manager at giving you a kick up the backside. You don't win a World Cup and go on to manage at a young age if you don't know the game.'

It would be an exaggeration, however, to suggest that everyone responded to a management style that some found unnecessarily abrasive at times. 'He would bollock people when they needed bollocking and praise them when they needed it,' says Knight. 'Some players would not agree because I know he fell out with some, but that is going to happen in football. He was a proper man's man, a footballing man. He didn't take any bullshit.'

Coach Graham Paddon, described by Hilaire as 'lovely and mild-mannered', was often left apologising for his boss's outbursts. Paddon would advise that 'he never meant that, so don't take it to heart', although, according to Hilaire, he excluded O'Callaghan and Dillon from that absolution because 'where those two were concerned, Bally meant every word'.

Dillon continues, 'He couldn't hold it back if we lost, but as long as you had put your work in he was fine.' One occasion when he was anything but 'fine' is remembered vividly by various players. After an overnight stay following a League Cup tie, Ball met his team back at Fratton Park before allowing them to go home. 'He ranted and raved for about five minutes, as he could do,' says Hardyman, who was at the club receiving treatment. Dillon continues, 'He said, "That is it, I am jacking it in," and he took his bag and walked out. Except it wasn't his bag, it was Kevin O'Callaghan's. He had to shout, "Gaffer, can I have my bag back?" Bally walked back in, got his bag and everyone cracked up. Later, a couple of the lads said I should call him because, although it was just a spur of the moment thing, he might feel he had to follow it through. Hopefully that helped and he stayed.'

Son Jimmy remembers that 'on Saturday nights we made sure the dog and cat were outside if we lost and that we were all quiet. But come Sunday morning it was done and he would be jovial in the pub at lunchtime. He was very emotional and I have never seen anyone cry like him – about football and people, not much else. But he would get emotional and worry about what he could have done and then it was done. He wouldn't dwell on things and always said he slept like a baby.'

Another aspect of Ball's management sticks with Dillon. 'He had a brilliant assistant in Lesley. She would come up in a lot of the team talks. "My wife was at the game on Saturday and she said this and that, and I agree with her." Some of the lads wondered what that had to do with anything, but Lesley was there every week, watching the game, talking about the game with him.'

That story surprises Jimmy, who says, 'I don't know if he would have quoted her,' but adds, 'She was extremely knowledgeable and had an opinion.' Meanwhile, daughter Mandy reveals a tactic her mother employed to assist during the games. 'Ladies weren't allowed in the board room at Portsmouth; they had their own room. The away team dressing room was next to the ladies' room toilet, so at half-time she used to go in and listen to what was being said and then run out and speak to Dad so they could change things around.'

On the Portsmouth training ground, Ball flourished, taking advantage of higher quality players than he'd had at Blackpool. 'I think he was one of the best, if not the best, coaches I ever worked with,' Quinn states. 'His methods and some of the stuff he did on a training field, it really was a joy coming in every morning.'

Dillon remembers the 'happiness and laughter' of training. 'It was always fun. His sessions were always good and competitive. I loved that. I didn't like it so much when it was just technical sessions, like passing drills. But there was always something on every session, like if you lost there was a forfeit.'

Another well-known new face became a part of those sessions during the summer of 1986, when Ball signed former England and Ipswich Town centre-forward Paul Mariner from Arsenal, replacing the now-retired Channon. 'People like Mariner and Swain were brilliant,' says Kennedy. 'Great, honest pros. They grafted and they loved the banter with the crazy, mixed-up 23-year-olds.'

Hardyman calls Mariner 'the best pro I ever worked with', while Dillon argues, 'Bringing in Mariner was the key. He wasn't as quick or as precise as he had been and didn't score so many goals, but he set them up and he was strong and powerful and was a good person to have around. Bally had an eye for a player and signed some good ones.'

Quinn felt like a marksman handed a fresh set of ammunition. 'Bally had worked out what he needed. I could get goals, but didn't build an association with anyone in particular. But then he signed Paul and we hit it off straight away. He would hold the ball up, little flick-ons, and I would get in the box and score the goals.'

Players believe that Ball's achievement in ensuring that they were motivated and prepared for another promotion challenge after two disappointments should not be underestimated. 'You wonder where you get the resolve from to get up, dust yourself down and go again,' says Swain. 'Part of it came from the more senior players thinking we have got a good side here, but credit to Alan Ball as well. He was passionate and driving them on every day.'

Kennedy adds, 'To miss out once and then do it again, it was incredible that Alan kept that spirit going. To come back and start pre-season and go, "Right, away we go again," that takes some management.'

Not that all was rosy between Kennedy and his manager as the new season began. 'I said, "Bally, I am going to captain this club to promotion." He said, "Mick, there have been changes. The board thinks your disciplinary record is not good enough." Kenny Swain was made captain. I wrote a transfer request and I never spoke to Bally for six months. Then one day I went to see him and said, "Gaffer, do me a favour and get me off that list." He gave the biggest smile I had ever seen.'

The first nine games of the new season brought five wins, four draws and only two goals conceded. Quinn's double against Birmingham City in the last of those games sent Portsmouth to the top of the table. There would be defeats to come, but this time Ball's team bounced back each time, avoiding the barren runs that had cost them in the previous two seasons. 'Our consistency has been marvellous,' he said as the season progressed. 'They are a smashing bunch of lads. To be kicked in the teeth twice and come out and grab this league by the throat again this year, to keep coming out and performing, shows great character.'

In December, however, Portsmouth made headlines for controversial reasons when Gilbert, Tait and Dillon – along with Sheffield United's Peter Beagrie – were all sent off before half-time in the first League match since 1955 to feature four dismissals. 'I couldn't believe what was happening. There was hardly room for me in our dug-out,' said Ball. Showing the kind of loyalty to his players that he'd admired so much in Sir Alf Ramsey, he added, 'I just asked my side to compete.'

Ball loved that his squad possessed a 'togetherness that was always going to hold out under pressure', adding with pride, 'They fought for me. They went in where it hurt and won matches. They could be frustrating at times, but I grew to love them all with all their idiosyncrasies.' At moments such as this he felt his own disciplinary record as a player coming back to bite him. The fact that people believed he would send his players out to deliberately play a dirty game clearly upset him. 'Because of how I was as a player, a bit naughty and always in trouble, people believe that is how I am now,' he said. 'What I do is tell my lads that they must compete for the right to play their football.'

Symes, who frequently found himself reporting on Pompey's latest misdemeanours, believes, 'They were thugs some of them. We even heard that he tried to sign Claudio Gentile from Italy and we couldn't understand why he would want a madman like that. For a player of such quality, I found it odd that he would want to go for thugs.'

Dale Tempest, a striker at Huddersfield during that period, adds, 'They had a lot of top players down there and a right hard bunch of bastards. All those boys were hard as nails and when you went down to Fratton Park you knew you were in for a battle. If you didn't roll your sleeves up you were in for a long afternoon.'

Alan Mullery, who managed south coast rivals Brighton, recalls that confrontation could even spread to the touchline. 'We were swearing at each other and this and that,' he says, 'and I got hold of him and threw him in the dug-out. He came out and went after me. They had to stop the game and sort us out.'

Knight insists that 'we always felt we could play a lot of football' and remembers Ball being angered by comparisons with Wimbledon, who had beaten them to promotion the previous year and, in a season's time, would win the FA Cup. 'Bally always felt they were more direct, while we were a more footballing side. When he saw what Wimbledon did I think it broke Bally's heart a bit. He wanted us to play football on the floor, in the right way. Yes, we had some supposed hard men, but that didn't detract from the fact that they were good footballers. Billy Gilbert was one of the best footballers you could wish for.' Blake describes Gilbert as a 'great technical player' and adds, 'I was the least effective player in the team. With Alan, I had to learn to play.'

Swain says, 'There was a great rapport and we looked at Wimbledon's Crazy Gang as apprentices. But Alan took pride in the way he liked football to be played and I found it quite easy coming from Forest and the way they played. We had a lot of good technical players.'

Quinn continues, 'We could play football, but we didn't get enough credit. Bally shopped for players who had a disciplinary record – criminal record some of them – and players that maybe other clubs wouldn't touch, but they could all play.'

The team's public image had hardly been helped, however, when Kennedy boasted to the *Sun* that he was the 'hardest man in football' and accused other players of being 'chicken'. Fining him £5,000, FA disciplinary chief Les Mackay said, 'It was one of the worst articles that has ever appeared in the press.' Three decades on, Kennedy explains, 'Bally was all about not getting beat. If it came to the crunch and we were getting beat 2–0 we had players who could change the game by getting the opposition wound up, the crowd wound up. Once they had changed it, the sensible people would say, "Job done, now keep your head," and if we came away with a point that might be enough to get you up.'

Ball joked that 'debt collectors, taxmen and bookies' all showed up looking for his players at various times, but things took a serious turn in January when Quinn was given a three-week jail sentence after being stopped by police for driving while disqualified. He had been banned for 12 months in April 1986 for a drink-driving offence in Liverpool. 'First of all, it was a joke that you got jailed for driving while disqualified,' Quinn maintains. 'It was embarrassment for my family, for the club and for Alan. They obviously wanted to make an example and it was my decision in the end to take prison rather than paying £10,000 and getting a longer ban. I had Alan's full support throughout.'

Ball recalled that it was important to him that he was the last person Quinn saw before he headed to jail and the first person to greet him on his release, while Lesley went to visit him during what ended up being 14 days in prison. 'Alan threw a surprise party when I came out,' Quinn explains. 'Not to celebrate, because what I had done was wrong. But it was also wrong to go to prison. He got my family down from Liverpool and we had a blow-out with the players and then it was back to business. I will always remember what he did for me. He was a special man in that sense, a family man. I couldn't have asked for a better man, as well as manager, to support me through that time. If you were loyal he would back it up.'

Ball explained simply, 'We loved the big fellow and all his daftness.'

With Quinn on his way to finishing with 22 League goals, Portsmouth ended up battling his former team, Oldham, for second place in the table behind Derby County. The introduction of promotion play-offs meant that only the runners-up spot would guarantee against a potential third season of heartbreak. After Mariner, with only his fifth goal of the season, and O'Callaghan secured a 2–0 win against Millwall, Portsmouth were just a single point away with two games remaining. After 87 minutes at Crystal Palace, a 0–0 scoreline meant that the 10,000 travelling Portsmouth fans were ready to celebrate their return to the First Division after a 28-year absence. Then Ian Wright scored from close range, Hilaire was sent off in the final minute and Portsmouth were left staring into the abyss of disappointment once more. 'It shouldn't happen to a dog,' said Ball.

All was not lost. Oldham needed to win at Shrewsbury Town the following night to take the contest to the final Saturday. While Deacon went to the theatre, Ball headed to Kempton races, hearing before he left for home that Portsmouth's rivals were losing but refusing to let his hopes run away with him. As he pulled up outside his house, a home-made sign on the front door told him all he needed to know: 'BALL'S UP!' Oldham had lost 2–0 and Ball and his family ended the night celebrating at the chairman's house. 'I'm so happy for everybody,' he told the TV cameras when his head had cleared the next day. 'It's been three years; we have been close so many times. This club's in the First Division where it deserves to be.'

A final home game against Sheffield United featured parachutists, pom-pom girls and pitch invasions, after which Ball was pictured celebrating in the stand with a tearful son, Jimmy, in his arms. 'When the final whistle went I was by the dug-out and everyone ran on, so I followed,' Jimmy laughs. 'A policeman grabbed me when I was running on and I completely bottled it and started crying and told them who I was. When all the players were up in the stand I was handed up to my dad and I was still blubbing my eyes out. Everyone thought I was crying through emotion, but it was from being grabbed by the neck by a six-foot policeman.'

The mood of celebration spilled on to the streets of Portsmouth when the triumphant players paraded on an open-top bus to a civic reception at the Guildhall. Addressing the tens of thousands gathered outside the building, Ball's words were barely audible over the din of those chanting his name. At one point he was even lifted up on the shoulders of one group of fans. Not bad for a 'scummer'.

Quinn believes Ball deserves every piece of adulation that came his way, the same kind of reverence he had inspired as a player at Goodison Park. 'Over three years, that team he created, the players he brought in and the vision that he had, they were as consistent as any team in any division around that time. At that time, he was brilliant as a manager – probably his peak looking back at his career. What he created, what he brought together socially and ability-wise, I don't think any other manager in my time could have done that with those players and that squad.'

Adrian Metcalfe, a former Olympic medal-winning athlete, might not have been directly responsible for Portsmouth's relegation in their first year back in the top flight of English football, but he does have a lot to answer for. As head of sport at Channel 4 when it launched in 1982 he had been responsible for finding new sports for a fledgling station with no existing contracts. As well as introducing American football to a UK audience through coverage of the NFL, he decided that Monday nights were crying out for live coverage of British basketball. It created a train of thought that basketball could be incorporated into the kind of super-clubs that existed at Barcelona and Real Madrid. Before long, Manchester United had taken over the Warrington Vikings, merged with the Manchester Eagles and had a team playing under their banner in the British league.

John Deacon liked the idea so much that, early in 1985, he bought the Telford Turbos, set them up with offices at Fratton Park and sent them on to the court at the Mountbatten Centre as Portsmouth FC. In 1985–86, they finished third in the league, before finishing first in the standings the following year, while his football team was winning promotion. In 1987–88, the clubs went in different directions, the basketball team again topping the table, while Ball's men spent the season fighting the drop. The truth was that the money was running out. As the season progressed, Ball felt that Deacon was prioritising the basketball team.

There had been money to spend early in the season, including £285,000 to Leeds United for striker Ian Baird; £200,000 to Brighton for another forward, Terry Connor; £60,000 on Wrexham midfielder Barry Horne; and £70,000 to Oxford United for centre-back Malcolm Shotton, whose debut coincided with a 6–0 thrashing at Arsenal. Kennedy recalls Ball sitting on the treatment table in the Highbury dressing room, pushing his flat cap up on his head and stating, 'Welcome to the First Division'. Kennedy adds, 'We were fit enough. We went to the navy every summer and they ran the bollocks off us for two or three weeks. It wasn't lack of fitness, it was pure ability.'

In January, with Ball still buoyant after a 2–0 win at Southampton lifted his team out of the bottom three, Deacon informed him that he needed to raise funds immediately to save the club from a winding-up order. Debts were estimated by reporters to be as high as £1 million as Kennedy was sold to Bradford City for £250,000.

'It was Tuesday and he had run the bollocks off us,' Kennedy recalls. 'Then we went in the gym and had a five-a-side. All you could hear was him shouting "feed the bear" with his squeaky voice. I was trying to kick the shit out of him, but couldn't get near him. He was that good even at that age. We went in and were debating which pub we were going to go to when Bally came down and pointed at me. "You're gone. The chairman has sold you." You could tell he was pissed off because he didn't want to sell me.'

Baird went back to Leeds for a cut-price £185,000 soon after and Knight states, 'Investing money in the basketball team made it difficult for us to compete in the First Division. They were great lads, but we could see the money being thrown at them and we knew they could not recover that with their gates. It didn't take a genius to work out that it must be draining Bally's resources. We were told that the basketball would be sustainable, but it did impact on us surviving.'

Quinn believes, 'It was in vogue to have a basketball team but it began to create a bit of needle. You know what footballers are like with wages and there was jealousy that the basketball players were earning more money than we were. The chairman couldn't afford both teams and he panicked and started selling players. I never understood the basketball thing. He had spent so much to get to the First Division, but now we were doomed.'

Ball had believed he was 'building for a brighter future' until the basketball team began netting all the club funds. But the manager was not blameless, according to Quinn. 'I don't think Alan spent wisely in the transfer market and he broke the promotion team up himself. The players that achieved promotion, some never really got a chance. I know teams change, but it was too drastic a change straight away. He didn't give that team from the year before the opportunity to see if we were good enough.'

Amid unfounded rumours that he might tempt Lawrie McMenemy to Fratton Park to work as director of football, Ball had begun the season by signing a new three-year contract and bringing in Peter Osgood to coach the youth team. Yet the arrival of his former Southampton teammate angered an old England colleague, Dave Thomas, who had been released from that position only weeks earlier.

The ex-QPR and Everton winger had played a handful of games under Ball's management before injury got the better of him, at which point Deacon had offered him the chance to coach the club's junior side. 'Bally was great to me in as much as he let me get on with the job,' Thomas told the *Portsmouth News* in 2015. 'If Bally had had his way he would never have appointed me. We got on all right, we played in the England team together, but we were complete opposites in character. He let me get on with things and was never nasty to me. But what really hurt was when he, Graham and the chairman said they were not going to have a youth-team coach because of financial cutbacks.'

When he heard of Osgood's appointment, Thomas concluded that 'it was all set up behind my back'. He continued, 'If Bally had said to me, "Dave, I am bringing Peter Osgood in," I would have accepted that because everyone picks their cronies in football. But from that day on I have never respected him and will never forgive him. I know he isn't here to defend himself, but he knew Osgood was coming. They were big buddies. It was quite hurtful really.'

The FA Cup provided much-needed respite in a troublesome campaign, wins over Blackburn Rovers, Sheffield United and Bradford City setting up a quarter-final on the artificial pitch at Luton Town, who were on their way to winning the League Cup. Having reached the last eight for the first time in 36 years, Portsmouth fell two goals behind before Quinn turned in Connor's cross before half-time. Yet Quinn was sent off in the second half and Ball was booked for dissent on the touchline as Luton completed a 3–1 win.

All that remained was the last rites of the League season. And as Portsmouth slid to a finishing position of 19th out of 21 teams, Knight remembers that 'it was obvious that Mr Deacon was going to have to sell'. It was Deacon who was the target of the fans' anger during a home defeat to Newcastle United that confirmed Portsmouth's fate. Chants of 'Deacon out', as well as pieces of pie, were hurled in his direction during a game that left Ball sitting disconsolately in the dressing room for an hour after its conclusion.

A week later, Deacon was gone, resigning his position and offloading his majority shareholding in the club for a reported £2 million to Jim Gregory, the former car trader who had been chairman of Queens Park Rangers for two decades until selling out a year earlier – on doctors' orders – for £5 million. A lifelong QPR fan, Gregory had left behind a string of discarded managers at Loftus Road. Tommy Docherty, who worked for him twice, explains, 'Where Jim was great was that if he wanted a player or he wanted you as a manager then no one would beat him. He always got who he wanted. But he was a crook, a gangster. Horrible.'

Gregory wasted little time in making his mark at Fratton Park, announcing plans to refurbish the ground and calling Ball to a meeting in which he told him he would now be known as chief coach rather than manager. He also told him to fire Osgood and demote Paddon to youth team coach in order to accommodate former England, QPR and Aston Villa midfielder John Gregory – no relation – as his new number two.

Unsurprisingly, a furious Ball admitted he had taken an instant dislike to his new boss, going as far as to write that he 'despised' him. He did at least have money to spend, including £350,000 on Aston Villa striker Warren Aspinall, although he claimed that the £100,000 signing of Queens Park Rangers full-back Warren Neill was purely the chairman's idea, along with the subsequent £175,000 spent on another QPR defender, Gavin Maguire. When the first three games of the new season were all won, Portsmouth were in first place and appeared to be picking up where they had left off in the Second Division two seasons previously.

They were top again mid-way through November, but Ball was naturally growing suspicious of John Gregory's presence. Gregory understood why 'Bally must have suspected a conspiracy theory', adding, 'He must have thought I wanted his job and I could tell by the way the coaches' room went quiet the moment I walked in.' Chairman Gregory had created a situation that was impossible for both men. While Ball recalled, with some satisfaction, that the reserve team under John Gregory struggled with results, Gregory responded by stating that 'I was happy to sit back and learn as much as I could from Bally . . . I don't think I learned that much'. There was never much chance that such a relationship would work out any other way.

Meanwhile, Ball was becoming involved in an increasing number of flashpoints with his chairman. He even recalled pushing him up against the boardroom wall after Gregory exploded at his public relations man. Injuries struck, results faltered and on 17 January, after a run of four League defeats that left Portsmouth 13th in the table and an FA Cup exit to Swindon Town, Ball was summoned to the chairman's office. 'It's time to call it a day,' he was told.

'Alan and I agreed to split,' Gregory told reporters. 'I hope it was a friendly parting.'

It hadn't been. A furious Ball had told Gregory what he thought of him and the way he had been treated, and warned him that he had better play straight when it came to paying up the remaining 18 months of his contract. 'I hope I leave the club with my credibility intact,' he announced before heading home to a family who had come to love life around the club and were 'devastated'.

Players to whom he had shown loyalty over the previous seasons were similarly dismayed. 'The reason I left Portsmouth was the way they treated Bally,' says Dillon. 'It was a disgrace. John Gregory went on to do good things, but he was at the wrong club at the wrong time.'

Quinn adds, 'Like any new chairman, they want their own people and have their own ideas. It was all change, but I was gutted to see Bally go. Forget what professional respect I had for him, as a man he was brilliant to know, and his family, Lesley and the kids. I will never forget what he did for me.'

Nor will Portsmouth fans who thrilled to the exploits of Ball's desperadoes.

16

RELIGHT MY FIRE

'We are all travellers in the wilderness of this world, and the best we can find in our travels is an honest friend'

– Robert Louis Stevenson

THE years encompassing Alan Ball's reign at Portsmouth, 1984 to 1989, helped to shape what English football would become in the 21st century. Caught in an intensifying downward spiral of stadium neglect, hooliganism and policing that focused more on stopping fights than ensuring safety, the sport hit its lowest point two months after Ball's departure from Fratton Park. Four years on from the heavy loss of life at Bradford and Brussels came the death of 96 fans at Hillsborough, forcing football to accept at last that it had to reinvent its image and rebuild its grounds. In Rupert Murdoch's Sky Television, launched in February 1989, it found a benefactor prepared to provide the gloss and underwrite much of the cost.

The birth of the FA Premier League in 1992 provided a welcoming home for Murdoch's millions and launched English football into a glamorous age unthinkable only a few years earlier. The trickle of exotic overseas players that had begun with Ardiles and Villa became a torrent. At the top end at least, English football was suddenly the place to be seen. Yet, sacked by Portsmouth two weeks before Murdoch's new broadcasting empire launched with its four channels, it would take a few years for Ball to find his way back to those bright lights.

His journey began only a few weeks after his departure from Portsmouth, at the team placed 92nd in the Football League. Jock Wallace, owner of a fearsome reputation and a stack of trophies from two spells as manager of Rangers, had accepted the daunting task of keeping Colchester United in the professional ranks after 18 months out of the game since his dismissal by Spanish club Sevilla. 'It is not

Alan Ball was something of an outsider during his early days with the Double-winning Arsenal team. Here he sets himself apart from teammates Charlie George, George Armstrong, Eddie Kelly, Peter Marinello and Sammy Nelson.

Father and son together after Alan Ball senior was fired as manager of Preston North End, a day Ball described as one of the saddest he could remember.

Ball comes under attack from a Scotland fan at Wembley in 1973, although he said that the invader was welcome to join him for a drink later.

The telegram Lesley sent to the Wembley dressing room on the night Ball first captained his country against West Germany in 1975.

Ball shows his delight after he and debutant Alan Hudson (left) helped guide England to a 2-0 win over world champions West Germany in his first game as captain.

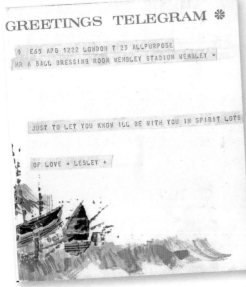

Ball returns to Blackpool's colours in 1980.

Returning to Division One with Southampton, Ball proves he has lost none of his competitiveness in a clash with Manchester City's Kevin Bond, a future coaching colleague.

Alan Ball found his feet as a manager at Portsmouth, leading them to promotion to the top flight after two near misses.

Matt Le Tissier describes Alan Ball as the only manager who ever really understood him after Ball built his Southampton team around him.

Former England teammate Francis Lee introduces Alan Ball as the new Manchester City manager in the summer of 1995.

Ball's run-ins with striker Uwe Rosler were typical of his relationship with many of the senior players at Maine Road.

A common image of frustration during Ball's term at Manchester City, a period that came to define his managerial career.

Ball accepts the Premier League's Manager of the Month award for November 1995, but the run of victories that earned him his prize could not be maintained.

His management career over, Ball casts an eye over David Beckham as he assists coach Arthur Cox and manager Kevin Keegan at an England get-together.

The 'forgotten five' World Cup heroes Roger Hunt, George Cohen, Alan Ball, Ray Wilson and Nobby Stiles finally receive official recognition with the award of MBEs in 2000.

Alan and Lesley at the wedding of daughter, Mandy. Family occasions would soon become milestones to achieve as Lesley began her battle against cancer.

The flat cap that became a feature of Alan Ball's managerial career sits atop the flag of St George as his coffin leaves Winchester Cathedral.

Members of the Ball family at Alan's induction to the Football Museum's Walk of Fame: Jimmy Ball, Keely Allan and Mandy Byrne, with Mack, Freddie, Louie and Jimmy.

This picture, taken during the 1970 World Cup game against Czechoslovakia, remains the Ball family's favourite photograph, encapsulating the passion with which their father played football and approached life. They even chose it for the front of the order of service at his funeral.

about the money,' he'd said. 'It is about wanting to become involved again.' Hoping that Ball would feel the same lure, he asked if he would join him as coach at a team that had won only three games all season. Ball was so keen that he even accepted less than his due from Portsmouth in order to tie up those loose ends and make himself available.

Colchester had begun 1988 top of the Fourth Division, only to win just five more games all season. 'We had been flying and won about nine out of ten games,' explains striker Dale Tempest. 'But about eight had been won by a single goal and we'd scored a lot of penalties, so we weren't actually that good.' As the new season unfolded, manager Roger Brown failed to survive an 8–0 beating at Leyton Orient in October and, a few weeks later, Wallace was enticed to Layer Road.

Former Arsenal defender Colin Hill, then in his second season at Colchester, recalls, 'A lot of the players couldn't have dreamt of being managed by Jock and coached by Bally. It was bad cop, badder cop – but on some days they were like a comedy act. Bally's coaching sessions were unbelievable. His intensity and enthusiasm for the game was frighteningly good. That was the way he lived. It wouldn't matter if it was Colchester United, Manchester United or the Prince of Wales pub.'

Under Wallace and Ball, players were encouraged to look beyond their position in the table and take pride in their abilities. 'Jock made sure we were always well kitted out,' Hill continues. 'We might be bottom of the league, but let's not look like that, let's look like a proper team. Those little things get in the players' minds. Bally would not go around shouting at players for doing things wrong. He would say you were unlucky and be encouraging. The atmosphere was stunning and that reflects on Bally's training. Jock would stand on the sideline like a sergeant major. Our playing style was possession-based. At that level, sometimes it is hard to believe that players can play because that division was renowned for lumping it up to the big man and fighting your way out of trouble. Bally said, "You can do that, but you can play a bit as well."'

Typically, Tempest recalls Ball's initial 'frustration' at the talent at his disposal. 'He couldn't get his head around the fact that we weren't that good. It was a shit-fight in that division and we were at a level he wasn't used to dealing with. He struggled with players' inability to get anywhere close to what he could see. But he still had that same fire in his belly.'

With five games to play, Colchester remained bottom of the table. And then they reeled off five wins, scoring 10 goals in the final three matches, to climb two places and finish eight points clear of doomed Darlington. Ball put the escape down to Wallace's unusual but effective powers of motivation, which included getting skipper Tony English to sing a battle anthem in the dressing room. Hill adds, 'It has got to be attributable to Jock and Bally. Every day it was a pleasure. Alan was brilliant to work with.'

Wallace asked Ball to stay on for the 1989–90 season, confiding in him that he was suffering from Parkinson's disease and would bequeath him the job in a year's time. Yet two months into the season, he was asked to release Ball to go and coach at Stoke City, where former England captain Mick Mills had been trying for four years to get the club back into the First Division, and had been spending heavily on his latest attempt. Peter Coates, who was just beginning his first spell as Stoke chairman and who returned to the same role in 2006, described Mills as 'being better without money than with money' and felt the board made a mistake in supporting his plea for more funds. One of the new signings had been striker Wayne Biggins, bought from Manchester City for £250,000. 'With the ambition we had it was all set up to be a good season,' Biggins recalls. 'Unfortunately it didn't turn out like that.'

Regardless of Stoke's poor start to their campaign, Ball found the temptation of an immediate jump of two divisions to a club where his father had once coached too strong to resist. He arrived at Stoke after the club had achieved their first win of the season at the 12th attempt. 'I want to be the greatest coach and manager in the country,' he announced. Yet he would recall that his first impression of the club was that 'there was rot everywhere from the rafters of the stands to the hearts and minds of the players'.

Mills declared himself 'delighted with the appointment' but when, four games and four defeats later, he was dismissed and Ball promoted in his place, it was impossible not to make comparisons with the situation Ball himself had faced with John Gregory at Portsmouth. Aware of the whispers, Ball argued, 'I came here to work with Mick. I have not been a vulture on his back.'

Biggins states, 'Bally was absolutely brilliant. He always had a smile on his face and was always joking. He wanted to be your friend as well. He was such a top man.' Both he and former Everton skipper Mark Higgins, another Mills signing, describe Ball's arrival as 'a breath of fresh air', with Higgins adding, 'His training was good, it was intense, and he had such enthusiasm. He made it fun and he got involved himself. You could see his passion in the five-a-sides; everyone wanted to be on the gaffer's side. I thought he would be a cracking manager.'

Ball's attempt to sort out the mess he found included bringing back some players discarded by Mills and signing trusted allies such as former Portsmouth stopper Noel Blake, who joined from Leeds United, Vince Hilaire, also from Leeds United, signed on loan before a permanent transfer a few months later, and Pompey defender Lee Sandford. 'I call Bally my football dad,' says former Portsmouth youth teamer Sandford. 'It could have been any club anywhere and I would have joined if he was manager.' Meanwhile, popular winger Pete Beagrie was sold to raise funds, which hardly endeared Ball to the fans of his new club, and midfielder Chris Kamara was allowed to join Leeds after requesting a transfer.

A 3–2 win against Brighton and Hove Albion in Ball's first game was a false dawn. Stoke never managed to lift themselves from the foot of the table. A run of 14 games without victory meant that their fate was sealed with several games still to play and they finished the season 13 points adrift from safety after winning only six matches. Which poses the question of what went wrong, especially if, as Biggins contends, Ball was doing a good job. 'It is down to the players,' says Stoke's top scorer that season. 'At the end of the day he can only do so much on the training ground and put us out on there on Saturday. We didn't perform for him. Even now we all hold our hands up and take most of the blame because day-to-day – his training and his attitude – it was all a pleasure. He could be a bit of a disciplinarian, but you always wanted to go training.'

Sandford suggests, 'As players we were not performing. Bally was still like the youth team manager; still wanted us to play the right way and with the right attitude. But some players didn't have the ability to do what he wanted and he got frustrated. Maybe he should have adapted more. But he wanted you to play football.'

The judgement on Ball from outside the dressing room is harsher than from within. Speaking to the *Sentinel* in 2015, Coates, who said the decision to appoint Ball had been easy for the board, said, 'He was an extremely likeable guy, a good man, but I would say Alan was probably the worst manager I had experienced.' Coates felt that Ball's inherent niceness meant he 'couldn't handle the pressure' of management.

One of Ball's attempts to instil a greater work ethic into his players bears out Coates to some degree. Locking his players in a pub all night drinking Calvados during a summer trip to Jersey hardly sounds like a method Jock Wallace or Harry Catterick would have used to strike fear into their players. When Ball let them out at 5am to witness the night fishermen returning home, he told them, 'Look at what they have to do to earn a living. Never will you lot have to work as hard as they do.'

The unorthodox nature of delivering his message via an all-night party was more memorable than the lesson it was intended to illustrate, and as the club faced up to only the second Third Division season in its history, Ball said that he sensed an 'unhealthy, uneasy feeling'. He'd seen comings and goings in the boardroom and feared that the directors were more committed to their business interests and personal status than they were to Stoke City. Nevertheless, he was bullish enough to be photographed placing a £25 charity bet on his team to win the title at odds of 12–1. Yet he also cautioned the fans against high expectations, a stance that couldn't help but confuse those frequenting the Victoria Ground. 'Our strength could become our weakness,' he said. 'We have fantastic support, but people expect us to go straight back up. I expect to do it and I am prepared to accept the consequences if we don't. But if the people of Stoke want promotion that badly it might start to affect the players. I'm not using that as an excuse, but we are under a great deal of pressure.' It was hardly the most cogent of mission statements.

Ball's team, which now included his old Pompey skipper Mick Kennedy, began the season by beating Rotherham United and Tranmere Rovers and by the time they had won at Bradford City on 24 October they were established in the promotion places. Yet they won only one of the next eight and Ball became so angry during a defeat at Preston North End just before Christmas that he kicked a hole in an advertising board. Kennedy, who insists that 'there is no way I would have gone to Stoke if not for Bally', says, 'He suffered because of the expectations that were put on him. He was given a licence to put a team together at Portsmouth but he walked in at Stoke and took over a team that wasn't sparking.'

When Stoke arrived at Wigan Athletic on 23 February they had gone another five matches without a win and were down to 13th in the table. What followed is generally considered by Stoke fans to be the most miserable day they can remember. Biggins was lost to injury early in the game and Stoke's five-man defence consistently, and hopelessly, left opponents unmarked as they went down 4–0 to a team below them in the table. Only the performance of goalkeeper Peter Fox prevented even more embarrassment. Ball would call it 'some of the most pathetic football I have ever seen'. Pages of the internet are now devoted to Stoke fans' painful memories of the match, described by one as 'one of the most ramshackle performances I had ever seen'. And that is one of the kinder comments. 'I had to persuade the police and stewards to let us out,' recalls a Stoke fan who left early, while another says, 'My lasting memory was my son asking me why on earth I supported that load of shit.'

On the day, and in Wigan's tiny ground, the response of the fans was even more vitriolic. Exposing their genitals while chanting 'Ball out' was one of the lighter moments. 'They spat, threw things and bawled the vilest abuse,' Ball recorded in his autobiography, adding that a boy of no more than 10 years old had spat at him. 'I think it would hurt anybody,' says Jimmy Ball. 'It was a young boy who had been pushed to the front of the stands by his father to do that. He couldn't deal with that because he was working his backside off to help this great club.'

Ball recalled witnessing similar invective directed at Mick Mills and coach Sammy Chung when he had first arrived at the club and had seen Lesley abused at home games. 'It was heartbreaking,' says Sandford. 'It was cruel the way the fans treated him, spitting at him and things like that. It wasn't his fault.'

Ball was in no mood to endure any more. Having been working on a month-by-month deal without a formal contract, he sought out Coates immediately after the game to resign. Coates was about to dismiss him anyway and asked the Wigan chairman for a room in which they could meet. 'I felt we had to do it,' Coates explained. 'It had been building, it wasn't just one game. It was the trend, which hadn't been good, and I felt Alan had been having a tough time and it wasn't for him.'

Jimmy Ball insists, 'When he realised he wasn't able to help the club any more he walked away. He was proud that he could always say to the fans there that he didn't take their money. It was foolish to do that, but it was honourable. Stoke fans were particularly hostile towards him, but the club was a juggernaut going downhill and I don't know if many people could have arrested it.'

Seeking out Graham Paddon to urge him to stay put as coach, Ball told the players he was finished. 'I am sure things would have got better in time,' says Biggins. 'It's a pity it didn't work out. Alan might have done things differently if he could have done it again, but I thought it was a brilliant time.'

Ball would have disagreed with that final sentiment. When he drove away from Stoke a few days after the Wigan match, disillusioned and dismayed, he wondered if he was done with football for good.

For the next few months, Ball attempted to prove to himself that he could live without the sport that defined him, teaming up with two friends to take over a pub near Ascot and turning it into a restaurant they called Winnigans. Yet for all the fun he had playing the host and all the money coming through the till, he realised he had been 'steeped in football from the womb'.

One summer morning, Stuart Dawe, the director in charge of football matters at Exeter City, called to introduce himself. The Devon club had been crowned champions of the Fourth Division 15 months earlier, but Ball was unaware of the unrest that existed at St James' Park. What was it about boardroom battles and Alan Ball? His managerial reigns at Blackpool, Portsmouth and Stoke had already been blighted by directors squabbling and swapping seats like children playing musical chairs. There would be more to come at future stops on his path through management.

To summarise the chaos at Exeter: In December, chairman Ivor Doble had been banned from football for a year for returning questionable numbers to the Football Grounds Improvement Trust. Two other directors, Muray Couch and Peter Carter, were also suspended, leaving president Clifford Hill to form a new board, while key players were sold off.

The fans were not happy. Not for them, though, protest through mere banners and chants. They had 'a plan to let Clifford Hill know that we wanted Terry Cooper as manager of our club', according to journalist and lifelong Exeter fan Simon Carter. 'We didn't have anything against Alan Ball, but his managerial record wasn't great then.' The fans' tactic would be to march across the pitch at half-time in a Friday night friendly against Millwall and occupy the seats in the directors' box.

Dawe, who had got to know Ball while serving as chairman of Plymouth Argyle, explains, 'They had a board meeting and the chairman said we would need somebody a bit special. I said, "I think I can get Alan Ball." We disguised him when he came to the game. At half-time there was a rebellion and the supporters came across the pitch and took over the directors' box. I remember the police sergeant saying, "It is not safe for you to go out there for the second half."' Meanwhile, the target of the protest, Hill, had not even attended the match. 'We went to a hotel in Exeter and discussed a deal,' Dawe continues. 'Lesley rang me and said, "Make sure you look after him." We became great friends. He used to go on holiday to Spain in my villa.'

If a directors' box sit-in on his first visit had not been bad enough, Ball was really wondering what he had let himself in for after a couple of weeks of the season. On the first day, his team shipped six goals at West Bromwich Albion. Then, after a home defeat by Brentford, they let in six more at Shrewsbury Town. Meanwhile, the midweek fixtures had brought a 5–0 aggregate loss in the League Cup to Birmingham City, now managed by Cooper.

Yet things were to improve to the point where Ball would recall his time at Exeter as 'convalescence', in the bosom of a homely club that turned out to be populated mostly by those who cared deeply about the team and its fortunes. He described his contract as 'a pittance', but quality of life had always been more important to him than money. Renting a converted barn in the village of Shobrooke, he felt his infatuation with football being restored.

After those initial setbacks, Ball announced, unsurprisingly, 'I am not happy with the squad. I have had a look at it for five games and not seen any improvement. I don't think this club is good enough, so I have gone to my board of directors and they have said, "Get on with it," which is smashing. There is money there, but I have also got to wheel and deal.' In the end, five men who appeared during the first five League games under Ball did not play for the club again.

Still waiting for his debut, defender Dave Cooper earned a reprieve by challenging his new manager. 'He stuck a load of us on the transfer list,' he recalls. 'Several of us were in his office and everyone stood there accepting it. But I went back and banged on the door and said, "How can you put me on the transfer list? You don't know who I am yet." He said, "Fair play, son. I will give you a chance." I think he appreciated what I'd done because he'd have done the same.'

Cooper, who would play regularly in Ball's second season, continues, 'He wanted the best for you and knew what was best for you. I remember not playing very well in a reserve game at Plymouth and at a team meeting, the day before we went to Rotherham, he had a go at me. We drove up to Rotherham and he woke me up in the room I shared with Ronnie Jepson and said, "The reason I had a go at you is because I want you to do well and I know you can take it." To be fair, he was right. I loved working under him.'

Exeter rose to fifth in the table with a run of nine unbeaten matches, including Tom Kelly's injury-time winner against local rivals Torquay United and a victory against Darlington in which Steve Moran scored all four goals. Moran was one of two former Southampton colleagues

Ball had taken to Devon to assist in his rebuilding project, along with midfielder Steve Williams, who had been at Arsenal and Luton Town since leaving The Dell. Also joining him would be Eamonn Collins, a midfielder he had first known at Southampton and then taken to Portsmouth and Colchester, and Vince Hilaire, signed for the third time in his career,

'If he wanted a player, I used to go scouting with him,' says Dawe. 'Managers think directors know nothing, but Bally knew I had a football brain and that is why we got on. Whatever he wanted to do or whatever I thought would be good, we listened to each other. Nine times out of ten we would agree.'

Ball made Williams his player-coach, although their relationship became strained over time. Moran recalls there being two factions in the boardroom and, while Ball remained an ally of Dawe, Williams was closer to a director called Allen Trump. 'It was a shame,' says Moran, 'because Steve had been one of the players Bally had taken under his wing as a youngster at Southampton.'

Cooper adds, 'The gaffer and Steve clashed a bit. They were both strong characters and I don't think you can always be in perfect harmony.'

Meanwhile, Dawe remembers the fans quickly getting over the loss of Terry Cooper. 'They had white caps made with "Bally" written on them. He had a terrific rapport with the supporters and they loved him to death. He produced good football. He wasn't a kick and run man, and the fans stood by him.'

Carter recalls, 'It was obvious that Cooper had left a squad that was not that good. Within five or six weeks, Ball had to bring in half a team and there was a remarkable transformation. He swapped Darran Rowbotham, who had been top scorer when we won Division Four, for Peter Whiston from Torquay. Darran was a hero and when he went to Torquay in exchange for a centre-half, people started to question things. But Whiston was a very good player and Rowbotham's best years had been and gone.

'So he quickly won the fans around. His enthusiasm was infectious and his passion is a cliché really, because everyone says the same thing. I ghosted his newspaper column for three or four years later in life and I had spoken to him as an Exeter fan, but he didn't change, whether he was talking to a journalist or the man in the street. He wasn't a big-time Charlie and, looking back now, Exeter fans have a greater respect for Ball than they have for Terry Cooper.

'He didn't have to come and manage Exeter City. He didn't do it to stroke his ego or for the money, and a lot of fans were impressed that he took it on. I met him a few times in the sponsors' lounge and there are not many managers who would stand around having drinks with fans. He was a true man of the people, which is another massive cliché. He came across as someone who came off the terraces. One of my friends used to watch the youth team regularly on a Sunday morning and Bally would ask my mate and a couple of other people to come to the pub, and sometimes he would invite them into his house and Lesley would cook a meal and Bally would be drinking beer and talking football. That kind of nature won the fans over.'

In the midst of researching his book *Everton Greats*, Ken Rodgers of the *Liverpool Echo* visited Ball in Exeter and found him coaching some young forwards. 'He was right in the heart of it, demonstrating, cajoling, inspiring people who were not fit to lace his boots,' said Rodgers, who described himself as 'mesmerised' by Ball's efforts. 'It didn't matter to Alan that this was Exeter. It didn't affect his drive and passion one jot.'

Former Norwich City, Manchester City and Southampton defender Kevin Bond, who would begin his professional association with Ball by signing to play for him at Exeter, explains, 'He was a humble man and he never gave the impression he thought he was too good for the level he was at. He rolled up his sleeves and got on with the job. He was absolutely mad about football and would talk to you about it all day. Everybody had the utmost respect for him for that and he was a delight to work for, a players' manager.'

Alan Tonge, a midfielder signed by Ball after being released by Manchester United, says that Ball reminded him of Sir Alex Ferguson. 'He was very passionate, football daft, and wanted to play it the right way. A lot of managers in the lower leagues just want to lump it forward into the box. He wanted to maintain his philosophy of playing football and, like Sir Alex, he wouldn't hold back if he felt standards weren't as good as he wanted.'

Results remained sporadic, although Exeter reached the third round of the FA Cup, where they were drawn at home to Portsmouth. It was a big game for both manager and his players, and Ball attempted to ensure that his men were not awed by the occasion. 'You don't need to be afraid today,' he told them. 'I will tell you what fear is. Fear was Mexico 1970 World Cup, the heat of the afternoon, sun blazing down, England against Brazil. There we were in all white. I had my shorts pulled down to my knees, socks pulled up over my knees, covered totally in factor 40. Then fear is going out and seeing all these glistening Brazilians: Carlos Alberto, Rivellino, Tostão, Jairzinho, Gerson and, of course, Pelé. Them looking down at you. That is fear – not facing this lot today.'

Regardless of what Moran recalls as 'a brilliant team talk', Exeter were knocked out and ended up needing to win the final game of the season at already-relegated Darlington to ensure Third Division survival. Hundreds of fans made the 300-mile trip to see their team lose 5–2. But they ended up carrying Ball shoulder-high from the field after news that Bury had lost to ensure they, not Exeter, occupied the final relegation place. Carter calls it 'a surreal moment', as fans chanted Ball's name after his team had 'capitulated spinelessly'.

By this time, Ball was back in an England tracksuit, if only on a part-time basis. As manager Graham Taylor looked to fill the vacancy on his coaching team created by the departure of Steve Harrison, assistant manager Lawrie McMenemy thought of his old Southampton favourite. 'I suggested to Graham that it would be good to get him involved. I thought he would be a good person to have on the staff. Graham and I had been successful managers, but hadn't played at such a high level and we thought that to have a World Cup winner around would be good for the atmosphere. He was delighted to do it and pleased to be back at the level he was used to.'

Ball admitted to being 'taken aback' when Taylor called him before the pre-Euro 92 friendly against France. 'Just the thought of helping prepare an England side is smashing. I feel like I'm a kid again,' he said. He remained part of Taylor's staff throughout the unsuccessful European Championship finals in Sweden, with young centre-forward Alan Shearer remembering that Ball encouraged him to confront the manager in the build-up to ask whether or not he was in the squad – a bold move that Shearer believed Taylor admired. Even though England were eliminated in the group stages, McMenemy states, 'He was a good person for the players, especially the younger ones, to have a chat with. Some of them would have idolised him.'

Back in Exeter, Ball's second season with the club began with two League defeats and another loss to Cooper's Birmingham City in the League Cup, all without finding the net. After the defeat at Blackpool, Ball admitted being 'shell-shocked' and 'alarmed' by his team's dismal performance. And then, in the second leg against Birmingham, Exeter went to their Second Division opponents and won 4–1, with Eamonn Dolan scoring twice against his former team.

It didn't exactly signal a resurgence. Another season of what could at best be described as sporadic results ensued. At least a 3–0 win at Peter Shilton's Plymouth Argyle on 10 April completed the double over their relatively expensively-assembled rivals and left Exeter apparently out of harm's way in 15th place. But, as they had done a season earlier, they went into meltdown over the closing weeks, failing to win any of the final six games. They ended up only two places and three points clear of relegation, their safety in the balance until Preston North End's defeat at Bolton Wanderers on the final Saturday.

Meanwhile, Ball came close to returning to Wembley, albeit in the somewhat unglamorous Autoglass Trophy, contested by teams from the third and fourth tiers – Divisions Two and Three as they had become following the launch of the Premier League that season. Having reached the Southern final, Exeter lost 2–1 in the first leg at Port Vale, and could only draw the return match 1–1.

A couple of weeks later, when the same opposition returned to St James' Park for the penultimate match of the League season, Moran's goal appeared to have given Exeter the win that would have ensured survival. But with the game in injury time, Vale were awarded a spot-kick for the most innocuous of shoves. Ball would call it 'the worst penalty decision I have ever seen' – although, typically, he mistakenly wrote about the incident as having occurred in the semi-final match. At the final whistle, he raced on to the field and had to be restrained by his coaching colleagues and skipper Whiston. Meanwhile, fans charged towards the match officials and one of them knocked referee Bob Hamer to the ground.

'Of course I regret running on the pitch,' Ball said. 'But this is my life, my club's future. People's lives hinge on these 90 minutes and again it's been shown that amateurs have an enormous say in this lovely game of ours. It's far too important not to get annoyed about.' Ball ended up being fined by the FA for bringing the game into disrepute, but escaped a ban.

After two seasons of marginal achievement, Ball and the Exeter fans might have been expected to consider whether their relationship had gone as far it could. Yet as the 1993–94 season began, Alan Crockford, a regular contributor to Exeter fanzines, wrote a piece for *When Saturday Comes*, explaining the bond between fans of the Grecians and a manager who, as it appeared to those outside Devon, had done nothing other than almost get them relegated in consecutive years. Crockford noted how outsiders would inevitably ask, 'Alan Ball . . . do you actually like him?' and added, 'People just cannot believe that anybody might actually have a good word for Bally.'

The Exeter fans had seen for themselves the ill-feeing that existed towards Ball from Stoke City followers when his former club visited St James' Park in November 1991 for a goalless draw. Carter remembers Ball being spat at again and having hot drinks thrown over him by the away fans. Yet the goodwill extended to him by the people of Exeter was rationalised by Crockford:

In a recent survey of City fans, even those who doubted Ball's tactical ability or cited various inadequacies amongst his squad were prepared to admit that he has been an honest and hard-working manager. And that's important following the revered Terry Cooper's defection to Birmingham . . .

Alan Ball's achieved plenty in those two years. Indeed, for a club who have finished as one of the top 20 lower division sides only 16 times in 62 League campaigns (Liverpool have won the Championship more often), 20th and 19th place can be seen as comparative success. And last season the French onion soup of League survival was merrily sprinkled not only with the croutons of cup success but also the grated parmesan cheese of a glorious double over the ghastly Plymouth

Argyle. Reaching the Autoglass Trophy Southern Final (stop snigger-ing, Premier League fans) and the 4–1 Coca-Cola Cup win away to Birmingham were both wonderful, but it was the two wins over Plymouth which really served to highlight Bally's qualities.

As the two-page article wrapped up, Crockford wrote, 'So, Bally bashers, feel free to carry on giving The Fiery One as much stick as you want – just don't cite Exeter as "another one of Alan Ball's failures".'

And then along came the new season; same as the old season. The first three League games were all lost, including a 6–0 thrash-ing at Bradford City. Then seven games unbeaten, followed by a bizarre few weeks in which Exeter lost 6–4 at home to Reading, won by the same score against Fulham and were visited by the comedian and Evertonian Freddie Starr with a view to buying the club – which he didn't. The FA Cup brought wins over Farnborough Town and Leyton Orient, sending Exeter into 1994 looking forward to a home third-round tie against Aston Villa, who were managed by Ron Atkinson and included players such as Dean Saunders, Ray Houghton and Steve Staunton. The allure of two big-name bosses and a potential upset tempted the BBC cameras to St James' Park, but they had to settle for a 1–0 win for the Premier League team via a Saunders penalty. It was Ball's final game in charge of Exeter City.

Two days later, Southampton, near the bottom of the Premier League with only five wins in 24 games, fired manager Ian Branfoot after a turbulent two and a half years and set in motion events that led to Ball's return to The Dell. The first step was confirmation of Lawrie McMenemy as general manager at the club he'd left in 1985 for a two-year stint at Sunderland. Speculation immediately centred on either Shilton or Ball being summoned from Devon to join him. Dawe, who had agreed that Ball would be free to leave if a Premier League opportunity arose, recalls, 'When the Southampton vacancy came through there was no doubt about Alan getting the job because he would be working with Lawrie.'

When Ball was officially confirmed as manager of the club he'd graced as a player during two spells, he declared, 'I am leaving a piece of my heart in Exeter. I feel I did a good job considering the position we were in when I took over.' But now the stakes would be higher; the rewards greater and the scrutiny more intense. Ball was entering the glamorous, intense new world of the Premier League. And starting at the bottom.

17

LEAVE IT TO LE TISSIER

'When a true genius appears in this world, you may know him by this sign; that the dunces are all in confederacy against him'

– Irish author Jonathan Swift

I T must have felt like a recurring nightmare: his teams, wearing their red and white stripes, struggling season after season to stay clear of the fiery pit of relegation. Stoke City, Exeter City and now Southampton. But this was real life, not just fantasy. Alan Ball was staring into the abyss once more.

When he had last been employed at The Dell more than a decade earlier he'd been part of a team that had spent several weeks on top of the old First Division. Now, even after winning their only League game between Ian Branfoot's departure and his arrival, he found the Saints in the Premier League relegation zone and out of the FA Cup at the hands of Port Vale.

Nothing had deterred him from taking the job, though: not the suspicion that he and Lawrie McMenemy were having to share the salary that Branfoot had received; not the fact that he had recently bought into another pub in Devon; not even that he had, that very week, completed the sale of the family's former home in Chandler's Ford, Hampshire, and now had to begin house-hunting all over again. He remembered being offered £60,000, plus a £10,000 bonus, which placed him near the bottom of the Premier League in terms of managerial salaries, but insisted, 'I would have signed anything just to be back at The Dell.'

Local journalist Pat Symes says eyebrows were raised in his circles that Southampton had been willing to pay compensation to acquire a manager who 'hadn't done very much at all' at Exeter and might even have been fired before long. Yet Saints midfielder Neil Maddison recalls it differently. 'We'd heard stories that he was a good man manager and a good coach. There was a lot of excitement and we were looking forward to being coached by him.'

Two days before his first game in charge, at Newcastle United, Ball met his players for the first time. He gave them the usual 'Alan Ball expects' speech and then, in a tale that has become almost apocryphal but is vouched for by everyone present, pointed a finger at Matthew Le Tissier. 'He is the best man at this club by a million miles,' he declared. 'His record of making goals and scoring goals will keep us up.'

Le Tissier, the 25-year-old from Guernsey, had been dropped earlier in the season, his languid-looking individuality apparently desired no more by Branfoot than by the England managers who had been resisting his charms and picking Carlton Palmer instead. He laughs wryly at memories of his years under Branfoot and admits, 'They weren't the happiest of my career, it is fair to say. It was a brand of football that was alien to what I had played my whole life. It came as a shock to have a manager who seemed just wanted the ball smashed in the corners and to play for set pieces. It wasn't conducive to how I wanted to play and probably the only reason I played so much under Ian was fan pressure.'

Dave Merrington, the reserve team manager who had nurtured Le Tissier while in charge of the youth side, explains, 'When Ian dropped Matty we tried to tell him it was a bad idea. I said, "You have to understand he is a player who plays in fits and starts, not a player who plays 100 per cent for 90 minutes." You had to live with that because he had a touch of genius. Branny said he was not fit and passed him back to me. I said, "Let me handle him my way." Matt was worried I was going to run the balls off him, but we put on sessions like one-on-one, two-on-two, where you had to finish with an end product on goal. He loved it, but he worked hard in those sessions.'

Le Tissier returned with a sparkling two-goal display against Newcastle. 'That kind of cemented my place,' he says, 'and about eight weeks after that he made me captain at Everton. I had gone from being persona non grata to captain in a few weeks, which was probably Ian's final attempt to keep his job.' Even when he was restored to the team, Le Tissier had found himself playing wide, but at that famous first encounter with Ball he discovered that the new manager had other plans for him.

Le Tissier explains, 'Alan always had a reputation as a manager who wanted to play football so when his name was linked to the job it was exciting for me. He and Lawrie were both down on the pitch and Alan was putting everybody in their positions, picking out the shape of the team in the centre circle. He picked three at the back, said these four would be in midfield and had two lads up front. At that point I thought, "I am not in this team," but then I realised he had only picked 10 players. He put his hand on my shoulder and put me in the middle and went, "This is your best player. This is your best chance of getting out of relegation. Every time you get the ball, look for him. That is your first thought." I stood there and thought, "Fucking hell, this bloke's won the World Cup and he thinks I am a good player." From that minute, my confidence went through the roof.

'He said to me, "I know you can't defend; we don't want you to do that. When we are defending you just find a bit of space so that when we get the ball back we can find you." That was brilliant. I don't even have to try to defend, which I am shit at. I was trusted by a manager to do what I felt was needed.'

Remembering Sir Alf Ramsey's discussion of dogs playing fetch, Ball announced that other players would be selected to win the ball and give it to Le Tissier. 'Those who scrap and fight and dig and run and head it will be picked, but the main man will be you, Matt.' He even told centre-forward Iain Dowie to win the team some free-kicks, because Le Tissier would score from plenty of them.

Far from being bowed by the weight of expectation, Le Tissier bore it eagerly. 'The more pressure you put on me on a football pitch the better I responded to it. Some of my best performances were when we were up against it in terms of relegation and needed a win. I liked the situation where you could be a hero.'

Ball's first game brought him into competition with his old buddy Kevin Keegan, manager of Newcastle. 'As visits from old friends go, it was as welcome as a random mugging,' wrote James Lawton in the *Daily Express* after Southampton came away from St James' Park with a 2–1 victory. The match began with Ball plonking himself on the bench in the dug-out, slapping his assistants Lew Chatterley and

Merrington on the back and chewing intently as photographers' flash-bulbs popped in his face. And then, within five minutes of his first taste of life in the Premier League, he was on his feet cheering a goal. 'Tiss put over a corner and I scored,' says Maddison – and it really did appear that simple. After an Andy Cole equaliser, the winner was scored by the liberated Le Tissier with a free-kick into the top corner after 83 minutes. 'To see Alan after the game, it was something special' recalls Maddison. 'He and Lawrie McMenemy were absolutely delighted.'

'Never underestimate Alan Ball's powers of persuasion,' stated tele-vision commentator Clive Tyldesley as the final whistle sounded. Ball, meanwhile, felt a surge of relief along with understandable elation, his approach vindicated. Le Tissier recalls, 'It cemented people's belief that this was the right thing to do. The lads were really support-ive of me and I had a good relationship with the other guys. We had a tight-knit group and that was one of the things that made it work.'

Maddison continues, 'Tiss was just unbelievable. I have never known another manager believe in what Tiss was all about, as we did as players. Alan told us to give him the ball wherever he was on the pitch and he would hurt teams. We worked our socks off and Tiss did the business. He was ridiculously good and Alan was the only manager I worked with who understood him. To be fair to Alan, it wasn't just about Tiss, but Tiss absolutely loved him because he made him feel special. And he was. He was so talented.'

After defeat at Oldham Athletic, Ball's first home match in charge brought the old enemy, Liverpool, to Southampton. This time, Le Tissier scored inside half a minute and finished with a hat-trick as Saints won 4–2 after racing to a 3–0 half-time lead. 'In many ways he reminds me of Bobby Charlton,' Ball gushed. Then Le Tissier scored the only goal against Wimbledon. Four games under Ball and the mercurial forward, considered an enigma by managers and media, had scored six goals.

'When Bally came I told him Matty loved working with the ball,' says Merrington. 'That was what Bally wanted. They had a great rapport.' And the teacher still had the odd trick to impart to his star pupil. Le Tissier remembers, 'You could still see in the five-a-sides that his awareness and his one-touch passing was pretty good. I was a player who got the ball and had a little dribble, but I learned that sometimes that it is pretty effective to play a bit of one-touch as well.'

After a run of winless games, however, Le Tissier had added only one more goal and Southampton were back down in 21st place with six matches to play. Before the last game in that sequence, at home to Manchester City, Ball had warned, 'Lose that and we are dead and buried.' But he reckoned without Le Tissier, who scored another hat-trick in a remarkable 5–4 victory at Norwich City, where Southampton came back from 3–1 and 4–3 down to score the winner in injury time via a Ken Monkou header. 'That was a massive result,' says Le Tissier. 'It gave us belief again because we had been struggling.'

Then came a 3–1 win against Blackburn, defeat at Tottenham and a 4–1 defeat of Aston Villa, with two more for Le Tissier. Losing against new champions Manchester United left Southampton needing something from their final fixture at West Ham to stay up. 'By the time we got to the last game we'd had a couple of decent results and were pretty confident that we were going to be OK,' recalls Le Tissier, who obliged by scoring two more goals and setting up Maddison for another in a 3–3 draw as Southampton achieved safety on a day remembered by many for Ball's beloved Everton staging a remarkable comeback from 2–0 down to beat Wimbledon and ensure their own survival. 'The lad has been the catalyst of everything we do,' said Ball of Le Tissier, scorer of 15 goals in 17 games since Southampton's change of manager.

Yet such was Ball's fire and competitiveness that he managed to put a cloud over what should have been a day of undiluted happiness for his team. When a pitch invasion by West Ham fans halted play with two minutes left, Ball's team had been 3–2 ahead and they discovered during the hiatus that safety had been guaranteed by Sheffield United's loss to Chelsea. They promptly went out and conceded an equaliser in the remaining moments. Ball was fuming. A win was a win in his book, not something to be carelessly given away, even when the table suggested it didn't matter. It was the West Ham goal rather than the Southampton achievement he focused on in the dressing room, forcing one of his players to snap back, 'Gaffer, give it a rest.' Le Tissier acknowledges, 'If you are a manager and your team gives away a sloppy goal you are always going to be disappointed, even though the ultimate aim of staying up was achieved.'

Maddison is another who finds it easy to forgive Ball. 'I was so pleased he was there. He was a great man manager and he got the best out of players. I fell out with him once when he took me off in a [League Cup] game at Huddersfield, but he explained that he was protecting me. He was the best coach I ever worked under. He knew the game, understood players, loved hard workers and he wanted to pass the ball and play good football. He gave players lots of encouragement and belief and I trusted everything he did. And he was a great enthusiast. He joined in five-a-sides on the Friday before a game and he hated getting beat. He put that sort of philosophy into our games. But if you didn't get on with him you were soon out of the football club. You had to take to his ways and embrace what he was trying to bring to the club.'

Similarly, Le Tissier admits, 'There were some people who didn't buy into everything; the lads who were not playing in the team, especially the more senior ones who didn't play every week. He dropped Iain Dowie on occasions and Iain was a very strong character, one of the louder people in the changing room, and if he was not playing he would kick up a bit of a stink. So there were some he didn't have quite the same effect on as me.'

Meanwhile, Merrington had quickly come to enjoy the energy and fun Ball had instilled into the backroom staff. 'He was a terrific lad, very funny at times and he just loved working with the players. He would ask your opinion, listen to what you had to say and respond to suggestions. He was bubbly and it rubbed off on other people. You want players to come to the training ground not knowing what they are going to do, so that they are kept on their toes. Everything he did was with the ball, even fitness training, and the players responded.'

Yet not everything had been going as smoothly as Ball expected. While he happily allowed former Saints manager Ted Bates to chat with him after matches and offer occasional advice, Ball was finding working with McMenemy, the club's director of football, harder than he had imagined. 'It struck me that he probably had too much time on his hands,' Ball said, telling McMenemy to stop questioning his managerial decisions and activities with members of the coaching staff.

Recalling one such incident, Merrington says, 'Lawrie came down after I had spent half an hour with Alan picking the reserve side. I had the team pinned on the board and Lawrie said, "No, change that and put him in and him in." I said, "Lawrie, with no disrespect to you, I have spent half an hour with the manager picking the team and you are coming down and changing it. Can you two get your act together?" Bally went ballistic and he had it out with Lawrie. You have to mark out the lines of demarcation.' Ball recalled a 'major row' with McMenemy and added, 'He took it on board.'

Forward Nicky Banger says that the Ball–McMenemy dual leadership could be 'very dysfunctional' and offers his own evidence. 'Alan had an office above the club shop and Lawrie had one above the club offices. I got dropped again after scoring two goals in the first four games of the 1994–95 season and decided I wanted to go on loan and wrote a letter to all the Championship clubs. One day Lawrie said, "Oldham have come in for you and I want to know your decision by three o'clock." I asked Lawrie if I was playing on Saturday and he said "no", but two days earlier Alan had started working with me, saying, "Keep your game simple, keep it to two touches." I had an outstanding game for the reserves and I think Alan would have given me a chance, but Lawrie told me I wasn't playing. I went on loan because I wanted to play football, not be fucked about.'

When Banger was subsequently offered the chance for a permanent move, McMenemy was 'adamant there was no future for me. I should have had that chat with Alan. He was brilliant for footballers and I wish I'd had more time with him. He would have made me a better player. He brought new dimensions to my game, helping me to simplify things and be more selective in my runs.'

The 1994–95 season saw Southampton flirt with relegation once more, mainly because of a three-month stretch from December to March in which they failed to win a Premier League game. It was their ability to avoid defeat – losing only three times in that period – that prevented them slipping further than 20th out of 22 teams by the time they won again versus Newcastle United. That was the first of six wins in seven games, a sequence that lifted them 10 places in the table. In the FA Cup, they lost a remarkable fifth-round replay at The Dell against Tottenham Hotspur, leading 2–0 at half-time before going down 6–2 in extra-time.

Le Tissier was again the team's outstanding individual, scoring 29 goals in all competitions. 'The 18 months Alan was my manager were the best of my career by a million miles,' he states. 'I played about 64 times under Bally and scored 45 goals. That wasn't even playing up front, so you can tell how much I enjoyed my football. It was the happiest time of my career. We had a good young team playing some really good football.'

Ball's great friend, Mick Channon, contends, 'That was when Bally was at his best as a manager. He gave Le Tiss the confidence to be a great player – he was the embodiment of Alan Ball in that team. Bally was a bloody good manager at Southampton.'

He had made some interesting additions to the squad, including Danish striker Ronnie Ekelund – loaned to the club as a 'gift' to Ball by his friend Johan Cruyff, manager of Barcelona – and 36-year-old goalkeeper Bruce Grobbelaar, out of contract after a medal-laden career at Liverpool. 'When Alan asked me if I would like to go to Southampton I agreed because I knew what he was like as a person and a manager,' says Grobbelaar, who as a young reserve goalkeeper at the Vancouver Whitecaps had babysat Ball's children. 'Other teams came in for me, including Manchester City, but Southampton was the easiest choice because of my relationship with Alan. He and Lawrie McMenemy made my transition very easy.'

The Zimbabwean's record was such that Ball knew there would be some eccentric performances along with the brilliance, but he had not bargained on a story in the *Sun* in November, in which Grobbelaar was alleged to have bragged to an undercover reporter about deliberately letting in goals on behalf of a betting syndicate in a pair of games, including Southampton's 3–1 win against Coventry City a few weeks earlier. 'I rang Alan and Lawrie and told them there was going to be something in the newspapers,' Grobbelaar explains. 'I aborted my flight for Zimbabwe, where I was supposed to be playing an international, but eventually left a couple of days later. On my return we were playing Arsenal.'

As reporters swamped the club's training ground, Ball called Grobbelaar into his office. 'He and Lawrie asked me six times, "Did you do it?"' I said, "No. I would never throw a game." Alan said, "That confirms it, you will be playing." Other managers would have wondered if my mind was right, but he knew my pedigree and knew where I came from. Alan and Lawrie saw it in my eyes and my demeanour. Who knows what other managers would have done? They might have made a different choice.'

With the world's media focused upon him, Grobbelaar went out and kept clean sheets in a victory over Arsenal and a draw at Crystal Palace, where even the home fans gave a heartfelt show of support for one of the game's most popular figures. When Ball decided to return to the safer option of Dave Beasant later in the season it was because Grobbelaar was becoming inconsistent on the field, not because of any fallout from the newspaper allegations.

In fact, when Grobbelaar went to court in 1997 to answer a charge of conspiracy to corrupt, Ball was eager to speak up on his behalf. 'I never asked Alan to give evidence,' Grobbelaar says. 'He came to give a character reference.' Ball said he felt like he was the one in the dock when asked to give technical evidence relating to the specifics of the Coventry match, but Grobbelaar and fellow defendants, ex-Wimbledon players John Fashanu and Hans Segers, were cleared when two different juries failed to reach a verdict.

Grobbelaar, who has coached in South Africa and Canada since losing a considerable amount of money in a messy libel action against the *Sun*, concludes, 'In the end, the court case looked like a farce, but it is in the past and I grew from that. I knew I had done nothing wrong. Alan Ball was instrumental in getting me to where I am today: working in football, not guilty and a free man.'

Despite the achievement of saving the Saints from relegation and turning them into a mid-table Premier League team, Ball was managing to upset some of those in the Southampton boardroom. McMenemy recalls the repercussions of the club issuing company credit cards to senior staff. 'The secretary said, "Have a word with Alan, will you? And get him to give me some receipts." There would be a fair amount on Alan's card. He would have gone up to QPR or Fulham reserves in midweek and taken a mate or two and then stopped on the way back to have a nice meal and bottle of wine.' McMenemy can laugh about it now, but he also admits that there was a serious element that was, perhaps, about to count against him.

Meanwhile, Ball had become great friends with Terry Hussey, who had been a licensee of various pubs and clubs, and Dave Hill, a man known to all as 'Big Dave', who had been a steward in the players' room back in Ball's playing days. The directors had voiced their disapproval to Ball of such acquaintances being admitted to the club's inner sanctum. 'Alan would get tickets for his friends in the room next to the boardroom,' says McMenemy, 'and because they had to wait for him to talk to the players and do the press they would have had a few drinks by the time he met them. I don't think that helped Alan in the eyes of some directors.'

Ball's daughter, Keely, recalls that Hill, who died in 2016, was much more than the ex-doorman that the directors saw. 'He was a big part of Mum and Dad's life. He would drive Dad everywhere and would drive us all to away games. He was there with the three of us on the night Dad died.'

Mandy adds, 'He was so big that people thought he was Dad's bodyguard. I remember us all going in a pub one day and somebody said something nasty to Dad as he walked in and Big Dave turned round and went for him.'

Nevertheless, McMenemy believes that minor irritations, such as Ball's choice of companions, made it easier for chairman Guy Askham to say 'go ahead' when his counterpart at Manchester City, Francis Lee, called in the summer of 1995 and asked for permission to make Ball an offer to manage his club.

Ball had concluded the season by meeting Askham to discuss extending a contract that had one remaining season and to ask about pay rises for his support staff. The club's reluctance to take either step – although they did offer to increase Ball's annual salary to £72,000 – was not what Ball felt was deserved. He departed for his summer holiday with the new deal unsigned. He barely had time to slap on his sun block before Askham called to explain that he had told Lee he could discuss the City job with him. Stuart Dawe, Ball's old Exeter ally, recalls, 'Alan was with me on holiday in Spain when he got the call from Franny. He was shocked. It was a hell of a good offer. His salary was going to be at least twice, probably a bit more, what he was on at Southampton.'

Lee expressed to Ball his surprise at how happy Askham had been to allow them to talk, while Ball recalled Lee suggesting he would offer him four times what Southampton were prepared to pay him. Lee urged Ball to travel to Manchester immediately to discuss a deal.

Also taken aback were daughters Mandy and Keely, who were preparing to fly to Spain to join the family holiday. 'I spoke to Dad on the phone and asked him what was happening,' says Mandy. 'There were reports on the radio already saying he was going to be manager of Manchester City. When he met us at the airport in Spain, wearing his Southampton FC shorts, he said he was going to take us to where we were staying and then he was coming back to the airport to fly home. He said, "I think I will be City manager by the end of the day."'

Even McMenemy had been shocked to hear of developments. 'I was abroad and Alan rang me and said, "I am leaving,"' he explains. 'I didn't know what was going on because, as I was on holiday, Franny Lee had rung the chairman. When I got back it was too late. Alan was hurt by the fact that Southampton didn't try to stop him. That is how he was. And if the board had said it was anything to do with his pals, I would have said that was rubbish and I would have got him to put his friends in the players' room. But I didn't realise any of that until it was too late. I think everybody loved him and the football was great, but it was little things like that and the credit card receipts. He needed to get that side of management right and he would have had more success.'

Running into Ball at Ascot races, Channon asked him, 'Are you sure? I think you are better off at Southampton. Don't go for the dough.' But he recalls, 'Money didn't matter to Bally. It was the last thing on his mind because he could always earn it. He needed Askham or someone to put his arm around him and say, "You stay here and we will look after you."'

'It was heartbreaking for him,' says son Jimmy. 'He would never have left that club if Southampton had said they didn't want him to go. He could have been there for another 10 years. The fact that City's approach was accepted hurt him.'

Ball was duly introduced as City's manager and delayed his return to Spain for long enough to deny claims that he had deserted Southampton, which was how the story was being portrayed. 'When Southampton fans were calling him a Judas, he cried,' Jimmy recalls. And when a stone was thrown through the window at the front of his home, Ball added, 'I just pray the whole thing will die down.' Describing himself as 'shocked and bewildered' by the events of the previous couple of days, Ball said, 'I've been painted as the villain who walked out on the club he loved, but that's not the case.' Meanwhile, Askham insisted, 'The decision was entirely Alan's.'

It was a decision that hit the Southampton dressing room hard – 'a real downer for us', according to Grobbelaar. 'We were on such a high. We had come 10th, one of the highest places they had ever had. Alan was a very good man manager. He knew when to put an arm round a player and when to scold a player and he was a very good tactician. We were going to kick on and improve.'

Maddison adds, 'I was absolutely devastated. The fans loved him, we as players loved him.'

None more so than Le Tissier, who argues, 'I knew he wasn't on a great deal of money, probably on less than me, so you could understand him wanting to go and sort out his financial future for his family if he was being paid three or four times as much. It was only later I learned that Southampton hadn't tried very hard to keep him, which was disappointing.'

Ball had weighed his love of Southampton and his belief that he and Lesley were done with moving homes against Manchester City's money, the apparent lack of interest of Askham and the challenge of restoring the fortunes of a club against whom he had battled as a player for the biggest honours in the game. The salary ended up being less than he had first believed, but, he explained, 'I signed for Francis Lee as much as anyone.'

What could possibly go wrong?

18
DON'T LOOK BACK IN ANGER

*'And maybe, you're gonna be the one that saves me. For after all, you're
my Alan Ball'*

— Manchester City fans to the tune of 'Wonderwall' by Oasis

I T seemed like the perfect fit. Going to manage one of the biggest
clubs in the country and working under an owner in Francis Lee
with whom he had been an England teammate. Even the fact that
Manchester City in the mid-1990s were known as much for being the
favourite team of Oasis, the hottest rock group in the country, as they
were for their on-field achievements appeared portentous when the
words of Noel Gallagher's anthem, 'Wonderwall', could be so easily
adapted by the fans to salute the new boss.

Yet Alan Ball's year or so at Manchester City ended up being the
butt of his own after-dinner jokes and has come to dominate popular
perception of his entire managerial career. His friends, family and
fans might want to skip the next few pages.

Lee had taken charge at Maine Road early in 1994, converting the
money he had made from a successful toilet paper business into the cash
required to buy the club and replace the unpopular Peter Swales, whose
two decades as chairman had brought a League Cup in 1976 and nothing since. The barrel chest that is usually referenced in any description
of Lee as a dynamic, darting forward who won League Championships
at City and Derby County was suitably puffed out as he announced,
'This will be the happiest club in the land. The players will be the best
paid and we'll drink plenty of champagne.' When Lee dug further into
the club's accounts, however, he discovered that there was a lot less
money available for salaries and celebrations than he'd imagined. 'The

club owed fortunes when I went there,' he reflects. 'I spent the first two years paying off debts they had accumulated over four or five years.'

Niall Quinn, who had been at the club since an £800,000 transfer from Arsenal in 1990, remembers, 'Franny was a hero who was coming back to take the club to a better place and even rival the club down the road. It felt like this was a magic wand.' As midfielder Steve Lomas adds, 'Franny was portrayed as the saviour on the white horse.'

Quinn recognised that Brian Horton, the former Oxford United manager who had been appointed by Swales in 1993, was working on borrowed time. 'He was a decent, honest man, but he wasn't Franny's man. The team was struggling and Franny wanted to bring to the club what he had as a footballer. Brian was trying his best and one night we were beaten 2–0 by Wimbledon. Brian was about to deliver his post-match talk and the dressing-room door burst open and he was told to sit down because Franny was taking the team talk. We were all aghast and we couldn't believe that Franny, knowing as much about football as he did, would do that. Whatever he said, we didn't remember because we were all in shock. We knew the writing was on the wall. It was difficult playing for a manager who has a date with the hangman.'

Failure to win more than four of the final 25 games of 1994–95 saw City drop from sixth to 17th in the table and was justification for Lee to make a managerial move, firing Horton and hinting at a big-name replacement. 'Colin Barlow, the managing director, said we were going to get an absolutely incredible manager that would stun football,' explains Gary James, renowned Manchester football historian and lifelong City fan.

Quinn remembers, 'Word had gone around that Franny had mentioned a World Cup winner and it didn't straight away get people thinking of Alan Ball. The word around Manchester was that it was going to be Franz Beckenbauer. I can remember radio stations ringing to say Franz was coming, so when we found out it was Alan, I wouldn't say it was a let-down, but it was different to where people thought they were going.'

James continues, 'George Graham had been mentioned as well, so when Alan Ball was unveiled we were like, "Well, what has he done as a manager?"' Or, as author Steve Mingle wrote in his memoir of following City, *Lows, Highs and Balti Pies*, 'We were gobsmacked. Alan Ball!'

Yet defender Ian Brightwell states, 'I was looking forward to it. I knew what a fantastic player he had been and Southampton had a good side under him for a small club. We always found it hard going down there.' And Quinn says, 'There was still a lot of optimism in the air. The Franny bandwagon could take place now because he had got his own man in.'

Lee admits that Ball had not been his first choice, revealing that 'we thought we had the perfect man to come to City'. Preferring to save the identity of his target for his own memoirs, he explains, 'He buggered me about for three or four weeks and then said, "They want me to stay here." We had shook hands on the deal, but then he said, "I really haven't got the courage to tell the chairman I am going to leave now." I said, "If you think you are ever going to be a big football manager and you can't make that decision, you've got no fucking chance." And he has still never been a good manager.'

Lee subsequently found himself announcing Ball's three-year contract. 'He was used to fighting with his back to the wall,' he says. 'Southampton had a wonderful player in Matt Le Tissier and I got someone to ask Matt what he thought of him. I did my homework.'

Ball's first impression of his new squad was the sheer number of players. 'He phoned me and said it was like watching an army coming home when they came back from a run,' daughter Keely laughs. It meant Ball was fully supportive of Lee's declared intention to reduce the playing staff to 32. He didn't realise, however, the extent of City's economic challenge, admitting that he'd made no real effort to find out and claiming that he had allowed his friendship with Lee to 'obscure the reality'.

The signing of Dinamo Tbilisi forward Georgi Kinkladze for £2 million masked the fragile finances. Dark-haired and mercurial, the 22-year-old had been called 'The Rivera of the Black Sea' by Italian media after they had seen a video of him starring for Georgia against Moldova. Lee had watched the same film, which he then showed to Ball, as well as seeing him star in a 5–0 win against Wales.

Yet Kinkladze's arrival would be followed by a steady flow of departures. Full-back Terry Phelan was sold to Chelsea and striker Paul Walsh returned to Portsmouth as Gerry Creaney moved in the opposite direction, a signing Ball would come to describe as 'a bad blooper'.

There appeared to be some kind of *Star Trek*-style transporter between Maine Road and Fratton Park, with Kit Symons beamed up from Ball's former club and forwards Carl Griffiths and Fitzroy Simpson heading south. Before the season was up, Garry Flitcroft, who had emerged as one of the most promising young midfielders in the country, was sold to Premier League champions Blackburn Rovers for a fee approaching £3.5 million. By the time Lee's four-year rule came to an end in 1998, new chairman David Bernstein was describing the club as having been 'under-capitalised and over-borrowed' for years.

He might not have studied the balance sheets, but Ball did come to believe early on that too many City players had become complacent because of their long and lucrative contracts. He would recall that he saw 'few signs of willingness and ambition' among parts of his squad. Son Jimmy claims, 'He couldn't wrap his head around the fact that some of these lads were on unbelievable money. Some had bonuses in their contract even if they got relegated. He agreed not to talk about that stuff. He got offered six figures by newspapers after he left, but respected the agreement he had with Franny Lee not to talk about it.'

One week before the Premier League season began, a foretaste of the trauma ahead was offered by an embarrassing 5–1 thrashing at Hearts. 'We got trounced,' according to defender Alan Kernaghan. 'We were absolutely garbage. We couldn't compete with Hearts at all. A lot of that epitomised the Alan Ball era. We had a lot of good players, but there was no cohesion between the team, there was no togetherness.'

Ball responded by signing Symons and, with Andy Dibble and Tony Coton both battling injuries, acquired German goalkeeper Eike Immel from VfB Stuttgart.[1] The new recruits made their debuts in a 1–1 home draw against Tottenham Hotspur in the Premier League

---

1 Another player who received a call from Ball was a man he'd already signed three times in his career, Vince Hilaire. 'Every time I was struggling he took me to clubs,' he says. 'I had been released by Exeter and all of a sudden the phone rang and I heard, "All right, little man?" I thought, "It's Bally. He has gone to Manchester City and he is going to give me one last hurrah." He said, "What do you think about a summer season at Butlin's? I can't do it now, but I thought of you straight away. It is £100 an hour." I said, "Where do I collect my red coat?" That was the last job he got me.'

opener, a game that was followed by a club-record eight consecutive defeats, during which City scored only twice. A second point, against Leeds United, preceded two thrashings in four days at Liverpool, 4–0 in the League Cup and 6–0 in the Premier League. The League Cup had previously offered a brief respite with a 4–0 win against Wycombe Wanderers, but even that had followed a disappointing 0–0 draw in the first leg, where travelling City fans ended up adapting the words of their 'Blue Moon' anthem to, 'One shot. We only had one shot.'

The mood around City was changing. 'There were all those songs like "Alan Ball is a football genius," and "Wonderwall",' recalls Matt Dickinson, then the Manchester football reporter on the *Daily Express*. 'They were sung with a straight face to start with, but quickly became parodies and piss-takes.[1] Ball started off full of enthusiasm, which was his calling card, that endless chirpiness. It soon turned.'

With Walsh gone after only three matches and winger Peter Beagrie done for the season because of a knee injury, Ball had turned to a proven ploy. In Kinkladze, he saw the kind of talisman Matthew Le Tissier had been at Southampton. Former City player Ken Barnes, who was on the City scouting team, even said of Kinkladze, 'If you'd put him in the United team at the time, fucking hell, they would have won everything, including the Grand National.'

Ball issued familiar instructions. 'It all centred on Georgi,' Quinn recalls. 'The team talk was, "Give it to the little genius and the rest of you cover if he goes wandering." You had players in certain areas who knew what they had to do, but then Georgi would come in from the left, drift across the pitch, beat four or five players and stand on the ball. Alan would be screaming at me, the centre-forward, to cover the right-back so they couldn't break. I found it difficult.'

Brightwell adds, 'I had to play left-back at Blackburn and everything was coming down their right hand side with Stuart Ripley. There was no help for me whatsoever. I kept thinking, "Where's Georgi?" They ran riot.'

Quinn says he 'wouldn't ever argue about the value of Georgi because the punters loved him and they needed a hero at a difficult

---

1 Various alternative versions of "Wonderwall" ended up being sung on the terraces – for example, 'Maybe, we could have got Liam Brady. But after all, we got Alan Ball.'

time'. But he observes, 'It worked brilliantly with Le Tissier, but at Southampton he probably had a more robust unit who'd combined well over the years. He didn't have to make wholesale changes like he had to at City. He was right that Georgi had the ability to do something brilliant; it was just that the rest of us had to completely change our approach. I was one of the worst affected because I was a 6ft 5in centre-forward who thrived on crosses and he certainly didn't cross it.'

Le Tissier, an interested observer, suggests, 'It went the other way at City because the other players rebelled against it. Some people looked at Kinkladze and thought, "Can we really trust him to go and win football matches?" whereas the lads at Southampton were really supportive of me.'

Lee admits, 'We had some big-name players – big names rather than big players if you understand what I mean – and they didn't want to be part of this. They wanted to continue running the team and running the club. It was a very difficult situation for Alan.'

Ball admitted that 'we had to mollycoddle' Kinkladze, flying his mother in to cook for him as he struggled to settle in a country where he spoke little of the language. In later years, Walsh would describe Kinkladze as 'the catalyst for City's problems', adding, 'Georgi had amazing individual ability and if you put his top five goals on YouTube they'd rival any great player. But Ball indulged him.' Walsh's verdict was that Kinkladze 'didn't score enough goals, didn't make enough goals, didn't tackle, didn't head it and his overall contribution wasn't enough'.

Striker Uwe Rösler would recall 'a lack of understanding in how we played as a team', while midfielder Nicky Summerbee retains few good memories of this period at the club where his father Mike had been a hero. Describing to author Colin Shindler the dressing-room's response to the reliance placed on Kinkladze, he stated, 'Some hated Alan Ball for doing that.' In Shindler's *Fathers, Sons and Football*, Summerbee explained, 'The problem with Georgi was that you couldn't play 4-4-2 because to get the best out of him you wouldn't want him playing a conventional running midfield game. [Ball] changed the formation all the time, a sure sign you don't know what you are doing.'

Lomas believes that a method could have been found that better accommodated Kinkladze's game. 'I have the utmost respect for Alan and he was a terrific coach, but I always felt we would have been better playing 3-5-2, keeping two up front and Georgi in behind. There was a big demand on the midfielders when you tried to give Georgi that freedom. He was a fantastic player, but the team Brian Horton had been building had goals from everywhere, with people like Beagrie, Walsh, Quinn, Rosler, Summerbee – and me and Flitcroft weighing in for a few. We became a one-man team and, even though he played very well in the second half of the season, ultimately it didn't work.'

Brightwell describes Kinkladze as 'one of the best I have played with or against', but adds, 'Alan didn't find a system where we could accommodate him. He couldn't play up front on his own and he wasn't a worker. He only worked when he had the ball.'

Quinn suggests that 'there could have been a better way', but Ball was unable to identify it. 'When the going got tough there wasn't the ability to change from the Plan A of Georgi. He might do well and get a goal and we still lost. For a period of time City fans had never seen anything like Georgi, but it wasn't going to last forever. I haven't been very public about this, but a couple of years later Joe Royle was trying to tell them, "This fellow is killing you." I would say I saw the start of that and it culminated in them dropping two divisions – not just because of Georgi, but there is reason to believe that the belief in Georgi was misplaced.'

City finally achieved their first win of the season via Summerbee's goal against Bolton Wanderers. Following a draw and three consecutive 1–0 wins, City were up to 15th position and Ball had accepted the manager-of-the-month award for November. Kinkladze had finally recorded the first of only four goals he scored during the season to secure victory against Aston Villa.

After the last win in that sequence, defender Keith Curle declared that 'sheer hard work' had created the change in City's fortunes. 'Every day in training the manager hasn't relented and wasn't going to give up until we started to play football the way he wanted it played. He has always kept a smile on our face.'

The upturn in fortunes was only temporary – two wins in the next 14 games – and modern opinions of Ball at City are nowhere near as flattering as the post-game PR-friendly version offered by Curle. According to club stalwart and former manager and captain Tony Book, who was still part of the backroom staff, Ball made 'some mistakes regarding the players and how to handle them'.

Lee concurs, describing it as 'one of the problems we had with Alan'. He explains, 'He used to confide in me and say he wanted to do this and that and I used to say, "Leave it. Don't fall out with him because he is friendly with two or three other people who [think they] run the club and we have to gradually get rid of them over a period of time." He said thanks for the advice and said he would do that and the next day he would have a row with one of them. He had gone home and talked to Lesley, who was a very strong character who influenced him a lot, and gone to the ground and done what Lesley said. He had singled them out and had a go at them. In the end, I feel if we hadn't got relegated that year he could have come through it because we would have got rid of those players and had a fair old chance.'

Book felt Ball had blundered from the start in introducing himself to the players with a talk about his own struggles to reach the top as a player. 'The lads didn't really want to hear about that or what he had achieved in his career. The players already knew he was a World Cup winner and I think they just wanted to hear about how they themselves could improve or what he had in mind for the coming season.' Book concluded that Ball 'never quite had the dressing room from there on in'.

Interestingly, Quinn offers a more positive memory of the same event. 'He brought up the World Cup in his first speech, but it was very impressive. I remember Tony Coton and me speaking about it and we didn't feel like he was using his medal. He said what he had done, but then he said, "I have got a World Cup medal in partying as well."' The point Ball made, Quinn recalls, was that the trappings of success and fame, rubbing shoulders with famous faces at parties, was there to be attained by anyone who worked hard. 'I will take you to some of those parties myself, but you must do it for me,' he told the players. Quinn continues, 'He brought up the World Cup, but in such a way that there was a bit of class about it. None of us walked out saying "who does he think he is?" We were really buoyed by what he had to say.'

The memory of Ball's opening speech highlights an issue I have been waiting to raise its head. As a journalist on a national newspaper sports desk in the mid-1990s, the gossip I heard was that no player would have to wait more than a few seconds on meeting Ball for him to mention the World Cup. Defender Richard Edghill even wrote about Lesley attending Ball's first day at the Platt Lane training ground and 'flashing his medal about like Tessa Sanderson at the Olympic Games'.

Dickinson suggests, 'The contrast with United was stark on so many levels. The whole place there was under the control of Fergie, but Platt Lane was where you would go to loiter around and grab players. As a journalist it was great because it was chaotic, the easiest club I have ever been involved with just to get leaks and stories. It is slightly sad to recall how the players said they used to take the mickey behind Ball's back about how often or quickly he would mention 1966. It was a standing joke. I didn't get the chance to ask him whether he did it and, if so, whether it was done out of glory or frustration or whatever, but it was certainly muttered about by the players.'

Jimmy Ball has heard the accusations, both in relation to management and day-to-day life, but says of his father, 'He wasn't a boaster. He understood if he was out that people would want to talk about the World Cup and he understood his responsibility to tell the story, to honour what it was.'

Brightwell remembers two specific occasions when the World Cup was brought up at City. 'He mentioned it when he sat all the players down in pre-season. He didn't need to do it because everyone knew who he was, but maybe he thought the younger ones wouldn't. Then he came out with it one Monday after we had lost and he didn't think we had put everything in. He also said he'd played 700-odd games and was scoring goals from midfield and you could see some of the older players putting their heads down and thinking, "What are you saying?"'

No one from Ball's other clubs I have spoken to for this book have brought up 1966 as an issue, even when asked directly. The closest comment of that nature I heard was Southampton player Nicky Banger's description of Ball's first day as manager at The Dell. 'He walked in and said, "If you are wondering why I don't have AB on my tracksuit it's because you all know who I am." Some said it was arrogant; some thought it was just confidence.' Ball would have said it was all part of the set-up for his 'Alan Ball expects' shtick. More typical is the assertion of Lee Sandford, a player under him at Portsmouth and Stoke. 'He never bragged about his medals,' he insists, 'He just had high standards.'[1]

Perhaps that contradiction illuminates the doubts and insecurities Ball experienced going into a club such as City, where his players – for the first time in his career – were mostly highly-paid household names. For all his outward displays of confidence, Ball had admitted to such feelings on occasions during his playing career, most notably when entering the Everton dressing room for the first time. Without the managerial trophies to establish his credentials perhaps he sought to win players' trust via the one achievement none of them could match. If so, he judged it all wrong. The City players were too sophisticated, and cynical, to offer their loyalty so easily. They needed something more substantial. They needed results, not reminiscences.

There were other points of conflict. Lomas admits that Ball 'put a lot of senior players' noses out of joint' with his approach, while Rösler would write, 'There were some big characters in our dressing room . . . and it's fair to say they didn't see eye-to-eye with Ball.' The German striker also told the TV cameras of a 'massive problem' between him and his manager after being left on the bench for the Manchester derby. James recalls that 'Rösler supposedly threw his boots in the direction of the manager after the defeats against Liverpool, and he was loved by the fans. He was our star man.' Beagrie, meanwhile, was hurt deeply by Ball's suggestion that his ongoing knee injury might be a mental problem rather than a physical one.

---

1 A more affectionate citation of Ball's supposed preoccupation with 1966 was offered by journalist Jim White in his *Daily Telegraph* tribute following Ball's death. Explaining that Ball told him that someone mentioned the World Cup to him every day, White added, 'Though with Bally you always got the feeling that if it was approaching midnight and no one had raised the subject he would have collared a passer-by and done so himself.'

Given that he was asking his players to subjugate themselves to the cause of Kinkladze, Ball might have realised that he needed to make greater effort to nurture their self-esteem and ensure they felt good about their value to the team. Instead, according to Summerbee, he preferred to spend his time berating them in training. 'As a manager your job is to encourage players and he rarely did that,' he said, adding that 'if he had slated Georgi all day he wouldn't have got much out of him'.

A more forgiving Brightwell says, 'As long as you gave Alan everything he did not have a problem. If he didn't think you were shirking and not giving 100 per cent he wasn't frightened to tell you. As a football manager you have to be ruthless and have a thick skin. If he had a go at a player, 99 times out of 100 it was deserved in my opinion.'

The arrival of former England striker Nigel Clough from Liverpool was no miracle cure for City, who also suffered the pain of FA Cup defeat at Old Trafford. But when Kinkladze's double, including one brilliant individual effort, earned a 2–1 win against Southampton they were still three places above the relegation zone with seven games to play. And then Lee instructed Ball to phone Blackburn manager Ray Harford and negotiate the £3.5 million sale of Flitcroft, the player Ball considered his 'diamond in the dressing room'. Without that money, Ball was worried that the bank would foreclose on the club. His painful task of breaking the surprising news to the player was made somewhat easier by his understanding of Flitcroft's situation. He had been on that side of the desk in Harry Catterick's office in 1971.

Ball explained to the press that it had been a good deal for the club and hoped that Lee would further explain the reasons for the transfer. No word was forthcoming and Ball called it 'the only time I felt let down by Francis'.

Lomas suggests, 'Maybe Alan's friendship with Francis didn't help him. He had to go along with a lot of stuff that he wouldn't have gone along with had he not had a close bond with the chairman.'

Brightwell argues, 'They took a gamble and sold Garry, but why didn't we just keep him for another six weeks? Surely the club couldn't have been that desperate. You can't sell one of your best and most influential players at that stage of the season. It was madness and if

Garry had stayed I think we would have stayed up.' Lee states now that Flitcroft was selected as the player who the club would cash in on because there was a need for more goals from the team's attacking midfielders.

Four more games without a win and a pair of 1–0 successes brought City to what would prove to be an unforgettable final day of the season. 'We were always playing catch-up,' says Brightwell, 'but we were all confident. In the second to last game we beat Aston Villa with a Steve Lomas goal and we came off the park thinking that would be enough, but the other teams down there had also won.'

To stay up, City now needed a better result at home against Liverpool than that achieved by either Southampton or Coventry City against Wimbledon and Leeds United respectively. Things began badly when Steve McManaman's cross was diverted into his own goal by Lomas. Even though Liverpool had an eye on the FA Cup final the following week, things got worse for City when Quinn and Rösler hit the woodwork and Ian Rush's shot deflected past Immel off Curle's boot. 'It wasn't the Liverpool you expected,' says Brightwell. 'They had nothing to play for, but before we knew it we were 2–0 down.' Yet a second-half fightback saw Rösler convert a penalty, won by Kinkladze, before Symons fired in at the far post to level the score at 2–2 with 12 minutes to play. 'We were right back in it,' Brightwell continues, 'and thought, with the crowd going, we could get another goal.'

Then, approximately five minutes from full-time, came the fateful misinformation, delivered by a spectator close to the tunnel area, that Southampton were losing to a late goal. Ignoring the fact that such news, if true, would have been expected to spread quickly on a wave of excitement, Ball seized upon it like a drowning man finding a piece of driftwood. He instructed his men to ensure they didn't blow the point that would save them. Lomas was ordered to dribble the ball into the corner, leaning against the flag post and thrusting his backside towards his opponents in an effort to kill time. 'If your manager tells you to do something, you do it,' says Lomas ruefully. 'Next thing, Quinny is running up the touchline.' With the benefit of watching television coverage in the dressing room after being substituted, Quinn knew it was still 0–0 at Southampton and that it was City's own survival hopes that were ticking away. He ran up the tunnel in his yellow shirt and beige trousers and charged along the sideline, urging his teammates to go forward. Ball could do nothing but look pained and embarrassed. The final whistle condemned City to relegation. 'Alan apologised to me afterwards,' says Lomas, 'which was the mark of the man.'

Ball would never live down this day. 'The whole City thing was so conflicting,' says Dickinson. 'He turned up as a World Cup hero and that deserves respect, but by the end he had become a bit of figure of fun and it was clear he was having a miserable, wretched time. It felt like there was enough talent and know-how there that, even if they were not competing for trophies, they shouldn't have been relegated. The final game did feel all too emblematic. There was enough chaos that it felt somehow appropriate.'

Pained by criticism, Ball wrote in 2004, 'Did people think I would be telling them to play keep-ball in the corner at 2–2 if I knew we still needed to win?' Of course not, and no one ever suggested that. But fans, angered by the direction in which their club was heading, had a right to expect that Ball would have ensured his information was correct before basing his tactics on it. Yet his exasperation was directed at the mickey-taking wider football public as much as those in Manchester, whom he found it easier to forgive. Despite the antipathy that Maine Road fans developed towards him, Ball would insist, 'I had never met supporters as steeped in their club as those who followed City.'

A couple of decades later, Ball might have expected to be fired within minutes of completing his post-match interviews. Instead, he was kept on, with instructions from the board that the club's biggest earners had to be sold. Club captain Curle was offloaded to Wolves for £650,000; Quinn to Sunderland for £1.3million.

Ball was allowed to sign Arsenal striker Paul Dickov for a reported £750,000 and came close to being reunited with Bruce Grobbelaar, released at Southampton by his old Liverpool teammate Graeme Souness, who had taken over from Dave Merrington as manager. 'Alan called me in Zimbabwe, where I had gone back to play in the

African Nations Cup,' Grobbelaar explains. 'It was coming up to the beginning of the season and I didn't have a club. He said, "There is a problem, though. The board haven't signed off on it yet and if there is one black ball you won't come in."'

Grobbelaar flew to Manchester, where Ball met him at the airport with the words, 'I am very sorry,' and explained that one director, Stephen Boler, had vetoed the move 'because of the court case'. Instead, Grobbelaar drove to Plymouth, signed for manager Neil Warnock and kept a clean sheet the next day in a 1–0 win against City in a Home Park friendly. 'I walked into the directors' room to see Steve Boler,' Grobbelaar recalls, 'and said, "That is for you, for not signing me."'

Off the field, Ball had recruited Kevin Bond to work with City's reserve team after a chance meeting at Royal Ascot. 'I bumped into Alan in one of the car parks after the races,' Bond remembers. 'He said, "How would you fancy coming to City and taking over the reserves." I had finished playing and said it sounded like a great idea and he said to leave it with him. A few days passed and I remember saying to my dad, "What would you do?" It was the end of the day, he might have had a few drinks and it was spur of the moment and I didn't know how serious it was. But, sure enough, I got a call and he took me up there. That was my first real opportunity in that side of the game and I will be eternally grateful for that.'

A former City player, Bond returned to Maine Road to discover 'a difficult club at a difficult time; Bally was doomed to fail'. Ball felt he was suffering continued criticism from the media without any protection from those directors forcing him to sell the club's assets. As Dickinson observes, 'Franny Lee obviously didn't want to advertise the difficulties.' All of which left Ball recalling, 'Nobody above me was prepared to put the supporters in the picture. It was a chairman's responsibility but there were no explanations.'

Lee, however, says he 'totally disagrees' with Ball's summary of the situation. 'I used to go out and speak to supporters' clubs and answered questions,' he recalls, adding that, in spite of the financial problems at the club, he had always managed to furnish his managers with a transfer budget. 'We spent a lot of money on players, but we had to move some on because these were the troublesome ones. I used to say to Alan, "If you want to get rid of him, shift him." When Frank Clark came we gave him 12 million quid to spend, which in those days was a lot of money, but what did he buy? It is all right the managers saying, "We didn't do this and it was a difficult club to manage," but it was a bloody difficult club to be the chairman of. It was bloody difficult to pay all the debts off and look people straight in the eye when you have owed them 150 grand for two years. And when you know what has gone on at the club, it was a nightmare.'

Ball did have some sympathy with Lee, acknowledging that he was another victim of years of 'feeble mismanagement'. And he would write, 'My fondness for Francis is undiminished. He was good for the club.'

His final meeting with Lee as his boss was approaching. Having begun the season with a win against Ipswich, City lost at Bolton and at Stoke, where Ball sat alongside his chairman to remain beyond the range of any home fans wanting to spit at him again. He still had to endure supporters of both teams chanting 'Ball out'. Bond was at the game and recalls, 'It was terrible. The Stoke fans were giving him all sorts of abuse and he was taking stick from City fans as well. It was coming from both ends of the stadium.'

Two days later, Ball was summoned to Lee's home, despite newspaper reports anticipating the chairman's continued support. 'I always said there was no point us kidding one another,' says Lee. 'And Alan always said, "If I am not doing my job, just tell me and I will be off." We used to call him the "red fox" and I said, "Fox, you better come and see me." He said, "Is it what I think it is?" He came down and we had a chat and I paid him off. He was always appreciative that I treated him well and we were able to remain good friends.'

Dickinson recalls that he and a colleague, the *Daily Mirror*'s Steve Miller, visited Ball's house after the news broke. 'This is journalism as schoolboys, but we basically drew lots about who was going to try to get him out. Steve drew the short straw, knocked on the door and got chased off the premises by his wife, while I hid behind a hedge laughing.'

Ball's biggest challenge in management, at least in terms of the size of the club, had not gone well. 'On paper I am the man who took them down while selling their best players,' he offered in his autobiography – a pretty accurate summation of how history would recall his year in Manchester. 'That is a hell of a statement to live with and it is quite unfair.'

'History treats him a little bit unkindly,' says Brightwell. 'There were things he didn't need to do, but there were a couple of decisions where, if he had got it right, it would have been a totally different story.'

Admittedly, he didn't help himself with signings such as Martin 'Buster' Phillips, a youngster he'd had at Exeter and whom he bought in November 1995 for £500,000. His proclamation that 'he will be the first British £10 million player' did nothing to ease the pressure on the player or convince anyone of the shrewdness of his judgement. Phillips would end up playing only 15 times for City before joining Portsmouth in 1998, for one-hundredth of Ball's predicted fee.

'There was something a bit Keeganesque about Ball,' says Dickinson. 'That same trait of excitability which carried him for a little bit, but needed more depth of thought, more rigour and planning. It was not the easiest job, in the sense that the whole club needed an overhaul, but Ball never felt equipped to reboot the club.'

James argues, 'With Alan Ball, it seemed like every purchase was worse than the player who had been let go. We were downsizing. Whether it was his fault or the chairman's, I don't know. As far as the fans were concerned, it was the manager. I have more sympathy with Franny Lee because he had so many fires he had to put out, but that first managerial appointment was his biggest mistake. The early 1990s were a period where no team dominated and we finished fifth two years running, so our ambition was to qualify for Europe and maybe win a trophy. But suddenly we were regressing. Fans were totally disillusioned by the way our hope had turned into despair. We felt we were a team heading for the top, not heading for relegation.'

Quinn concludes that Lee might have found the perfect manager for City had he taken a look in the mirror. 'Franny probably should have managed the thing himself,' he suggests. 'If he had taken it for a year or two and then brought in Alan Ball maybe things would have worked out better. What he wanted Alan to do he could easily have done himself. Alan got taken away from a kind of a spiritual home at Southampton and exposed to a regime that was in need of a complete reshuffle and a man who should really have done it himself. Alan was the wrong man at the wrong time.'

19

FINAL SCORE

'I should have realised when I went back to Portsmouth the second time how perilous football management was when I went to my office and found my name in chalk on the door. It wasn't that I was bothered about – it was the sponge underneath'

– Alan Ball during one of his after-dinner speeches

SINCE the departure of Alan Ball, Portsmouth had reached the FA Cup semi-finals under Jim Smith in 1992, come close to Premier League promotion a year later, seen plans for a new stadium blocked by the Department of the Environment, and passed from the control of Jim Gregory, suffering from ill health, to his son, Martin. By the beginning of 1998, Terry Venables had been and gone as chairman after briefly owning 51 per cent of Gregory's shares, debts were mounting and crowds were dipping below 7,000. American business-man Vince Wolanin and Pompey fan Brian Howe, the rock singer who once fronted Bad Company, had discussed plans to buy the club and Terry Fenwick was fired as manager.

Ball was no stranger to boardroom upheaval – he'd lived through changes of chairmen at the majority of his clubs – but perhaps he should have heard alarm bells when Howe, despite not yet having tied up his deal, announced Ball's return as manager after a defeat at Oxford United, a result that left Portsmouth bottom of the 24 teams in the First Division, the second tier of the English game. According to the official club history published later that year, 'Gregory was extremely unhappy at having the credit for Ball's appointment being, as he saw it, stolen from him.'

Ball had been contacted by Howe in Barbados and told that the purchase of the club was as good as finalised. Even so, Ball's instinct told him that this was a 'complete no-win situation' and that

Portsmouth's position was irredeemable. Before long, he was called by club director Terry Brady, on behalf of Gregory, confirming that the takeover was imminent and reiterating a desire to have Ball manage the club. Working for Howe was one thing, but serving under the Gregory family again was not something he wanted to consider after his experience of a decade earlier. Yet the pull of the dressing room was strong enough that, with reservations, he allowed himself to be announced as the new boss in February 1998. And then, as someone less impetuous than Ball might have expected, Gregory turned down the Wolanin–Howe offer, retaining his 97 per cent shareholding. 'I was faced with the prospect of working with the son of the father I despised,' Ball lamented.

After a year and a half out of the game, football had undeniably got back under his skin. There were only so many race meetings to attend and foreign holidays to take. A club close to his heart saw him as their salvation, and Ball loved nothing more than being wanted. He agreed to stay until the end of the season, admitting that 'I let my heart rule my head'.

Ball's opening lecture to the team was not, according to the memory of Swedish striker Mathias Svensson, a resounding success. Condemning most English managers as knowing 'diddly squat about football', he said of Ball, 'All the players were just laughing at him. The only thing he had going for him was that he won the World Cup in 1966 as a player.' In the same 2005 interview, however, Svensson dismissed Patrick Vieira as a 'dirty player', called Roy Keane 'psychotic' and labelled William Gallas a 'psychopath', so it might not have been the most considered assessment ever delivered.

It certainly doesn't mesh with the memory of forward John Durnin, who had been at the club since 1993, but had frequently found himself playing out of position. 'Bally was great for me because he allowed me to play up front,' he recalls. 'His first team talk was inspirational. He kept us waiting to go out to training for about an hour and a half while he spoke about the people of Portsmouth and what they expected of us.'

Ball had been here before, of course, invoking the spirit of Portsmouth's sea farers to save its team. 'If you have the right people and the right character around you it works,' says striker Steve

Claridge, who was on loan from Leicester City. 'Alan got everyone together and reiterated what a proud club it was, with a fantastic history. He said, "Be aware of what you are representing when you put your shirt on."'

Andy Steggall, Meridian TV's sports reporter at the time, remembers, 'Alan was a bolt of energy. He wished all of his squad lived within the locale of the ground because if they went out for a pint on Sunday they had to look the fans in the face. If players were from all over the place, they didn't look at the hurt in the fans' eyes or see the joy and how intoxicating that could be. He tapped into that family, that community; something that was so essential and vital to Portsmouth. The town has a huge island mentality. It has always been them against the world.'

Defender Adrian Whitbread adds that 'Alan galvanised the club, the players and supporters', although it still took Portsmouth until their fourth match under Ball to record a win, Claridge scoring his first goal for his hometown team as they beat Stockport County 1–0. Durnin continues, 'For the first few weeks, Bally was trying to get players to do things they couldn't do because they weren't as good as he had been. He was open to senior players like me giving an opinion and I felt we needed to be more direct, knocking the ball forward quickly into the final third and fighting for the ball there. We started to turn things around.'

There were three more clean-sheet victories and the unbeaten run eventually extended to six games as those fans whose support Ball valued so highly created a din of drumming and singing at every match. Yet eight games without a win meant Portsmouth needed six points from their final two fixtures to stay in the First Division, at which point Robbie Pethick, Andy Thomson and Durnin scored in a 3–0 home win against Huddersfield Town. 'We got ourselves into a position where it was in our own hands,' says Durnin, who, at almost 33 years of age, felt Ball's management was adding years to his career. 'He was great with me. He gave me days off and would always ask me how I was feeling; if I was up to it. Sometimes he made me take a day off when I wanted to train.'

On the final weekend of the season, 4,000 Pompey fans followed their team on a trip north to Bradford City's Valley Parade, a ground at which their team had not won for 72 years. 'We went up the day before,' Durnin recalls, 'and all went to a match at Sheffield Wednesday. It was all very relaxed and Alan wanted to distract us from our own game.' Whitbread, who missed the match because of a knee injury, adds, 'The whole squad went up. We used to have a bottle of whisky in the dressing room and used to have a little nip before going out on the pitch. The guys that weren't playing put some of the whisky in a Lucozade bottle, but then we were scared that the players would be drinking out of it on the pitch. I am sure Alan was aware of it.'

Durnin remembers taking the field convinced that Portsmouth would win. 'You just have days sometimes when you feel there is no way you can lose; just like there are some games you know you won't win. Everything went right.'

Andy Steggall, who made the trip to report for Meridian, recalls, 'Because of working in Southampton, Pompey fans always called me a "scummer". At one point I had to take a battery around to the away end for my cameraman and the whole end was chanting "scummer" and the noise was getting louder and angrier. The police were getting twitchy because they didn't know where it was coming from, so I found the copper with the most braid on his shoulder and said, "Serious apologies, it is me. I am the reason. I will give my battery to my cameraman and walk the other way as quickly as I can.'

On the field, buoyed by their pre-game snifter, Portsmouth had the ball in the net early on – Svensson's effort ruled out for handball – and then Bradford hit the woodwork twice in a single attack. But Portsmouth took the lead after 35 minutes when home keeper Gary Walsh made a hash of a clearance and Sammy Igoe was able to square the ball for Durnin to slide into an empty net. Portsmouth withstood pressure either side of half-time and when left-back Matt Robinson pulled the ball back for Igoe to shoot first-time into the roof of the net the visiting fans behind the goal were ready to celebrate survival. Durnin headed in a third goal with 15 minutes remaining, disappearing under a pile of jubilant teammates, and not even a late consolation goal by the home team could change the course of Portsmouth's destiny.

The final whistle brought most of the travelling fans on to the field, lifting their heroes to their shoulders while they tried to rip shirts from their backs as souvenirs. Eventually, the players climbed into the stands and threw articles of equipment to the crowd below while Ball raised both arms to the skies as if giving thanks to a divine force. In future years he would say it was impossible to describe the elation he felt. For now, looking drained and emotional, he told Steggall, 'These people are fantastic. They are great people and I have got a certain amount of love and passion for them. They have pulled our club through when everything looked lost.'

Whitbread continues, 'It was euphoria at the final whistle. It was like winning promotion. People look back at highlights like getting into the Premier League and winning the FA Cup, but this was one of the special moments that memories of a football club are made of. If we had not stayed up, you don't know which way the club would have gone.'

The irony of Stoke City and Manchester City, the clubs where his associations were most painful, both falling out of the division while Portsmouth survived was not lost on Ball, but son Jimmy insists, 'It didn't please him at all that they both went down. He never held animosity towards any club.'

Ball would say later that the achievement of rescuing Portsmouth from relegation meant that 'all the pain of Manchester City had gone away'. Yet discomfort of a different kind was on its way. The club was under mounting financial pressure, the most immediate impact upon Ball being that the £25,000 he had been promised for keeping Portsmouth up failed to materialise.

Early in December, with the club reported to be £5million in debt and losing a further £40,000 a week, Gregory told Ball he had to make the entire squad available for sale. Australian centre-forward John Aloisi was the man likely to attract the highest fee, but Ball responded, 'He isn't my prized asset, he's the chairman's' – a milder version of what he'd told his boss during a blazing row. 'If my phone rings and another manager asks me if a player is for sale, I'll say "no". But if the chairman's phone rings it might be a different story.' Gregory subsequently took a call from Coventry City and struck a deal for £650,000.

'Initially, Alan tried to keep the problems away from the players,' says Whitbread, 'but you become aware of it when you stop getting paid on time, or only part paid, and then the whole squad is made available for transfer. At one game, the players went out for the warm-ups with white T-shirts showing how much they could be bought for, like "50 pence per pound."'

Asked on a daily basis about the potential sale of players, Ball told television reporters that Gregory had assigned that particular role to football agent Athole Still. 'That is the most ridiculous thing I have heard in quite a while,' he argued. 'If managers start ringing this guy up, I will be very surprised. I have stuck up for the football club and I thought he was wanting to sell players for the wrong reasons. I might suffer for that, but if you believe in something you see it through.'

When fans chanted 'Gregory out' and demonstrated on the Fratton Park pitch, Ball voiced his support for them, taking the microphone at the end of one game and assuring them that 'no one is going anywhere'. Unlike at Manchester City, his record of relative success at Portsmouth and his rapport with the supporters – not to mention that he'd had enough of playing the patsy for anyone – emboldened him to say, 'If I have to put my head in the lion's mouth then so be it, but I don't care because he is wrong.'

This time it was Ball who outlasted his chairman. With the Aloisi deal done, Gregory resigned, revealing that he had received death threats against his wife and children. Two months later, the club went into receivership, further negotiation with Wolanin and Howe having failed to produce a sale. Staff were released across all areas of the club, players agreed to forgo win bonuses and were asked to pay for their own boots, while travel expenses were cut to a minimum. Jimmy Ball, coaching the club's youth team, recalls, 'As a coaching staff we had a percentage of our wages taken away because Dad told the adminis-trator, "No one is losing their job, everyone is getting something."'

Kevin Bond, appointed by Ball as first-team coach, adds, 'I remem-ber them taking away Alan's club Mercedes. He just got on with it and, before long, the Mercedes people said they felt sorry for the way it had been dealt with and gave him the use of another one. It was a shame that Alan was always firefighting.' Against this backdrop, Portsmouth managed no better than 19th position in 1998–99, Ball describing his team as 'pathetic, abysmal, gutless and disgraceful' after a Boxing Day defeat at Ipswich Town, although his words did preface an unbeaten run of eight matches.

Claridge, who had finally completed a permanent move to Fratton Park, believes Ball's own part in the team's struggles should not be overlooked. 'I have got to be honest, I had a terrible relationship with him when he was at Portsmouth with me, but a fantastic one when we both left. As a manager, he wasn't very good. He was excellent as a coach, but tactically he wasn't very good. Unfortunately, he had his favourites and if you were a favourite you were fine. If you weren't then it didn't matter how good you were, you were going to struggle. I got goals for him, I did well for him, but for some reason he just pushed me away and I have no idea why. I desperately wanted him to like me. A perfect example was that we had a boy called Rory Allen, who he bought from Tottenham for £1 million. He was always injured. We had both been injured, which meant you trained before the first team, the fit lads. We had done our bit and both sat down, sweating profusely, and he walks out and goes up to Rory and says, "Can't wait to have you back, you are going to be brilliant," – eulogising over him. Then he looked at me and never said a word; just walked away.'

Yet Claridge continues, 'I temper that with that, when we both left the club, we lived quite close to each other and I would see him a lot at various things. I had a benefit game and the fellow absolutely fell over himself to help me. He managed the side and helped me in every way he could.'

With the season over, Milan Mandarić, who had owned the San Jose Earthquakes, Belgian side Charleroi and, most recently, OGC Nice, bought the club. Immediate crisis was averted. The new owner even gave Ball the survival bonus that was a year overdue. Yet it was one extreme to another. While Ball promoted an approach of steady, sensible building, Mandarić, perhaps understandably for a new man in charge, was determined to make a splash and had no patience with bad results, of which there plenty.

Three wins and three draws in the first seven games of the 1999–2000 season hinted at an upturn in fortunes, but by the time Portsmouth lost at Sheffield United in the first week of December they had won only twice more in 15 matches and were down in 20th place, one point above the drop zone. It was Ball's final game in professional football. 'I knew he was getting restless,' he recalled of Mandarić, who fired him five days later.

Meridian TV reported the sacking with a tribute to the departing Ball that closed by describing him as 'the man who saved the club'. Yet the chairman, in a damning indictment of the manager he was dismissing, announced, 'I believe we have a lot of good players, but we don't have a good team yet.' The comment upset Ball, who felt steady progress was being made and had become suspicious of the presence at the club of his former Arsenal teammate, Bob McNab, as the owner's advisor. Yet he recognised the genuine desire Mandarić held for the club to succeed and appreciated his private thanks for all Ball had contributed to the history of Portsmouth and the assurance that Fratton Park would always offer him a warm welcome.

Alan Ball's four-decade career in professional football was done; a World Cup triumph, a League Championship and seven stops on a managerial career that still divides opinion all now a matter for the record books. Little further assessment or endorsement of his playing days is needed beyond the details and tributes contained in the first half of this book. For evidence in motion, YouTube hosts vast amounts of video to bring Ball back to life.

Greater evaluation is required, however, before accepting the widely depicted image of Ball as an unsuccessful manager. His endeavours remain contentious; judged by most according to geography and team loyalties. Former Stoke City player Wayne Biggins, for example, says, 'I have been back there for evenings and dinners and every time you mention Alan you can see the reaction there is, "Whoa!" It is probably unjustified because he was as good as anybody.' Similarly, good luck trying to find a kind word about him, even now, on websites inhabited by Manchester City fans.

Elsewhere, though, Ball was guaranteed a different reaction. 'I was hosting the hospitality rooms at Southampton before he died,' says Lawrie McMenemy. 'The MC would introduce me and a couple of guests and I would talk with them and the punters. The Saturday before he died Alan was my guest. I said, "Well, I have one guest here today, but we don't need any more." They loved him. And it was the same at Portsmouth.'

Ball ended his career being adored by fans of three of the six teams he managed; and of the others, Blackpool supporters forgave him because they still revered him as a player. Outside of the great leaders of his own playing days – Clough, Shankly, Revie, Busby – and giants of the Premier League era, such as Ferguson and Wenger, Ball's approval ratio is not uncommon among managers. It is, after all, a profession where most jobs end in failure and the sack.

His record as a manager amounts to this: a mix of clubs, a mix of divisions, a mix of achievement and failure. A journeyman, if you like, and there is nothing wrong with that. Unless you have conquered the world as a player. Unless your triumphs on the field are the yard-stick against which your future efforts are gauged.

Had they measured up, Ball, winner of 72 caps, would have achieved what no Englishman has ever done. Of the eight former England international players to be champion managers in their home country, none has done it with more caps to his name than Alf Ramsey's 32. None of the 24 players who have played as often for England as Ball has won a major trophy in management. The cliché of the great players not necessarily making great managers is only hackneyed because it is largely true.

As anyone who has studied English football over the past half-century can tell you, the boys of 1966 have become labelled as under-achievers as managers, or bearers of some kind of jinx. Ball actually over-performed in that context. Of the World Cup final line-up, only six managed professionally and only two – Ball and Jack Charlton – ever held permanent positions in the top flight of English football. Widening the sample to the squad of 22 brings the list of those who managed to 11, but adds only Jimmy Armfield to those who did so full-time at the highest level. Charlton, who led the Republic of Ireland to the World Cup quarter-finals, is the only one generally considered to have achieved in management anything remotely approaching what he did on the field. Out of 22 men, only Ball, Charlton and Stiles can honestly be said to have forged a second career in coaching or management, that is to say that they stuck at it for more than 10 years. Most merely dabbled or were overlooked entirely. The 1966 World Cup squad produced more insurance sales-men than international managers; its members going off to post letters, bury the dead and sell fish and chips.

There is an interesting comparison to be made with the next all-new England squad to perform in the World Cup finals, Ron Greenwood's side of 1982. Of their number, 17 took charge of teams in English professional football, with 11 of them managing in the top flight. Even allowing for the advent of greater coaching opportunities, such as specialist goalkeeping roles, the fact that 15 of Greenwood's men forged coaching careers spanning at least a decade, compared to three of Ramsey's, is a stark contrast. The 1982 squad even produced two England managers, Glenn Hoddle and Kevin Keegan.

All of which is to illustrate that if Ball's managerial career can be considered a failure it is only in relation to his previous feats and his own hopes and expectations. History certainly doesn't assume that he should have accomplished more on the basis of his playing record.

Equally, to pretend Ball's management was without flaws would be misleading. Son Jimmy says that management, for his father, was 'a splinter that he couldn't pull out'. In seven managerial engagements in England, only twice did Ball win more competitive matches than he lost, in his first spell at Portsmouth and at Southampton. Throughout this book players have struggled to explain why he didn't win more often, given that many enjoyed working under him, thought him a skilled coach and found him an inspirational figure to play under. The views emanating from Manchester City over the years are not fully representative of the majority offered for this book, even allowing for the nature of biographical research and the reluctance of people to speak ill of the dead.

Some have suggested that Ball, despite his ability as a technical individual coach, could be limited as a tactician. He prepared his players with passion more than he armed them with sophisticated playing patterns, and he failed, as we have seen, to hit upon an alternative strategy at City, for example, when his 'give it to Kinkladze' approach failed. If good players needed extra belief and motivation, Ball could deliver; if what you needed was an intricate game-plan you might have wanted to look elsewhere.

'This is my analogy,' Steve Claridge offers. 'If you were in a trench and you had 300 people against 30,000 and he was with you, that is a perfect situation for him. If he had 30,000 people and was attacking 300 he wouldn't know what to do. He was very good at rousing people, working on emotion. He had the personality and love of the game to be a coach, but as a manager, absolutely not.'

Additionally, Ball's recurring struggle to understand that not everyone could play in the manner he craved created frustrations all round. 'There were clubs where it didn't work out for him and I could probably look at the way he managed and understand why,' says Le Tissier, perhaps the most gifted individual to play under him . . . 'He expected people to be at his level and was asking stuff of players that they weren't capable of.' Yet, ironically, it was the lower, less successful players who responded best to Ball's stature as a World Cup winner, whose respect for him was highest. Further up the ladder of football fame and fortune, he found that it counted for less. You certainly would not have found many at Manchester City echoing McMenemy's testimony that 'the players had to listen to him because they couldn't argue with what he knew and what he had done.' Maybe that is why his best fit was at Portsmouth, where the players were closer to the technical level required to realise his game-plan, yet not so elevated in status that his motivational methods fell on deaf ears.

Another paradox of Ball's managerial efforts was the issue of his 'interpersonal skills', to use the language of modern employment appraisals, although that is an area where individual experience and circumstance makes it difficult to secure an objective view. Micky Quinn suggests, 'I don't think his man management was the best. I think that probably held him back in going on to become a top-class manager.' Others feel differently. Noel Blake, who played for Ball at two clubs, insists, 'I went to Stoke for no other reason than him. I played for him, but I actually loved the fella – and I am not embarrassed to say that – for what he did and how he helped me as a person on and off the field, and how he believed in me.'

Mick Channon Jr, who was released by Ball at Southampton, suggests in his book, *How's Your Dad?*, 'He was brilliant at encouraging young people, inspiring people whom he believed in. It seems strange that he fell out with so many of the established professionals he managed in football, because with youngsters he was as good as anyone I could imagine.'

In other words, if you were at the stage of your career when learning was the most important thing, then you were likely to enjoy an easier relationship with Ball than if you were an experienced player concerned about selection and agitating for profile, playing time and potential financial reward. That is hardly a revelation. The same could be said of most managers. Jimmy Ball points out, 'At least players knew where they stood with him. His heart was on his sleeve and if you needed telling, that was it. But then he would say, "Right, do you want a pint?"'

'When you look back you are surprised he wasn't a better manager,' says Simon Carter, who ghost-wrote newspaper columns with him after he left the game. 'Alan spoke more sense than anyone I have known involved in football. His name carried gravitas, but what he said was invariably correct.'

Yet, to prove how personal perspective can create polar opposite opinions, another journalist, Pat Symes, says, 'God bless him, because as a newspaper man I loved the way he came up with his hyperbole. It was often just nonsense really. He made so many extravagant claims and his judgement of a player was very weird. Harry Redknapp told me he thought Bally was a bad punter; one of those who instinctively go for a horse and didn't think carefully enough about it. He was exactly like that in football.'

Mick Channon – who, when asked what he remembers of his great friend's eye for a horse, calls it 'fucking useless' – is another who saw him making instant assessments. 'Someone would do something good, and he would be very impressed and would immediately like him. The same if they fucked up. He didn't suffer fools.' Symes concludes that Ball 'would make up his mind that some players were excellent and others were not good and there were no grey areas'.

No grey areas. It could perhaps have been the title of this book. It suits Ball's personality and outlook and, typically, reflects how most people remember him as a manager. Some bad, some good; masking a truth that probably resides somewhere in the middle.

An interesting take comes from Kevin Bond, who worked under Ball in various capacities at three clubs, was the son of a successful manager in John Bond, and went on to form a famously close working bond with Harry Redknapp. He believes Ball's most meritorious achievement as a manager doesn't show up in the record books. 'When you become a manager, amid all the pressure, the game changes you,' he states. 'I have seen it with nearly all of the people I have worked with. But in all of that, Alan never lost his perspective, his generosity, his humour or his values.'

Son Jimmy says that 'it is sad that only the failures, if you like, are highlighted when people talk about his management because he had some amazing achievements in his career'. But here's the thing. Two decades of ups and downs as a manager is not what defines him. Ball's other achievements live on more robustly and were the reason for pull-outs in national newspapers and memorials around the country when he died. By retiring as a manager he gave himself back to the nation. He was no longer Alan Ball, manager of 'insert divisive club name here'. He was, once again, Alan Ball, England World Cup hero. He could live with that very happily. Fate, however, had other plans.

20
'P.S. LOOK AFTER YOUR DAD'

'They were so strong together. I think that if Mum was going to die, then he was, too. She would have looked down and said, "You are not doing very well on your own, are you, mate?"'

– Alan Ball's daughter, Keely Allan

THE red hair that marks her out unmistakably as Alan Ball's daughter falls over her face as Keely Allan's head drops to her chest and she warns, 'I am going to get upset now.' For half a minute she gives in to tears before continuing the story of the event that denied her father the happy family retirement that was due to a national hero.

Lesley Ball died on 15 May 2004, three years after being diagnosed with ovarian cancer. The loss of his childhood sweetheart, the woman to whom he had been married for 37 years, broke Ball's heart. Perhaps literally. After three years of washing back and forth on a tide of grief, emotion, hedonism – maybe even self-destruction – Ball collapsed and died in his back garden.

According to journalist Jim White, writing on Ball's death, 'His life seemed to come to an end the day [Lesley] died.' It was that obvious, even to detached observers, how much his world had been torn apart.

Keely's tears arrive while she is describing how her mother relayed her final wishes to the family from her hospital bed. 'One fortunate thing about knowing you are dying is that she was able to say everything to us and to him,' she remembers. 'And she wrote us all a letter, telling us what she wanted.' Each of those notes, written inside identical floral cards, ended with a heartbreaking footnote: 'P.S. Look after your dad.'

He would make it an impossible task.

Ball's life after full-time football had begun with a brief, uplifting, return to the training ground in his country's cause. Shortly after his departure from Portsmouth, he was asked to help out his old friend Kevin Keegan, then in his second year as England manager and preparing for the European Championship finals. According to Jimmy Ball, it was his dad, while assisting at Keegan's England get-together, who first had the prescience to propose David Beckham as a future captain.

More national recognition was on its way – albeit belatedly. After England won back the Ashes in 2005, it took only a few months for their cricketers to be honoured en masse with the award of MBEs. In 2000, five players who had helped to achieve the most famous victory in English sporting history at last followed the remainder of their teammates in making the trip to Buckingham Palace. It had taken 34 years.

While various honours were bestowed upon six of the 1966 World Cup team – including Bobby Charlton and Geoff Hurst's knighthoods – Ball, George Cohen, Roger Hunt, Nobby Stiles and Ray Wilson had gone unrecognised by officialdom. A clamour among various people in football, along with the increasingly populist nature of the Honours Lists, combined to ensure that the unsung heroes finally got to dress up and collect their medals. 'They give them away like buttons now,' says Cohen. 'You look at some and say, "What did he do to deserve that?" Alan was on top form that day, very bubbly. He was making jokes all the time, saying that Nobby couldn't possibly wear morning suit because the tails would drag along the carpet.'

Jimmy Ball calls it 'a proud moment for him, being stood in front of the Queen – up there with winning the World Cup'. But he adds, 'For his family, and I am not ashamed to say it, I think it is a disgrace that they were not all knighted. I know there has been a campaign, but I have been told that my dad and Bobby Moore won't ever be knighted because they only do it posthumously for the military. I have to emphasise that he was never bitter about it. It wasn't in his nature and he was delighted to have an MBE because he loved his country.'[1]

1 Mick Channon recalls an occasion during the Australian summer of 2006–07 that illustrates Ball's great patriotism. 'We had a box for the Test match in Sydney when we lost the Ashes 5–0. Freddie Flintoff was coming to our party one night and Bally said, "Right, Mick. We know what they are going through. They have

With management behind him, Ball appeared happy to remain on the fringes of professional football. He was busy enjoying life in the home he and Lesley had moved into in the southern Hampshire village of Warsash in 1998, a property of which he said, 'After living in 24 different houses throughout my career, this one seemed as if it was telling me to stop the wandering.'

He spent Saturday afternoons working for BBC Radio Solent, where he co-hosted a pre-game phone-in, and had a weekly column in the *Evening Echo*, where Simon Carter, who had been one of the protesting fans when Ball arrived at Exeter, was his ghostwriter. 'We used to go to Bally fairly regularly and then he started doing his column,' Carter explains. 'You could always get him on a good rant about agents and players having too much power. But he didn't come across as an 'in my day' man. His passion for the game shone through – and his love of England. He was worried about too many foreigners in the game and its effect on the England team.'

Asked if he ever got the sense that Ball regretted being out of the game he loved, Carter replies, 'None whatsoever. The feeling was that he was glad. He always said managers needed three years, but Saints were changing managers about every six months.' Ball himself spoke of the 'huge amount of relief' that came with the acceptance that he was done working in football.

Yet Mick Channon believes that the apparent disaffection with modern football was all a front. 'Personally, I don't think that was true,' he argues. 'If someone had offered him another chance, I think he would have taken it. He died at only 61, still a young man.'

Jimmy Ball is of a similar opinion. 'Football is a love affair that never ends. Maybe he knew his stock was such that he wouldn't get another job, so he was guarding against disappointment. He would have been happy just working with kids. Why he wasn't in that role with the England set-up I just don't know. Why weren't all the 1966

---

been up against it, they have had a hard time with the press, so we won't talk cricket." Well, Freddie walked in the door and Bally has gone, "That fucking Pietersen. How can you have him in the team?"' Channon's son, Mick junior, adds, 'We are all looking at Alan and thinking, "What the fuck?" He couldn't stop himself. He was such an England fan.'

lot? You talk about pressure; how about playing against Germany 20 years after the war at Wembley in a World Cup final? No, let's not draw upon that knowledge, that experience.'

If there was one job that Ball would have loved more than any other, it was at Everton. 'He always said he would have run there with a nail in his shoe,' says Jimmy. 'There is a rumour that [Everton chairman] Bill Kenwright called him before David Moyes [in 2002] and no one answered the phone. Upon hearing that story, he was very emotional and was devastated that he didn't pick up the phone that day – if it happened. If he had managed that club, I think it would have been the pinnacle of his football life. It would have eclipsed winning the World Cup.'

Outside of his media work, Ball earned renown as one of the funniest, most fluent after-dinner speakers on the sporting circuit. He also became a patron of British European Soccer Training, a youth coaching programme based in the United States; and, of course, enjoyed days at the racecourse, where a grey gelding called Pic Up Sticks put him back in the winner's enclosure as an owner. He loved getting together with his old football pals, frequently accepting invitations to attend 1966 dinners and cruises, where Sir Alf Ramsey's boys were guests of honour. 'Bally loved those reunions,' says Cohen. 'He filled them with his infectious laugh and was a great fun guy. He never really talked about his management career. It was something he saw as his own problem and when things had gone wrong nobody was to blame but him.'

Then, in the space of a few weeks in the spring of 2001, the core of his happy existence was ripped out. Travelling home from the golf course, Ball took a call from Lesley telling him that Mandy, their elder daughter, who had not long given birth to their first grandson, Louie, had been diagnosed with breast cancer. On the same day, Lesley began suffering from a pain in her groin. While the family focused on Mandy's recovery from an operation to remove a tumour, and preparations for her follow-up sessions of chemotherapy, Lesley – unknown to her husband – began seeing specialists to ascertain the cause of her own discomfort. 'I cannot believe even now that Lesley kept secret all the things that were happening to her,' wrote Ball, who was eventually confronted by the news that his wife had ovarian cancer. 'It was the start of years of helplessness,' he recorded.

"He buried his head in the sand,' says Keely. 'He couldn't face the thought she might not come through.'

The routine of normal life helped to protect him, with Tristan Pascoe, his radio partner, remembering, 'It was a difficult time for him with Lesley being so ill. The show provided a little light relief for him, talking football with his pals. He often came to the studio from her bedside and returned there straight after, and I know the show meant a great deal to him.'

Ball watched with a mixture of helplessness and admiration as chemotherapy and Lesley's own indomitable will pushed her towards, and beyond, a series of family landmarks that became personal challenges. There was a round-the-world trip in early 2003; Keely's wedding to John and the birth of their first child, Jimmy; the marriage of son Jimmy to his own Lesley and the arrival of granddaughter Lacey; seeing Mandy, now recovered, and Jimmy run the London Marathon in aid of the Bobby Moore Fund for Cancer Research.

'She was strong,' Ball recalled. 'She was a battler. There were times when her spirit was simply unbelievable.' Yet one final family holiday in Spain had to be curtailed when Lesley took a turn for the worse. Even her remarkable resolve could not combat the cancer's cruel, relentless march and she died on a spring Saturday in 2004.

'The night before she died, I woke up in the night and drove to the hospital and sat with her,' Jimmy recalls. 'She woke up and panicked and said, "Why are you here? Am I dying" She had this thing about me driving tired, so I said I was driving home to London and had gone in in for a kip. I thought, "She knows." I went home for a while and before I got back she slipped into a coma. We rang everyone. Dad was playing golf, which sounds odd but he was in denial and had kept saying, "She will be fine." And he had made a promise to his friend, who was running this golf day. He ran off the course and turned up at hospital in his golf shoes. Mum came round for two or three minutes and drifted off again and, two or three hours later, she died. As soon as she took her last breath, my dad said, "Come on, let's go. She is not here anymore. She's gone." He ushered us all out the room.'

'Dad sat with her until the end,' says Mandy. 'It was horrendous to see the devastation in his face, while handling your own grief.'

Interviewed after his wife died, Ball said, 'I won't marry again because for Lesley, and for me, our marriage was forever.' Yet it was clear to all that he faced a tough road ahead without her to guide him, as she had done throughout his adult life. 'Losing Lesley hit him hard,' says Channon. 'He was devastated. He was very lonely.'

As long ago as his diary of the 1978–79 season, Lawrie McMenemy had observed, 'Bally needs people a lot more at times than they need him. The worst thing that could happen to him would be to be left on his own. That is probably why he is such a good family man.'

'Mum was just the rock of our family,' says a faltering Mandy, 'and to lose her . . . I can't even talk about it. I ache for her every day. He hated going back to an empty house. He was a lost soul. He said, "Life is never going to be the same again." He couldn't cope.'

Keely continues, 'He wasn't meant to live on his own without her. I remember him getting cross on the phone, saying, "I can't get this damn washing machine to work." He had put the tablet in with the wrapper still on and it had jammed up. When Mum died, he didn't even have a bank card. She did everything financially.'

Mandy relates another painfully sad story. 'Just after Mum died, he took us to Ascot, where he had a horse running. It was a beautiful day and we were all drinking champagne. Dad sat down and someone said, "Alan, what are you wearing?" He didn't have any socks, so he had put on a pair of Mum's pop socks because he didn't know what else to do. He laughed it off, but that really upset me.'

With heavy hearts, Ball's children explain that his way of coping with the family's great loss was, inexplicably, to put an increasing distance between him and those he loved the most. 'He took big holidays,' says Keely, 'going off to Australia and Barbados for three months, totally out of character. Mum was such a driving force and so strong that when she died it pulled us all apart. Me, Mandy and Jimmy got a lot closer, but Dad went. We understand it. He couldn't stand being sat around the table on Sunday without her, but we were all craving that.'

'He was running away,' adds Mandy. 'He couldn't cope with seeing us all together. He couldn't cope being in the same places without Mum. I wrote him a letter when he decided to go to Australia for Christmas. There were things he had done since Mum died that I didn't agree with and he was becoming aloof. I said, "This is hard enough for us as it is; you can't leave us as well." He was slipping away. He rang me and we had a good chat. He said, "I am doing what I can to keep my head above water." It was really sad because we needed him.'

Keely shares similar memories. 'I had a few run-ins with Dad over the last three years of his life. It was purely the emotion of what was happening to us as a family.' Three weeks before he died, as part of 'a very frank and open conversation', Ball apologised and told her, 'I was clasping at straws. I was lost. I didn't know what I was doing and I have made some mistakes. It was just to avoid everything and stop me rattling around on my own.'

Jimmy's verdict is, 'After Mum died, he was on a bit of a mission to live, maybe to die. He was going for it in every sense: trips around the world, the Ashes in Australia, racing in Dubai, going out and drinking. He just wanted to have a great life and he wasn't bothered how long he had. He just wanted to live, and maybe hurry up and die.'

An old school friend of Lesley's, Valerie Beech, shared some of those trips. 'Mum wanted Dad to have another life,' says Keely. 'She would want him to find another companion and he had a few over time. That wasn't a problem; it was the segregation from the family. I remember saying to him, "I remember when you knew all the words to the *Teletubbies* song," because that was the kind of granddad he was. They were great grandparents. After Mum died, that didn't happen and the other grandchildren didn't get as much of that. He couldn't deal with any of that. That first Christmas was just cringe worthy. Bless him, without Mum there were these little presents under the tree. It was heartbreaking. He just didn't know how to deal with it. His way of dealing with it was to go away. Which was fine, we wanted him to do that. But not all the time.'

Three years after Lesley's death, Ball was set to sell the family home in Warsash to move into a rented property close to Channon's racing stables. 'The house was massive and it was Mum's house,' Jimmy recalls. 'I think it was depressing him.'

'The idea,' says McMenemy, 'was that every morning he was going to cycle to the stables to get his fitness back.'

Channon explains, 'He would come up here and take the piss out of me. He would ring and say he was passing and he used to love to come and watch the horses. We would watch the two-year-olds, have a bit of lunch in the pub down the road. It was a way of life. He was moving into the next village in East Ilsley. It was close to the motorway and it meant he could easily get to wherever he wanted. The night before he died, he called me at about six and said, "Mick, this moving house is the hardest thing I have ever done in my life." Lesley had always done everything for him.'

Mick junior continues, 'The day before he died, I'd helped him move some stuff in; some furniture and his player-of-the-year trophies.' One thing that had not been among the remaining memorabilia was Ball's World Cup medal. He had auctioned that for £164,000 at Christie's in 2005, along with the related England cap, which had fetched £43,200. 'I have three children and three grandchildren,' he'd explained. 'The most important thing for me is to make sure they are looked after as well as possible.'

Keely admits to mixed feelings about her father's proposed move. 'He could have gone to see Mick in the mornings and it would have been good for him, but the time we would have had with him would have been even less. That whole segregation after Mum died, we struggled with it, and now we all had young children and didn't have that family thing.'

The move never happened. Alan Ball died in the final minutes of 24 April 2007, the second member of the 1966 World Cup team to lose his life, following Bobby Moore's death from cancer in 1993. In preparation for changing home, he had lit a bonfire in his garden that day to dispose of some rubbish and was getting ready for bed in the belief that it had burned itself out. 'I had spoken to him that evening,' says Jimmy. 'A short conversation about football. He had been raving about a Paul Scholes pass that set up a goal for Manchester United in the Champions League. We had a short chat, said "love you" and that was it.'

'We all spoke to him the night he died,' adds Keely. 'I had one of the best conversations I'd had for ages. We had organised a van because he was moving and I said, "See you in the morning," and he said, "Love you, Princess." He was happy and affectionate.'

With midnight approaching, Ball noticed that the embers of his bonfire had reignited and there was a danger of the garden fence catching fire. He rushed outside and, while attempting to douse the flames, suffered a fatal heart attack. 'I laugh about it now,' Jimmy admits. 'Any other person would phone the fire brigade. Not him. He had a bucket and a jug from the kitchen and he was running up and down from the fire to the tap. He had worn out a strip in his garden. I can hear him talking to himself, saying, "Come on. You can win this." It tickles me. There was a hose around the corner and he knew it was there because he loved his garden. Mental.'

Ball was discovered after neighbours, seeing the fire growing and receiving no reply from his house, telephoned the fire brigade. 'The firemen were about to leave,' Jimmy continues. 'They had put the fire out and found him on the ground in the dark.' The smashed nose and bruising around the eyes helped to establish that Ball had lost consciousness immediately, unable to break his fall. 'I asked the coroner if he'd been lying there dying,' Jimmy adds, 'and he said he would have been dead before he hit the ground.'

The greater question that his children continue to ask themselves was whether Ball had any inkling that time was running out on his own life. 'Mum had even started getting a bit worried about him before she died and was trying to get him to lose weight,' says Mandy, while Jimmy adds, 'There are indications that he potentially knew, when you look back at that three years he had after Mum died.'

Meanwhile, it was Mandy who received the call from the police and summoned family and close friends. Keely admits, 'I freaked a bit. I was screaming at the police, "How do you know it was even him?" They said, "Because he's Alan Ball."' Once the family had gathered, they contacted friends in the media to help announce the story that would dominate the news over the next 24 hours. Andy Steggall, who had covered Ball's managerial career at Southampton and Portsmouth for Meridian TV and was a regular Sky Sports News presenter, remembers Jimmy phoning at 6am and telling him, 'Dad really respected you. I think we need you here with us.'

Steggall continues, 'What a way to find out what Bally thought of you. While he was thoroughly lovely and we got on famously, that was not the way you wanted to find out you were held in that kind of esteem. I remember walking through the door of the house, and there was his golf bag and his sweater hung over it because he was obviously going to be playing golf that morning. I went further into the house and there is the family and Sky Sports talking about the death of Alan Ball. It was the most surreal and saddest experience. I was hit by the enormity of what happens when you are on the receiving end of being close to someone so famous, so acclaimed and the publicity that comes your way. As a journalist, I had been on the outside of that, throwing stuff out on air.

'How Jimmy had the forethought to call me, or anyone, was extraordinary. It must have been the most appalling time for him, but he had the wherewithal to say, "We need someone here because it is going to come at us." I phoned Meridian, Sky and BBC and explained that Jimmy didn't want to do interview after interview, so would they be happy if I sat down and did one interview with him?'

What happened next brought back poignant memories for Steggall, who had been in the same situation after Lesley's death three years earlier. 'Alan did an interview with me and I barely breathed because of what he said and how he said it. If I had breathed, I might have broken the moment. Now, blimey, I am in the same damn place again and Jimmy has to go through it. I don't know how they summoned the courage, but it was a requirement in their mind to do this well. It was like an obligation as leader of the family; that homegrown, deep-rooted family thing. It was appalling for them, but with some bloke from the TV and a light on you, the interview had to be fulfilled in honour and respect to the person who had died. It was extraordinary, a very powerful feeling. Where did that strength come from? How many people could do that? You knew Jimmy was in a state of shock and you were painfully aware that he knew that whatever he said would have to stand afterwards. You wanted to make sure he was happy with what he said. He was incredible.'

Keely adds, 'Jimmy was amazing. He sat there and spoke and how he did it I will never know.' Her brother's commitments were not yet over, however. Jimmy continues, 'Several hours later, when we had all cleared our heads, we went out and I addressed the press. I can't remember what I said. All I remember is putting on a suit and then putting on Dad's favourite tie. It was a crazy thing to think about at a time like that.'

While media and fans – bearing tributes of shirts, flowers and photos – had been gathering outside the Ball home, those closest to him had been receiving the shocking news. 'Jimmy phoned me,' recalls Mick Channon junior. 'He didn't phone my dad because he didn't want to be the one to tell him.' McMenemy was another on Jimmy's call list. 'He said, "It's Jimmy here. My dad's dead." I thought I was dreaming. That day, would you believe it, Alan, Hughie Fisher and I were going to be playing a charity golf tournament for Wessex Heartbeat.'

Joe Royle remembers, 'I was doing a day skipper's badge on the Mersey when my wife called and told me the news. I couldn't believe it. I just turned off the phone and I lost a day of my life. It was pretty damn horrible.' Former colleague Kevin Bond adds, 'He was such a vibrant character, loving life. He thought of everything in terms of football and I remember him saying, "I reckon I have four World Cups left," meaning he thought he would last about another 16 years. I loved him.'

While fans around the country gave their own tributes over the next few days via minutes of applause at football grounds, others had the opportunity to put their memories into print. Everton chairman Bill Kenwright wrote in the club's next programme:

He didn't just epitomise everything that is good about our great football club, but also everything that is good about those sportsmen who achieve the elusive goal of reaching the very top of their chosen profession whilst somehow managing to retain a sense of humility, honesty and integrity. Alan Ball was special because anyone who came into contact with him was treated with great courtesy and anyone who knew him loved him.

Sir Bobby Charlton restated his argument that Ball was 'a sensational little player with great touch and vision', while Sir Alex Ferguson said, 'He was a fantastic footballer, but more than that he was a fantastic person.' Even Theo Walcott, who had not long moved from Southampton to Arsenal, recalled being coached by Ball as a young teenager. 'His enthusiasm for the game was obvious and I just tried to pick up on that,' he said.

A week after his death, Ball's funeral was held at Winchester Cathedral. Among almost 2,000 people inside the building were figures from the full chronology of his football life, from World Cup and club colleagues to opponents, those who played under him and others who simply wanted to pay their respects. The likes of Sir Bobby Charlton, Gordon Banks and Matt Le Tissier shared pews with then England manager Steve McClaren and Sir Alex Ferguson, who had flown back from Milan for the service. Outside, speakers were set up so that thousands of fans, decked out in a range of colours from Ball's career, could hear the proceedings.

According to Mandy, 'He'd always said that when he went we should just put him in the cheapest box we could find and burn him. He didn't want any fuss.' But the public demanded much more than that.

'I got a call from the chief of police,' Jimmy explains, 'asking where we were thinking of holding the funeral. I told him we were going to do it at the local church and he said, "You can't. We have had thousands of enquiries. It either needs to be Romsey Abbey or Winchester Cathedral." That is when me and the girls realised this was not normal. Then Sky and BBC started contacting us. Driving there, I am thinking that no one is going to be there, that people are not going to take a day off work and stand here. Then we hit the outskirts of Winchester and it was unbelievable. We still cannot believe the amount of people there. For me and the girls it is an amazing memory of a day that should be so painful. All this for my little old dad. It blew our minds. He would have had no clue whatsoever. If he'd been looking down on it he would have been absolutely gobsmacked.'

'Over the Rainbow' and 'Abide With Me' featured among the musical selections, while Nobby Stiles, Ball's 1966 roommate, was the first to speak. A tearful Frank McLintock thanked his old colleague 'for the contribution to our lives'. Leading the service, the Reverend Canon Michael St John-Channell reminded the congregation that Ball 'tucked into his life many things we only dream of'. Jimmy spoke on behalf of his sisters when he said that 'we have been very fortunate to have a mother and father as great as ours', before reading Rudyard Kipling's *If*. 'He loved the poem,' Jimmy confirms, 'especially the bits about walking with kings and not losing the common touch, and losing it all and not speaking about your loss. It encapsulated him.'

As a nod to Ball's great love of crooners such as Frank Sinatra, Nat King Cole and Tony Bennett, 'My Way' was played as the coffin exited the cathedral, after which Mandy, Keely and Jimmy made their way out to the mourners. 'We walked round the perimeter and shook hands,' says Keely. 'This old lady with two tears bobbed in her eyes said, "Your dad drove 400 miles to push over some pennies for my charity and he never asked for anything."'

Mandy reflects, 'I never realised how famous he was until he died. I can never look at Winchester Cathedral without remembering us in the car with a police escort and all the people there.'

The following day, the family held a private cremation, after which Alan's ashes were scattered along with Lesley's. But that was far from the end of it. The tributes kept coming. Books of condolence arrived at the family home, via everywhere from supporters clubs to the customers at Asda in the Walton district of Liverpool. So, too, did hundreds of letters, many addressed simply to 'the family of Alan Ball', trusting that the post office would know where to deliver them.

Some of those messages were tributes from afar, others were personal memories of how Ball had briefly touched people's lives, like the lady from Yorkshire who recalled him knocking on her door in Blackpool two nights after the World Cup victory because his team-mates had hidden his car keys as a prank. Others recalled purchasing white boots, or crying when Ball was sold by Everton to Arsenal. One remembered seeing Alan Ball senior marching purposefully along the road with little Alan trotting behind him, struggling to keep up as he maintained control of the ball at his feet. Ten years after his death, notes and photographs continue to drop through the letterbox, or are posted online on sites such as the Alan Ball Appreciation Society page on Facebook.

Writing in the *Liverpool Echo*, Ken Rodgers argued, 'There are footballers. There are heroes. There are legends. And then we have the immortals.' Of course, he was referring to Alan Ball. And he was not wrong.

During a year of researching this book, I attended Ball's introduction to the National Football Museum's Walk of Fame; saw a play celebrating his life; witnessed the award of a community service honour in his name; joined his family for a presentation at Blackpool

FC; and followed discussion of a statue of him, Colin Harvey and Howard Kendall being put up outside Goodison Park. Ball's daughter and grandson played key roles in the FA's official 50th anniversary celebration of the World Cup victory, although hopes of a memorial match at Everton remained unresolved at the time of writing. Others continue to remember Ball in their own way.

'In 1996, I dreamed up the idea of a footballers' golf classic,' says former Arsenal teammate Terry Mancini, who went on to achieve success in the sports travel industry. 'We held it in La Manga and Bally used to love coming. He was always top of my list. He was brilliant company and a competitive little bugger. Our practice round was always some kind of competition and when he died I asked Jimmy if I could put up a cup for the practice round and call it the Alan Ball Trophy. All the footballers want to get their name on it. They loved him as much as I did.'

When I interviewed Mick Channon for this book, he finished by throwing a final look in the direction of the photo of Ball that sits behind his desk and sighed, 'He left us wanting more, that's for sure.' The fact that we have all heard family and friends say similar things about departed loved ones made it no less poignant and painful.

Had Ball himself known he was departing at the age of 61, his only regret would have been for the years that would remain unlived; the occasions he would miss, however painful they had become since the loss of Lesley; the grandchildren who would only ever know him through photo albums and YouTube clips. He could have held no regrets about the years he had spent on this earth; the family he had nurtured and the fact that he had given everything to the game he loved. He had lived in the same way that he had played, leaving nothing out on the pitch, no cause for regrets over actions never taken.

Few in football can point to a contribution such as Ball's. He will forever be a part of an achievement that hastened his nation's awakening to the fact that the sport could be a communal, unifying event, in the manner of coronations and conclusions of wars. In the winning of the 1966 World Cup was the genesis of the fan zones and packed public houses that have come to characterise England matches in major tournaments, the beginning of an appreciation that the power of football extends far beyond the touchlines and the terraces. Timed perfectly in the wake of George Best breaking down the barriers between sport and celebrity, the victory that Ball did so much to realise saw football embark upon its acceleration from Saturday afternoon obsession to round-the-clock cultural phenomenon.

For that – and through the words of Kenneth Wolstenholme; and the fans who share videos and photographs in his memory; and through the monuments and memorials; even the debates about his management – Alan Ball remains a part of our national sport and our national history, his spirit and legacy as bright as those white boots.

ACKNOWLEDGEMENTS

The story of a character as vivid as Alan Ball is an amalgam of many people's experiences and memories. Thanks, therefore, is due to all with whom I have discussed his life and times, either specifically for this book or for one of my previous titles, most notably those about Arsenal and the North American Soccer League: Jimmy Armfield, David Armstrong, Jack Ashurst, Nicky Banger, Geoff Barnett, Wayne Biggins, Noel Blake, Kevin Bond, Ian Brightwell, Steve Burtenshaw, Simon Carter, Mick Channon, Mick Channon Jr, Martin Chivers, Steve Claridge, George Cohen, Dave Cooper, Carl Davenport, Christopher Davies, Stuart Dawe, Matt Dickinson, Kevin Dillon, Tommy Docherty, Alan Durban, John Durnin, Hugh Fisher, Gerry Francis, Ronny Goodlass, George Graham, Bruce Grobbelaar, Ray Hankin, Paul Hardyman, Wayne Harrison, Kevin Hector, Brian Hewitt, Mark Higgins, Colin Hill, Dave Hockaday, Norman Hunter, Sir Geoff Hurst, John Hurst, Jimmy Husband, Gary Imlach, Gary James, Glyn James, Kevin Keegan, Eddie Kelly, Mick Kennedy, Roger Kenyon, Alan Knight, Peter Lawson, James Lawton, Francis Lee, Matt Le Tissier, Steve Lomas, Neil Maddison, Terry Mancini, Barrie Martin, Roy McFarland, Frank McLintock, Lawrie McMenemy, Bob McNab, Dave Merrington, Steve Moran, Willie Morgan, Alan Mullery, Sammy Nelson, Graham Oates, Kenny O'Connell, Bobby Parry, Tristan Pascoe, David Peach, Derek Possee, Micky Quinn, Niall Quinn, John Radford, Joe Royle, Jon Sammels, Lee Sandford, Peter Simpson, Andy Steggall, Peter Storey, Fred Street, Kenny Swain, Pat Symes, Dale Tempest, Derek Temple, Alan Tonge, Paul Trevillion, Tony Waiters, Colin Waldron, Adrian Whitbread, Trevor Whymark, Bob Wilson, plus the late John Best, Graham Taylor and Phil Woosnam.

I was fortunate to have interviewed Alan Ball for previous books and found him to be engaging and helpful. It is his how the majority of people remember him – but not all. In football, as in life, no one will get along with everyone and Ball attracted his fair share of professional detractors, critics and those who simply didn't get on with him, including some teammates and those who played under his management. He once admitted, 'If you're passionate about something, then I'm afraid you're going to make a few enemies as well as friends.' It has been instructive as a biographer to note those who politely declined my request for an interview or left emails, text messages and phone calls unanswered.

Family was the area of Alan Ball's life of which he most proud and I would never have set off on my journey through his rich existence without the support of those closest to him: daughter Mandy Byrne, husband David and sons Louie and Freddie; daughter Keely Allan, husband John and sons Jimmy and Mack; and son Jimmy, wife Lesley and daughters Lacey and Bo. In thanking them I should acknowledge that their greatest gift was the freedom to write what I wanted and to encourage interviewees to say what they liked; such was their interest in having Ball's story told and their confidence that his achievements, personality and legacy would speak for themselves. Mandy, Keely, Jimmy and Ball's sister, Carol Cooke, gave their own time generously for interviews, and Keely, in particular, deserves special mention for the role she played in helping this project come together.

The roll call of others who have helped in a variety of ways is extensive and by producing it here I run the risk of missing someone out. But here goes: Paul Addison, Bobby Barnes, Georgie Bingham, Ben Cardwell, Ian Cheeseman, John Cross, Simon Crosse, Anthony Husband, Pat Labone, Josephine Long, Bob Lowe, Paul Mace, Pete Maxwell, Mel McCarthy, Mark Mothershaw, James Motley, William Nelson, Jake Payne, Nick Pike, Adam Pope, Rob Pritchard, Ian Rigby, Richard Smith, Tony Stevens, Colin Sutton, Mike Thew, Ben Thompson, Mike White, Jon Wyse, and the staffs at the National Football Museum, Blackpool Central Library, the British Library and West Ilsley Stables.

The bibliography that follows will identify those publications that have been of the greatest value in my research. My gratitude is due to all those authors and journalists. Also of great help was the amount of written material Ball himself delivered over the years. As well as autobiographical volumes, there were several years' worth of weekly columns in *Shoot!* and various pieces penned in his name for the *Alan Ball International Soccer Annual* and other publications. Even allowing for the uncontroversial ghostwritten nature of those articles, they have been useful in shedding light on Ball's reactions to the events of his life and, therefore, an enlightening source of reference.

Thank you, also, to the author of the poem whose extract kicks off this book. It was sent to the Ball family – they believe by a Portsmouth fan – shortly after Ball's death, although attempts to identify and track down the author have so far proved fruitless. We will happily rectify this in future editions.

My agent, David Luxton, needs no introduction to anyone who regularly reads the acknowledgements sections of sports books. His guidance and expertise has been a cornerstone of this endeavour and my thanks go to everyone at David Luxton Associates. It has been a privilege and a thrill to work with a publishing legend in Roddy Bloomfield at Hodder & Stoughton, along with his colleagues, Karen Geary, Jasmine Marsh, Fiona Rose and others. Thank you for making me feel so welcome. Thank you, too, to an old friend, Richard Whitehead, for being such a sensitive copy editor.

My daughters, Amy, Sarah, Laura and Karis, have no knowledge of the people I write about, but always express their pride whenever a new book comes out. It is nothing compared to my pride in them.

Over the years, my wife, Sara, has been forced to share me with battle-scarred rugby veterans; cricketers of both sexes and various ages; and footballers about whom I have become boyishly excited at the thought of interviewing. I realised how deeply I had become immersed in my latest subject when I noticed, just in time, that I had signed an email to someone 'Alan Ball'. The initials FAB, which as a lifelong *Thunderbirds* fan I hold dear, have come to have a whole new meaning in our house over the past year or so. That Sara has said them in a light-hearted manner as often as with exasperation says everything about the love and support she gives me, and which I can never possibly repay.

Finally, I dedicate this book to my mum, Eileen, and my late father, Ron, who never batted an eyelid and simply handed over the cash when I told them I needed some Alan Ball white boots in the autumn of 1971. Look what you started.

PHOTO ACKNOWLEDGEMENTS

The author and publisher would like to thank the following for permission to reproduce photographs:

Mirrorpix, PA/PA Archive/PA Images, Gerry Cranham/Offside, Mirrorpix, Rolls Press/Popperfoto/Getty Images, PA/PA Archive/PA Images, Gerry Cranham / Offside, Popperfoto/Getty Images, Gerry Cranham/Offside, Evening New/REX/Shutterstock, Colorsport, Peter Pittilla/Associated Newspapers/REX/Shutterstock, Mirrorpix, Colorsport, Peter Robinson/EMPICS Sport, Mirrorpix, Paul Popper/Popperfoto/Contributor/Getty Images, Colorsport, Mirrorpix, Colorsport, John Varley/Offside, Mirrorpix, Les Lee/Stringer/Getty Images, Peter Robinson/EMPICS Sport, Associated Newspapers/REX/Shutterstock, Colorsport, Paul Trevellion Collection, Colorsport, PA Images/PA Archive/PA Images, Geoffrey White / Daily Mail /REX/Shutterstock, Mirrorpix, Colorsport, PA/PA Archive/PA Images, Mark Leech/Offside, Phil O'Brien/EMPICS Sport, Mark Leech/Offside, Steve Morton/EMPICS Sport, Allstar Picture Library/Alamy, Mike Egerton/EMPICS Sport, Colorsport, Andy Heading/EMPICS Sport, Paul Marriott/EMPICS Sport, Paul Marriott/EMPICS Sport, Jamie McDonald/Staff/Getty Images, Jeremy Selwyn / Evening Standard /REX/Shutterstock, Gareth Fuller/PA Archive/PA Images, Mirrorpix.

All other photographs are from private collections.

BIBLIOGRAPHY

Armfield, Jimmy, *The Autobiography: Right Back to the Beginning* (Headline, 2004)

Bagchi, Rob and Paul Rogerson, *The Unforgiven: The Story of Don Revie's Leeds United* (Aurum Press, 2002)

Ball, Alan, *Ball of Fire* (Pelham Books, 1967)

Ball, Alan, *It's All About a Ball* (WH Allen, 1978)

Ball, Alan with James Mossop, *Playing Extra-Time* (Sidgwick & Jackson, 2004)

Banks, Gordon, *Banksy: The Autobiography* (Michael Joseph, 2002)

Barnes, Ken with Jimmy Wagg, *This Simple Game: The Footballing Life of Ken Barnes* (Empire Publications, 2005)

Berman, John and Malcom Dome, *Everton Greats: Where Are They Now?* (Mainstream, 1997)

Book, Tony and David Clayton, *Maine Man: The Tony Book Story* (Mainstream, 2004)

Brady, Liam, *So Far So Good: A Decade in Football* (Stanley Paul, 1980)

Brooking, Trevor with Michael Hart, *My Life in Football* (Simon & Schuster, 2014)

Calley, Roy, *Blackpool: The Complete Record* (Derby Books, 2011)

Carter, Simon, *Gus Honeybun, Your Boys Have Taken One Hell of a Beating* (Pitch Publishing, 2016)

Channon, Mick Jr, *How's Your Dad? Embracing Failure in the Shadow of Success* (Racing Post Books, 2016)

Charlton, Sir Bobby with James Lawton, *1966: My World Cup Story* (Yellow Jersey Press, 2016)

Charlton, Jack with Peter Byrne, *The Autobiography* (Partridge Press, 1996)

Cohen, George, *My Autobiography* (Greenwater Publishing, 2003)

Dawson, Jeff, *Back Home: England and the 1970 World Cup* (Orion, 2001)

Dickinson, Matt, *Bobby Moore: The Man in Full* (Yellow Jersey Press, 2014)

Edghill, Richard and Dante Friend, *Once a Blue, Always a Blue* (Pitch Publishing, 2014)

Endacott, Robert, *Disrepute: Revie's England* (Tonto Books, 2010)

France, David, *Everton Crazy* (Gwladys Street's Hall of Fame, 2016)

Gregory, John with Martin Swain, *The Boss: Out of the Shadows* (Andre Deutsch, 2000)

Harrison, Paul, *Keep Fighting: The Billy Bremner Story* (Black and White Publishing, 2010)

Hughes, Emlyn, *Crazy Horse* (Arthur Baker, 1980)

Hunter, Norman with Don Warters, *Biting Talk: My Autobiography* (Hodder & Stoughton, 2004)

Hurst, Geoff, *1966 and All That: My Autobiography* (Headline, 2001)

Imlach, Gary, *My Father and Other Working Class Football Heroes* (Yellow Jersey Press, 2005)

James, Gary, *Manchester: The City Years* (James Ward, 2012)

Jeffs, Peter, Colin Farmery and Richard Owen, *Portsmouth Football Club: The Official Centenary Pictorial History* (Bishops Printers, 1998)

Keegan, Kevin, *My Autobiography* (Little, Brown and Company, 1997)

Keith, John and Colin Harvey, *Colin Harvey's Everton Secrets* (Trinity Media Sports Media, 2005)

Kendall, Howard, *Love Affairs and Marriage: My Life in Football* (De Coubertin Books, 2013)

Law, Denis with Bob Harris, *The King: My Autobiography* (Bantam Press, 2003)

Macdonald, Malcolm with Colin Malam, *Supermac: My Autobiography* (Highdown, 2003)

McKinstry, Leo, *Sir Alf: A Major Reappraisal of the Life and Times of England's Greatest Football Manager* (HarperSport, 2006)

McLintock, Frank with Rob Bagchi, *True Grit: The Autobiography* (Headline, 2005)

McMenemy, Lawrie, *A Lifetime's Obsession: My Autobiography* (Trinity Mirror Sports Media, 2016)

McMenemy, Lawrie, *The Diary of a Season* (Arthur Baker, 1979)

Miller, David, *England's Last Glory: The Boys of '66* (Pavilion, 1986)

Mingle, Steve, *Lows, Highs and Balti Pies: Manchester City Ruined My Diet* (History Press, 2011)

Mingle, Steve, *When England Ruled the World: Four Years That Shaped the Modern Game* (Pitch Publishing, 2016)

Moore, Tina, *Bobby Moore: by the Person who Knew Him Best* (Collins Willow, 2005)

Morgan, Willie with Simon Wadsworth, *On the Wing: My Autobiography* (Trinity Mirror Sports Media, 2013)

Mourant, Andew and Jack Rollin, *The Essential History of England* (Headline, 2002)

Mullery, Alan, *The Autobiography* (Headline, 2007)

Neill, Terry, *Revelations of a Football Manager* (Sidgwick & Jackson, 1985)

Peters, Martin with Michael Hart, *The Ghost of '66: The Autobiography* (Orion, 2006)

Powell, Jeff, *Bobby Moore: The Authorised Biography* (Everest Books, 1976)

Quinn, Niall, *Head First: The Autobiography* (Headline, 2002)

Reedie, Euan, *Alan Shearer: Portrait of a Legend* (John Blake, 2006)

Rösler, Uwe, *My Autobiography: Knocking Down Walls* (Trinity Mirror Sports Media, 2003)

Ross, Ian and Gordon Smailes, *Everton: A Complete Record* (Breedon Books, 1988)

Royle, Joe, *The Autobiography* (BBC Books, 2005)

Sandbrook, Dominic, *State of Emergency: The Way We Were: Britain, 1970–74* (Allen Lane, 2010)

Sawyer, Rob, *Harry Catterick: The Untold Story of a Football Great* (De Coubertin Books, 2014)

Shindler, Colin, *Fathers, Sons and Football* (Headline, 2001)

Stiles, Nobby with James Lawton, *After the Ball: My Autobiography* (Hodder & Stoughton, 2003)

Storey, Peter, *True Storey: My Life and Crimes as a Football Hatchet Man* (Mainstream, 2010)

Taylor, Rogan and Andrew Ward, *Kicking and Screaming: An Oral History of Football in England* (Robson Books, 1996)

Taylor, Rogan and Andrew Ward with John Williams, *Three Sides of the Mersey: An Oral History of Everton, Liverpool and Tranmere* (Robson Books, 1993)

Ternent, Stan and Tony Livesey, *Stan the Man: A Hard Life in Football* (Blake Publishing, 2003)

Tossell, David, *Bertie Mee: Arsenal's Officer and Gentleman* (Mainstream, 2005)

Tossell, David, *Playing for Uncle Sam: The Brits' Story of the North American Soccer League* (Mainstream, 2003)

Turner, Alwyn W, *Crisis? What Crisis? Britain in the 1970s* (Aurum, 2008)

Vacher, Nigel and Ted MacDougall, *Macdou-Goal! The Ted MacDougall Story* (Pitch Publishing, 2016)

Westcott, Chris, *Joker in the Pack: The Ernie Hunt Story* (Tempus, 2004)

Wilson, Jonathan, *The Anatomy of England: A History in Ten Matches* (Orion, 2010)

Wilson, Jonathan, *Brian Clough: Nobody Ever Says Thank You* (Orion, 2011)

Winter, Henry *Fifty Years of Hurt: The Story of England Football and Why We Never Stop Believing* (Bantam Press, 2016)

Annuals (various years)

Alan Ball's International Soccer Annual, The Arsenal Football Book, Charles Buchan's Soccer Gift Book, Goal Annual, Rothman's Football Yearbook, Shoot Annual, Topical Times Football Book

Magazines and periodicals

Charles Buchan's Football Monthly, Goal, Match Weekly, Shoot!, Soccer Star, When Saturday Comes

Newspapers

Blackpool Gazette, Daily Express, Daily Mail, Daily Mirror, Daily Telegraph, Exeter Express and Echo, the Guardian, the Independent, Liverpool Daily Post, Liverpool Evening Echo, Manchester Evening News, Portsmouth News, Southern Evening Echo, Stoke Sentinel, the Sun, Sunday Express, Sunday Mirror, The Times

STATISTICS

CLUB APPEARANCES

	Played	Goals
Ashton United		
1960-61	7	1
Blackpool		
1962-63	5	0
1963-64	34	14
1964-65	42	13
1965-66	45	17
Everton		
1966-67	51	18
1967-68	40	20
1968-69	49	18
1969-70	41	12
1970-71	55	9
1971-72	18	3
Arsenal		
1971-72	27	5
1972-73	51	14
1973-74	40	13
1974-75	38	10
1975-76	42	9
1976-77	20	1
Hellenic (Loan)		
1976-77	4	*
Southampton		
1976-77	29	2
1977-78	48	5
1978-79	56	3
1979-80	28	1
Philadelphia Fury (Loan)		
1978	25	5
1979	8	0
Vancouver Whitecaps		
1979	15	8
1980	16	2
Blackpool		
1980-81	38	5
Southampton		
1980-81	10	0
1981-82	47	1
1982-83	16	1
Floreat Athena (Loan)		
1982	3	2
Eastern AA		
1982-83	12	*
Bristol Rovers		
1983-84	17	2
Totals	**977**	**214***

* Unknown

GAME	DATE	OPPOSITION	VENUE	COMPETITION	RESULT	NOTES
1	09-May-65	Yugoslavia	Belgrade	Friendly	Drew 1-1	Full debut
2	12-May-65	West Germany	Nuremburg	Friendly	Won 1-0	
3	16-May-65	Sweden	Gothenburg	Friendly	Won 2-1	First England goal
4	08-Dec-65	Spain	Madrid	Friendly	Won 2-0	
5	05-Jan-66	Poland	Goodison Park	Friendly	Drew 1-1	Home debut
6	23-Feb-66	West Germany	Wembley	Friendly	Won 1-0	Wembley debut
7	02-Apr-66	Scotland	Hampden Park	BC	Won 4-3	
8	26-Jun-66	Finland	Helsinki	Friendly	Won 3-0	
9	03-Jul-66	Denmark	Copenhagen	Friendly	Won 2-0	
10	05-Jul-66	Poland	Chorzow	Friendly	Won 1-0	
11	11-Jul-66	Uruguay	Wembley	WCF	Drew 0-0	
12	23-Jul-66	Argentina	Wembley	WCF	Won 1-0	
13	26-Jul-66	Portugal	Wembley	WCF	Won 2-1	
14	30-Jul-66	West Germany	Wembley	WCF	Won 4-2 AET	Youngest in team
15	22-Oct-66	Northern Ireland	Windsor Park	BC/ECQ	Won 2-0	
16	02-Nov-66	Czechoslovakia	Wembley	Friendly	Drew 0-0	
17	16-Nov-66	Wales	Wembley	BC/ECQ	Won 5-1	
18	15-Apr-67	Scotland	Wembley	BC/ECQ	Lost 2-3	First England defeat
19	24-May-67	Spain	Wembley	Friendly	Won 2-0	
20	27-May-67	Austria	Vienna	Friendly	Won 1-0	2nd goal
21	21-Oct-67	Wales	Ninian Park	BC/ECQ	Won 3-0	Penalty, 3rd goal
22	06-Dec-67	USSR	Wembley	Friendly	Drew 2-2	4th goal
23	24-Feb-68	Scotland	Hampden Park	BC/ECQ	Drew 1-1	
24	03-Apr-68	Spain	Wembley	ECQ	Won 1-0	
25	08-May-68	Spain	Madrid	ECQ	Won 2-1	
26	01-Jun-68	West Germany	Hannover	Friendly	Lost 0-1	
27	05-Jun-68	Yugoslavia	Florence	ECF Semi-Final	Lost 0-1	
28	06-Nov-68	Romania	Bucharest	Friendly	Drew 0-0	
29	15-Jan-69	Romania	Wembley	Friendly	Drew 1-1	
30	03-May-69	Northern Ireland	Windsor Park	BC	Won 3-1	
31	07-May-69	Wales	Wembley	BC	Won 2-1	

32	10-May-69	Scotland	Wembley	BC	Won 4-1	
33	01-Jun-69	Mexico	Mexico City	Friendly	Drew 0-0	
34	08-Jun-69	Uruguay	Montevideo	Friendly	Won 2-1	
35	12-Jun-69	Brazil	Rio de Janeiro	Friendly	Lost 1-2	
36	10-Dec-69	Portugal	Wembley	Friendly	Won 1-0	
37	25-Feb-70	Belgium	Brussels	Friendly	Won 3-1	5th & 6th goals
38	18-Apr-70	Wales	Ninian Park	BC	Drew 1-1	
39	25-Apr-70	Scotland	Hampden Park	BC	Drew 0-0	
40	20-May-70	Colombia	Bogota	Friendly	Won 4-0	7th goal
41	24-May-70	Ecuador	Quito	Friendly	Won 2-0	
42	02-Jun-70	Romania	Guadalajara	WCF	Won 1-0	
43	07-Jun-70	Brazil	Guadalajara	WCF	Lost 0-1	
44	11-Jun-70	Czechoslovakia	Guadalajara	WCF	Won 1-0	65th min sub
45	14-Jun-70	West Germany	Leon	WCF	Lost 2-3	
46	25-Nov-70	East Germany	Wembley	Friendly	Won 3-1	
47	03-Feb-71	Malta	Gzira	ECQ	Won 1-0	
48	21-Apr-71	Greece	Wembley	ECQ	Won 3-0	Replaced 75th min
49	12-May-71	Malta	Wembley	ECQ	Won 5-0	75th min sub
50	15-May-71	Northern Ireland	Belfast	BC	Won 1-0	
51	22-May-71	Scotland	Wembley	BC	Won 3-1	
52	10-Nov-71	Switzerland	Wembley	ECQ	Drew 1-1	
53	01-Dec-71	Greece	Piraes	ECQ	Won 2-0	
54	29-Apr-72	West Germany	Wembley	ECQ	Lost 1-3	
55	13-May-72	West Germany	Berlin	ECQ	Drew 0-0	
56	27-May-72	Scotland	Glasgow	BC	Won 1-0	8th goal
57	11-Oct-72	Yugoslavia	Wembley	Friendly	Drew 1-1	
58	15-Nov-72	Wales	Ninian Park	WCQ	Won 1-0	
59	24-Jan-73	Wales	Wembley	WCQ	Drew 1-1	
60	14-Feb-73	Scotland	Hampden Park	Centenary Match	Won 5-0	
61	12-May-73	Northern Ireland	Goodison Park	BC	Won 2-1	Away game
62	15-May-73	Wales	Wembley	BC	Won 3-0	
63	19-May-73	Scotland	Wembley	BC	Won 1-0	

64	27-May-73	Czechoslovakia	Prague	Friendly	Drew 1-1	
65	06-Jun-73	Poland	Chorzow	WCQ	Lost 0-2	Sent Off 76th min
66	03-Apr-74	Portugal	Lisbon	WCQ	Drew 0-0	76th min sub
67	12-Mar-75	West Germany	Wembley	Friendly	Won 2-0	Captain
68	16-Apr-75	Cyprus	Wembley	ECQ	Won 5-0	Captain
69	11-May-75	Cyprus	Limassol	ECQ	Won 1-0	Captain
70	17-May-75	Northern Ireland	Belfast	BC	Drew 0-0	Captain
71	21-May-75	Wales	Wembley	BC	Drew 2-2	Captain
72	24-May-75	Scotland	Wembley	BC	Won 5-1	Captain

Legend

BC   British Championships
ECQ European Championship Qualifier
ECF European Championship Finals
WCQ World Cup Qualifier
WCF World Cup Finals

MANAGERIAL RECORD

	Managed
Philadelphia Fury	
1978	15
Blackpool	
1980-81	34
Portsmouth	
1984-85	48
1985-86	52
1986-87	51
1987-88	47
1988-89	31
Stoke City	
1989-90	33
1990-91	37
Exeter City	
1991-92	56
1992-93	58
1993-94	31
Southampton	
1993-94	17
1994-95	50
Manchester City	
1995-96	46
1996-97	3
Portsmouth	
1997-98	19
1998-99	52
1999-00	97
Total	777

INDEX